Study Guide

CONTEMPORARY LINGUISTICS

AN INTRODUCTION

Study Guide

CONTEMPORARY LINGUISTICS

AN INTRODUCTION

Fifth Edition

Teresa Vanderweide
Mount Royal College

U.S. edition prepared by

Janie Rees-Miller
Marietta College

Mark Aronoff
State University of New York at Stony Brook

Bedford/St. Martin's
Boston ♦ New York

Manufactured in the United States of America.

9 8 7 6 5
f e d c b a

For information, write: Bedford/St. Martin's, 75 Arlington Street, Boston, MA 02116 (617-399-4000)

ISBN: 0-312-41765-9

EAN: 978-0-312-41765-9

PREFACE FOR INSTRUCTORS

The *Study Guide* that accompanies *Contemporary Linguistics* is designed to be more comprehensive than a simple workbook, and as such it includes summaries and reviews of important concepts found in Chapters 1 through 7 of the textbook as well as extensive supplementary practice exercises. It is particularly well suited to those undergraduate and graduate students with no prior knowledge of linguistics; it may also be profitably used by students who need additional self-study material, by professors who need supplementary lecture material, and by teaching assistants who need to organize recitation sections. Thus we are once again pleased that the Canadian editors of *Contemporary Linguistic Analysis,* upon which this U.S. book, *Contemporary Linguistics,* is based, have reissued the *Study Guide* to accompany the text.

Student-friendly features that distinguished the previous edition of the *Study Guide* have been retained in this edition:

- **Practice exercises** cover the major topics in each chapter and provide an intermediate step between explanation of linguistic processes and their application to more challenging problems.
- **Charts** summarize important concepts graphically and guide students through the process of problem-solving.
- **Cross-references** refer students to the appropriate sections and pages in the main text and to relevant pages on the Web site.
- **Reminder boxes** give helpful hints for understanding concepts and solving problems.
- **Review exercises** for each chapter consolidate skills acquired throughout the chapter.
- **Recap boxes** at the end of each chapter list important concepts covered in the chapter.
- An **answer key** enables students to check their own work.
- Each chapter ends with a space for students to jot down **questions** or **problems** that they want to ask their professor or teaching assistant about.

This new edition of the *Study Guide* has been thoroughly revised to reflect the contents and order of presentation in the fifth edition of *Contemporary Linguistics.* In particular, phonetic transcription in Chapter 2 has been revised to take account of the presentation of [ɹ] in American dialects and the principles for transcribing syllabic liquids and nasals presented in the main text. The presentation in Chapter 5 has been completely revised so that the X' schema is used throughout. In all chapters of the *Study Guide,* explanations have been revised for clarity where necessary, and practice exercises have been revised or added where appropriate to suit students' needs and to reflect the contents of the fifth edition of *Contemporary Linguistics.*

As with the previous edition, this *Study Guide* closely follows its Canadian precursor in its organization and layout. Each chapter begins with an overview of material and ends with a review list of concepts and skills. Chapters comprise summaries of important concepts and processes and include numerous practice exercises and reminder boxes. Some practice exercises have been specially written for the U.S. edition of the *Study Guide,* and sources for these exercises are listed in the back before the answer key.

We are grateful for assistance that we have received in preparing this edition of the *Study Guide.* We would like to acknowledge reviewers who gave feedback on the *Study Guide:* Janet

Cowal, Lynn Guindon, Sharon Hargus, Darya Kavitskaya, Saundra Wright, and Doug Wulf. We would particularly like to thank Carson Schutze for detailed suggestions that helped in the revision for this edition. At Marietta College, we once again acknowledge Richard Danford, who supplied linguistic data at a moment's notice. Our gratitude is also extended to the staff at Bedford/St. Martin's. Our editor, Joelle Hann, kept us on our timetable and coordinated the various stages of production. Harold Chester checked data and ensured accuracy in the final stages of production. Finally, we acknowledge the feedback from students, for whom the *Study Guide* is intended.

Janie Rees-Miller
Mark Aronoff

PREFACE TO THE CANADIAN EDITION

This workbook is intended to accompany the fifth edition of *Contemporary Linguistic Analysis: An Introduction.* It originally began as a series of worksheets distributed to students in class and gradually expanded to include brief explanations of text material and practice exercises, as well as review sheets. All of the material that came to be included in the workbook was either modified or designed to supplement the content in *Contemporary Linguistic Analysis,* the text being used for introductory linguistics. As the workbook evolved, it became more generic and, as a result, potentially useful to virtually any instructor of introductory linguistics using *Contemporary Linguistic Analysis*.

The workbook contains a preview of major concepts followed by six chapters that correspond to the core components of linguistics: phonetics, phonology, morphology, syntax, and semantics, as well as historical linguistics. These are the main areas in which students typically require a great deal of exposure to, and practice with, the methods of analysis used in that particular branch of linguistics. It is hoped that this workbook will help fulfill this need. Each chapter in the workbook begins with a list of the main topics and/or concepts found within. It then contains explanations of these important concepts followed by practice exercises. All chapters include reminders of important concepts that students need to be familiar with, and conclude with a review list intended as a study guide. Throughout the workbook, the focus is always on the content of the corresponding *Contemporary Linguistic Analysis* chapter. Finally, while every attempt was made to include as much language data as possible, the workbook does tend to emphasize Canadian English, the starting point for most students as they learn and become familiar with the methodology used in linguistic analysis.

I gratefully acknowledge contributions made by Carrie Dyck, Elaine Sorensen, Leone Sveinson, Joyce Hildebrand, and Lorna Rowsell, without whom this workbook would not have been possible. I would like to thank all the reviewers for their comments, especially Carrie Dyck and William O'Grady for their invaluable suggestions and advice, which have improved the overall quality of the workbook. Thanks also go to Elizabeth Ritter for using a version of the workbook with her students and providing valuable feedback. Finally, I extend my sincere thanks and gratitude to Michael Dobrovolsky for his continued inspiration, support, and encouragement.

Teresa Vanderweide

CONTENTS

NOTE TO STUDENTS: HOW TO USE THIS STUDY GUIDE

Welcome to the study of linguistics! For many of you using *Contemporary Linguistics* this is your first experience with the field of linguistics. Everyone speaks a language and has ideas about language, but using the analytical tools for the scientific study of language can at first seem daunting. However, with study and practice, you can discover beauty in the systematic ways in which human language behaves and be fascinated by the ways in which languages differ.

This *Study Guide* is designed to help you accomplish that goal. Since each section of the *Study Guide* is keyed to pages and sections of *Contemporary Linguistics,* you can use the relevant sections of the guide to review some of the important concepts and practice skills that you have read about in the text. For greatest benefit, we suggest the following procedure:

1. Read the appropriate section in *Contemporary Linguistics.*
2. Recall important concepts and terms, and try to explain them in your own words.
3. Read the review explanations in the *Study Guide.*
4. Work the practice problems.
5. Check your answers using the answer key in the back of the *Study Guide.*
6. List questions or problems on the last page of the chapter in the *Study Guide.*
7. Ask your instructor or teaching assistant for help with any difficulties and for explanations of concepts that are not clear.

This may seem like a lot of work, and it may indeed be time-consuming. However, learning the concepts and skills of a new discipline is a step-by-step process, and each step builds on the preceding one. We are confident that *Contemporary Linguistics,* complemented by this *Study Guide,* will give you the necessary foundation for understanding the principles and methods of linguistics.

one

Language: A Preview

The following are some of the important concepts found in this chapter. Make sure you are familiar with them.

Specialization
Creativity
Linguistic competence
Grammar parity

Specialization (Section 1, pp. 1–2)

Humans are specialized for language. The characteristics below illustrate some of the aspects of our special capacity for language.

- *Speech Organs*

  Our lungs, larynx, tongue, teeth, lips, soft palate, and nasal passages are used both for survival (i.e., breathing, eating, etc.) and for producing the sounds of our language.

- *Speech Breathing*

  We have the ability to breathe not only for survival but also for speech. Speech breathing uses a different set of muscles and different lung pressure and exhalation time than our normal breathing.

- *Specialized Brain Areas*

  The human brain is structured for language. Our brains appear to have specialized areas dedicated to language production and comprehension—areas that are not found in other species.

This specialization for language sets us apart from all other creatures.

Creativity (Section 2, pp. 2–5)

Human language is creative. That is, language does not provide us with a set of prepackaged messages. Rather, it allows us to produce and understand new words and sentences whenever needed. However, there are limitations on both the form and interpretation of new words and sentences. Linguists attempt to identify and understand these limitations.

PRACTICE 1.1: Creativity

1. Arrange the words *bird, worm, catches, early, every,* and *the* into an English sentence.

2. Write two other sentences using the same words.

3. Use the same words to create a "sentence" that is not an acceptable English sentence.

4. Compare the sentences you wrote in 1 and 2 with the sentence in 3. Why is the sentence in 3 unacceptable in English?

Linguistic Competence (Section 3, pp. 5–6)

Linguistic competence can be defined as subconscious knowledge that enables the native speakers of a language to produce and understand an unlimited number of both familiar and novel utterances. The **native speakers** of a language are those who have acquired it as children in a natural setting like the home rather than in a classroom.

Linguists divide the subconscious knowledge that the native speakers of a language share into the following fields of study:

1. Phonetics: the study of the sounds found in language, including the articulation and perception of speech sounds
2. Phonology: the study of how speech sounds pattern in language
3. Morphology: the study of word structure and word formation
4. Syntax: the study of sentence structure
5. Semantics: the study of the meaning of words and sentences

This subconscious knowledge allows the speakers of a language to produce an infinite number of sentences, many of which we have never uttered or heard before. This is often referred to as language **creativity**. We don't memorize language; we create it.

While we all have this unconscious knowledge of our native language, we often make mistakes when we talk. That is, our actual use of language does not always reflect our linguistic competence.

PRACTICE 1.2: Linguistic competence

Your linguistic competence allows you to decide whether new words and novel sentences are acceptable or not. Test your linguistic competence by answering the following questions.

1. Put a check mark beside those words that are possible English words.

   a. tlim ____________________ e. plog ____________________

   b. stuken ____________________ f. skpit ____________________

   c. tseg ____________________ g. ngan ____________________

   d. fomp ____________________ h. breb ____________________

2. Put a check mark beside those words that are possible English words.

   a. speakless ____________________ d. reglorify ____________________

   b. beautifulness ____________________ e. horseable ____________________

   c. unrug ____________________ f. weedic ____________________

   Why are some of the above not possible English words? (Hint: Think about the prefix or suffix and its contribution to the meaning of the word.)

3. Put a check mark beside those sentences that are possible English sentences.

   a. The building is swept yesterday evening. ______________

   b. The building is swept every morning. ______________

   c. Every child should obey his parents. ______________

   d. Somebody left their gloves in the theater. ______________

   e. George surprised Mary with a party. ______________

   f. Joe surprised the stone. ______________

   Why are some of the above not possible English sentences?

Grammar Parity (Section 3.2, pp. 7–8)

Grammar, to a linguist, refers to all the elements of our linguistic competence: phonetics, phonology, morphology, syntax, and semantics. In very general terms, grammar can be defined as the system of rules and elements needed to form and interpret the sentences of a language. The study of grammar is central to understanding language and what it means to know a language. This is because all languages have sounds, words, and sentences; all grammars allow for the expression of any thought; all grammars share common principles and tendencies called universals; and all grammars change over time. However, our grammatical knowledge is subconscious: we can decide what sounds right and what does not even though we may not be sure about why this is so. There are two different perspectives on grammar: prescriptive and descriptive. A **prescriptive grammar** gives the socially accepted rules within a language, while a **descriptive grammar** is an objective description of the knowledge that the native speakers of a language share.

Practice 1.3: Distinguishing prescriptive and descriptive grammar

1. Examine the boxes below (adapted from "The Verbal Edge," *Readers Digest,* August 1994), and see if you can tell which type of grammar is being exemplified.

WRONG: Between you and I . . .
RIGHT: Between you and me . . .

On an episode of the TV sitcom *Home Improvement,* handyman Tim Taylor said of competitor Bob Vila, "A lot of people think there's a big rivalry between Bob and I."

That may sound correct, but the pronoun *I* is wrong here. *Between* is a preposition, and prepositions are always followed by objects. *I* is a subject or nominative pronoun. So are *he, she, we,* and *they*. Objective pronouns that follow a preposition are *me, you, him, her, us,* and *them.*

Use the rhyme "Between thee and me" as a reminder.

WRONG: She is older than me.
RIGHT: She is older than I.

Unlike *between,* the word *than* is not a preposition; it's a conjunction—a word that joins two sentences, words, or phrases. In this case there are two sentences: (1) *She is older* and (2) *I am*—but the *am* has been dropped, and that throws people off.

In a comparison joined by *than* or *as,* just complete the sentence, and the correct word will be obvious. You wouldn't say "He is smarter than me am," so it must be *He is smarter than I.*

WRONG: Who do I ask?
RIGHT: Whom do I ask?

Who and *whom* will never stump you if you remember: *Who* is generally appropriate whenever you use *he, she,* or *they*; *whom* acts as a substitute for *him, her,* or *them.* Sometimes it helps to recast a question into a statement. In this example, you'd never say "I ask he," so the correct wording is *Whom do I ask?* ("But that sounds stuffy," you say. Yes—which is why the incorrect *Who do I ask?* is sometimes used in informal situations.)

WRONG: The demand for durable goods such as cars and home appliances were unchanged last month.
RIGHT: The demand for durable goods such as cars and home appliances was unchanged last month.

A CNN news anchor delivered this blooper, which goes to show that even professionals err. The mistake was mating a plural verb with a singular subject. And it often happens as it did here: the subject of the sentence, *demand,* was singular, but it got separated from the verb by the plural phrase *such as cars and home appliances.* Distracted by these particulars, the anchor forgot that she was speaking in the singular and used a plural verb. Keep your mind on the subject—what it is you're talking about.

The above are all examples of a prescriptivist view on language. While a prescriptivist grammar is useful in helping people learn a foreign language in that it contains the socially accepted rules for language use, linguists are more interested in descriptive grammar.

2. Each of the following aspects of linguistic competence contains two statements. See if you can identify which statement is prescriptivist and which is descriptivist. Do this by writing either P.G. (prescriptive grammar) or D.G. (descriptive grammar) beside each statement.

a. Sounds

_______________ The English words *Mary, merry,* and *marry* should be pronounced differently because they are spelled differently.

_______________ English contains over twenty different consonant sounds.

How many different vowel sounds are found in English?

Do all languages have the same consonant and/or vowel sounds? Think of a language that has different consonant or vowel sounds.

b. Words

_______________ The use of *has went* instead of *has gone* is an example of how change is causing the English language to deteriorate.

_______________ Many nouns in English are formed by adding the suffix *-ment* to words (e.g., *achievement, government, judgment*).

Why would no English speaker construct the word *chairment*?

c. Sentences

_______________ There are at least two ways in English to make a sentence refer to the future.

_______________ The auxiliary *shall* should be used with first person (i.e., *I, we*), whereas *will* should be used for second and third persons (e.g., *He will go, but we shall stay*).

Revise the following sentence in two different ways to make it refer to the future: *The horses eat hay.*

How do other languages make statements refer to future time?

d. Meaning

_______________ The word *cool* should only be used to refer to temperature.

_______________ Words often come in pairs of opposites (e.g., *hot/cold, light/dark*).

How is the meaning of a sentence different from the meaning of the words that compose it?

REMINDER

Linguistics is the study of the structure of human language. Linguists attempt to describe in an objective and nonjudgmental fashion the internalized and unconscious knowledge that the native speakers of a language share, which allows them to both speak and understand their language. While the primary focus of this guide is on English, many of the principles and theories discussed apply to all other languages as well.

Review Exercise

Each of the following statements illustrates a concept covered in Chapter 1. For each statement, determine which concept is being illustrated. Do this by writing the number of the concept beside each statement. The first one is done for you.

Concepts:
1. Linguistic competence
2. Prescriptive grammar
3. Descriptive grammar
4. Universality

Statements:

a. ___4___ All languages have a way of making negatives.

b. __________ Speakers of American English know that one way to make questions is to move an auxiliary verb ahead of the subject noun phrase.

c. __________ Many nouns in English are formed by adding *-ness* to an adjective, for example: *sadness, silliness,* and *happiness.*

d. __________ *Brung* should never be used as the past tense of *bring.*

e. __________ Every language has a set of vowels and consonants.

f. __________ Speakers of any language are capable of producing an unlimited number of novel sentences.

g. __________ In English, there is no theoretical limit on the number of adjectives that can occur before a noun.

h. __________ In the sentence *My friend is smarter than me, me* is incorrect because it is an object pronoun and this comparative construction requires the subject pronoun *I.*

i. __________ In English, the plural is formed by adding [-s], [-z], or [-əz] to the end of nouns.

j. __________ Every language has a way of forming questions.

k. __________ Speakers of American English know that the different vowel sounds in the words *bat, bet, but,* and *bit* are crucial to their meanings.

☑ RECAP

Make sure you understand these terms. (See also the Key Terms on p. 11 of the main text.)

- creativity
- descriptive grammar
- generality
- grammar
- inaccessibility
- linguistic competence
- mutability
- native speaker
- parity
- prescriptive grammar
- specialized brain areas
- speech breathing
- speech organs
- universality

Questions? Problems?

two

Phonetics: The Sounds of Language

Phonetics is the study of the articulation and perception of speech sounds. Following are some of the important topics and concepts covered in this chapter. Make sure you are familiar with them.

[vowkl̩ tɹækt]
[sawnd klæsəz]
[ɑɹtʰɪkjələtɔɹi dɪskɹɪpʃn̩z]
[plejsəz əv ɑɹtʰɪkjəlejʃn̩]
[əmɛɹəkn̩ ɪŋglɪʃ kʰɑnsənənts]
[æspəɹejʃn̩]
[fejʃl̩ dajəgɹæmz]
[əmɛɹəkn̩ ɪŋglɪʃ vawəlz]
[sɛgmənts]
[trænskɹɪpʃn̩]
[ʃɛɹd fənɛtɪk pɹɑpɹ̩tiz]
[supɹəsɛgmɛntl̩z]
[aɹtʰɪkjələtɔɹi pɹɑsɛsəz]

By the end of this section, you'll be able to translate the above phonetic transcription into standard English with ease.

In "plain" English, some of the topics we will be discussing in phonetics are:

Vocal tract
Sound classes
Articulatory descriptions
Places of articulation
American English consonants
Aspiration
Facial diagrams
American English vowels
Segments
Transcription
Shared phonetic properties
Suprasegmentals
Articulatory processes

Sounds and Phonetic Transcription (Section 1, pp. 16–18)

Human language contains a finite number of speech sounds, or **phones**. The speech sounds found in language are transcribed using the symbols found in the **International Phonetic Alphabet (IPA)**. Each symbol in this alphabet represents one and only one speech sound. Each speech sound found in language corresponds to one and only one IPA symbol. Since symbols represent sounds, the same symbols can be used in whatever language that sound occurs.

It is important to remember that IPA symbols represent sounds and not how that sound is spelled in a particular language. To indicate this difference, symbols are enclosed in [ ] brackets. Don't forget to use them.

Units of Representation

There are three units of linguistic representation that are relevant to the study of speech sounds. Segments are discussed in this chapter, features and syllables in the next.

Segments: A **segment** is an individual speech sound. Each symbol in IPA represents a segment.

Features: A **feature** is a single aspect of articulation. Individual segments are composed of a number of features. Taken together, these features make up the articulation of the segment.

Syllables: Segments can also combine with each other to form a larger unit called a **syllable**. Syllables, therefore, consist of one or more segments.

REMINDER

The focus in this chapter is on learning the IPA symbols corresponding to the vowel and consonant sounds of English. Many, but not all, of these sounds are found in other languages. In addition, there are many sounds that do not occur in English but that are found in other languages. For more information on some of these sounds, their descriptions, and their IPA symbols, please refer to

- Table 2.28 and Table 2.29 on pp. 48–49 of the text, and
- **bedfordstmartins.com/linguistics/phonetics** and click on **IPA vowels and consonants.**

The Vocal Tract (Section 2, pp. 18–20)

The **vocal tract** is the sound-producing system. It includes the lungs, trachea, **larynx, pharynx, velum**, oral cavity, and nasal cavity. Speech sounds are made as air passes through the vocal tract.

PRACTICE 2.1: Parts of the vocal tract

On the following diagram, label the lungs, larynx, pharynx, oral cavity, nasal cavity, and velum.

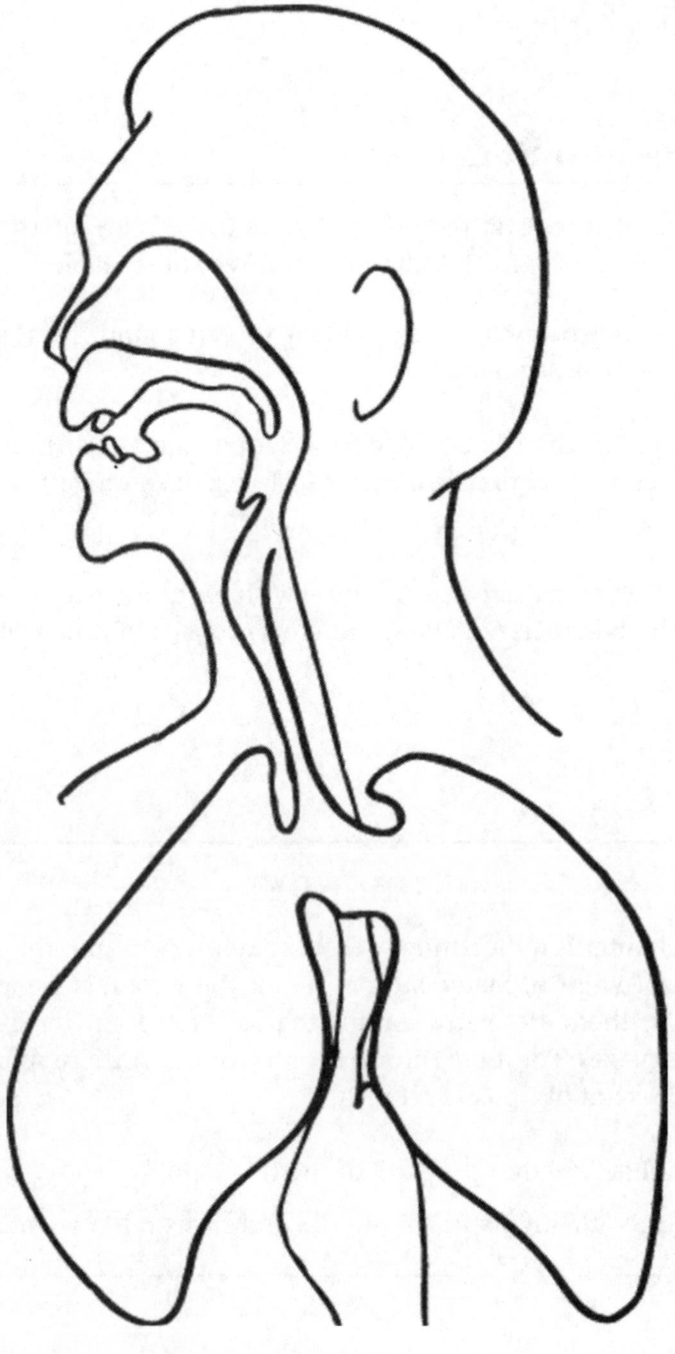

Sound Classes (Section 3, pp. 20–21)

Sounds produced with the vocal tract can be divided into three major classes: **consonants**, **vowels**, and **glides**. The defining characteristics of each class are given below.

- **Consonants.** Consonantal sounds are made with a narrow or complete obstruction in the vocal tract. Some of them come in **voiced/voiceless** pairs.
- **Vowels.** Vowel sounds are made with little obstruction in the vocal tract, and they are typically voiced. Vowels tend to be more **sonorous** than consonants. Vowels are also classified as **syllabic** sounds, meaning that they can function as the **nucleus** of a syllable.
- **Glides.** Glides are sounds that have characteristics of both consonants and vowels. They are sometimes called semivowels or semiconsonants. Glides are like vowels in their articulation, but they are like consonants in that they do not function as the nucleus of a syllable.

Practice 2.2: Identifying consonants, vowels, and glides

Each of the following words has one or more letters underlined. The underlined letters correspond to one sound. Identify this sound as a consonant, vowel, or glide. The first is done for you.

1. rottweiler consonant
2. through ____________
3. lovely ____________
4. year ____________
5. myth ____________
6. whistle ____________
7. suffer ____________
8. judge ____________

Articulatory Descriptions (Section 4.1, pp. 21–24; Sections 6.2–6.3, pp. 33–35)

All sounds, regardless of whether they are consonants, vowels, or glides, are described in terms of how they are articulated. This information is contained in the sound's articulatory description. Every sound has one and only one articulatory description. Every articulatory description corresponds to one symbol in the International Phonetic Alphabet (IPA). Consonants and glides are described differently than vowels.

Consonant Articulation (Section 4)

There are three parameters necessary to describe consonant (and glide) articulation:

- Glottal state (Section 2.1, pp. 19–20)
- Place of articulation (Section 4.2, pp. 22–24)
- Manner of articulation (Section 5, pp. 24–31)

Glottal state refers to whether a sound is voiced or voiceless. Place of articulation refers to where in the vocal tract an obstruction occurs. Manner of articulation refers to how the airflow is modified at the place of articulation.

Vowel Articulation (Section 6)

Four parameters are necessary to describe vowels: (Sections 6.2–6.3, pp. 33–35)

- Tongue height
- Tongue position
- Tenseness
- Lip position

Tongue height and tongue position are used to describe tongue placement. Tenseness refers to the amount of constriction in the vocal tract muscles when the sound is articulated. Lip position refers to whether the lips are rounded.

REMINDER

For every articulatory description, you need to be able to provide the corresponding phonetic symbol, for example:

voiceless bilabial stop → [p]

For every phonetic symbol, you need to be able to provide the corresponding articulatory description, for example:

[ej] → mid front tense unrounded vowel

Places of Articulation (Section 4.2, pp. 22–24)

Different places in the vocal tract can be modified to produce different sounds. Most of these places are found within the oral cavity, but there are two places of articulation outside the oral cavity.

PRACTICE 2.3: Locating places of articulation (See Figure 2.3 on p. 22)

On the following diagram, identify all the places of articulation.

American English Consonant Chart (Sections 5.2–5.8, pp. 24–31)

Consonant sounds are classified according to:

- where they are articulated (place of articulation)
- how they are articulated (manner of articulation)
- whether they are voiced or voiceless (glottal state)

Although the consonant chart looks daunting, you will find that completing it will help you remember each phonetic symbol.

Practice 2.4: Consonants (Table 2.12, p. 31)

Fill in the chart with the symbols corresponding to the consonant and glide sounds of American English. Put a box around the group of fricatives and affricates that are strident.

[redacted]		GLOTTAL STATE	PLACE OF ARTICULATION							
			Bilabial	Labiodental	Interdental	Alveolar	Alveopalatal	Palatal	Velar	Glottal
MANNER OF ARTICULATION	Stop	voiceless								
		voiced								
	Fricative	voiceless								
		voiced								
	Affricate	voiceless								
		voiced								
	Nasal	voiced								
	Liquid									
	a. lateral	voiced								
	b. retroflex	voiced								
	Glide	voiced								

To see a consonant chart that includes consonants for other languages, go to **bedford stmartins.com/linguistics/phonetics** and click on **other vowels and consonants.**

Aspiration (Section 5.5, pp. 28–29)

Sometimes when voiceless **stops** are pronounced, they are produced with a small puff of air. This puff of air is called **aspiration** and is represented as [^{h}]. Pronounce the words in the boxes below, paying close attention to the first sound, and see if you can tell when aspiration does and does not occur. You can feel this extra release of air by putting your hand close to your mouth as you produce the words. (It is easier to feel the puff of air with **bilabial** and **alveolar** stops than with the **velar** stop.)

ASPIRATED VOICELESS STOPS	
[p^h]	pit punk
[t^h]	take tab
[k^h]	kill car

UNASPIRATED VOICELESS STOPS	
[p]	spit spunk
[t]	stake stab
[k]	skill scar

Voiceless stops in English can be both aspirated and unaspirated. Aspiration occurs only when there is a delay in the voicing of the vowel after the voiceless stop. This delay occurs in words such as *pit, take,* and *kill* because there is not enough time after the release of the voiceless stop to vibrate the **vocal folds** for the vowel articulation. The vowel therefore is not immediately voiced, and it is this initial voicelessness that is perceived as a puff of air. In words such as *spit, stake,* and *skill,* there is no delay in voicing, and therefore no aspiration. The delay does not occur because the presence of an extra sound provides the time necessary to get the vocal folds into position to immediately start voicing the vowel when the stop is released.

Practice 2.5: Aspiration

Pronounce the following words, and put a check mark beside those words containing aspirated voiceless stops.

1. scratch ______________________
2. talk ______________________
3. segments ______________________
4. pending ______________________
5. stripe ______________________
6. careful ______________________

Facial Diagrams for Consonants

There are four important parts to completing or deciphering facial diagrams.

Voicing/Voicelessness. Voiceless sounds are represented by two lines shaped like an ellipse. Voiced sounds are shown by two wavy lines where the larynx would be.

Nasal Passage. For oral sounds, the nasal passage is closed; for nasal sounds, the nasal passage is open.

VOICELESS, ORAL

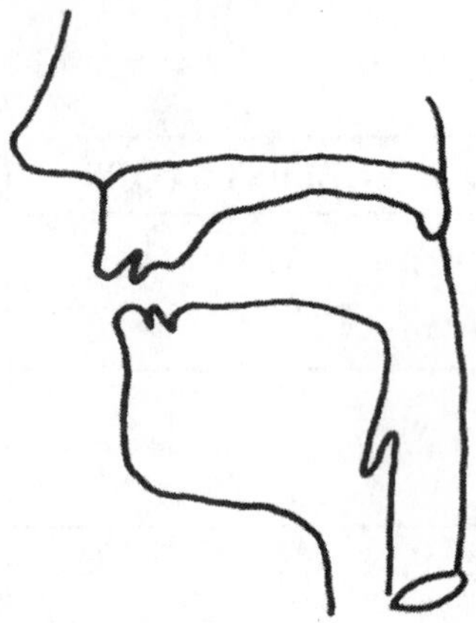

VOICED, NASAL

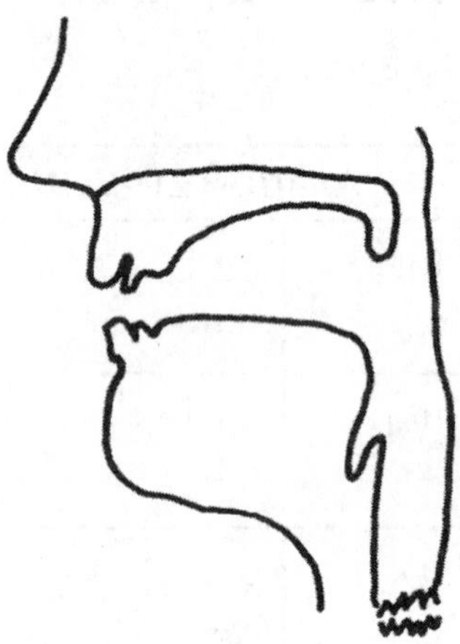

Place of Articulation. The narrowest point in the airstream passage is the **place of articulation.**

Manner of Articulation. If no air escapes past a given articulator (i.e., a stop), then the articulator must touch the place of articulation. If the air does escape (i.e., a **fricative**), then there is a space between the articulator and the place of articulation. If the sound is an **affricate**, then the diagram is shown with the articulator touching the place of articulation and an arrow indicating the direction in which the articulator moves.

STOP

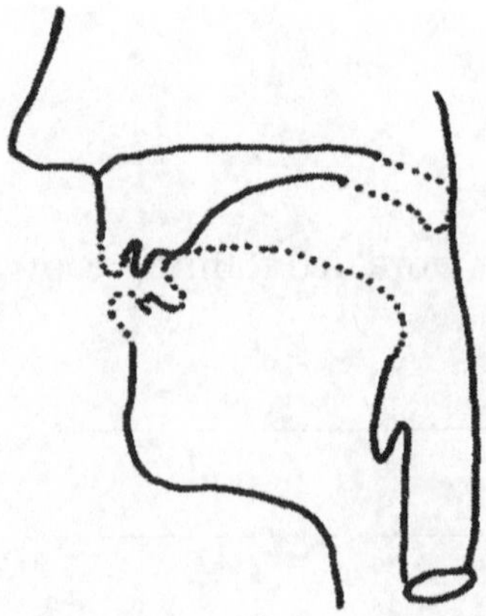

FRICATIVE

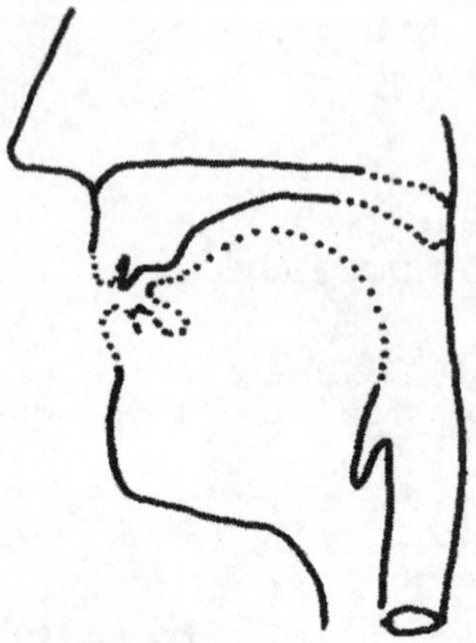

AFFRICATE

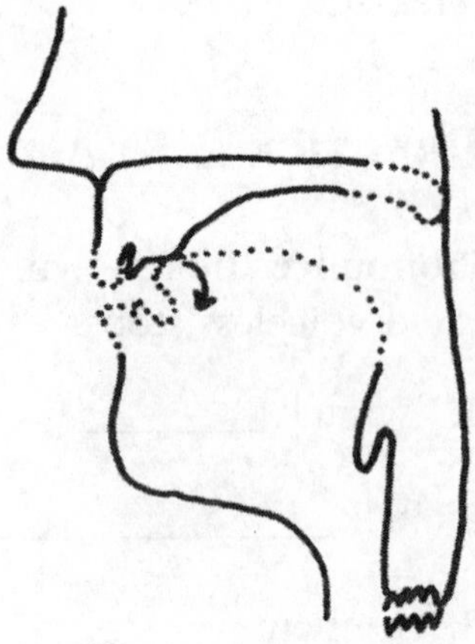

PRACTICE 2.6: Drawing facial diagrams

Complete the following diagrams so that each of the sounds listed below is depicted.

1. [s]	2. [b]	3. [dʒ]
4. [n]	5. [g]	6. [ð]

To complete the diagrams, you must:

- Draw in the lips: either closed or open.
- Draw the tongue to the place of articulation and to the manner of articulation.
- Draw in the velum: either closed or open.
- Draw in the glottal state: either voiced or voiceless.

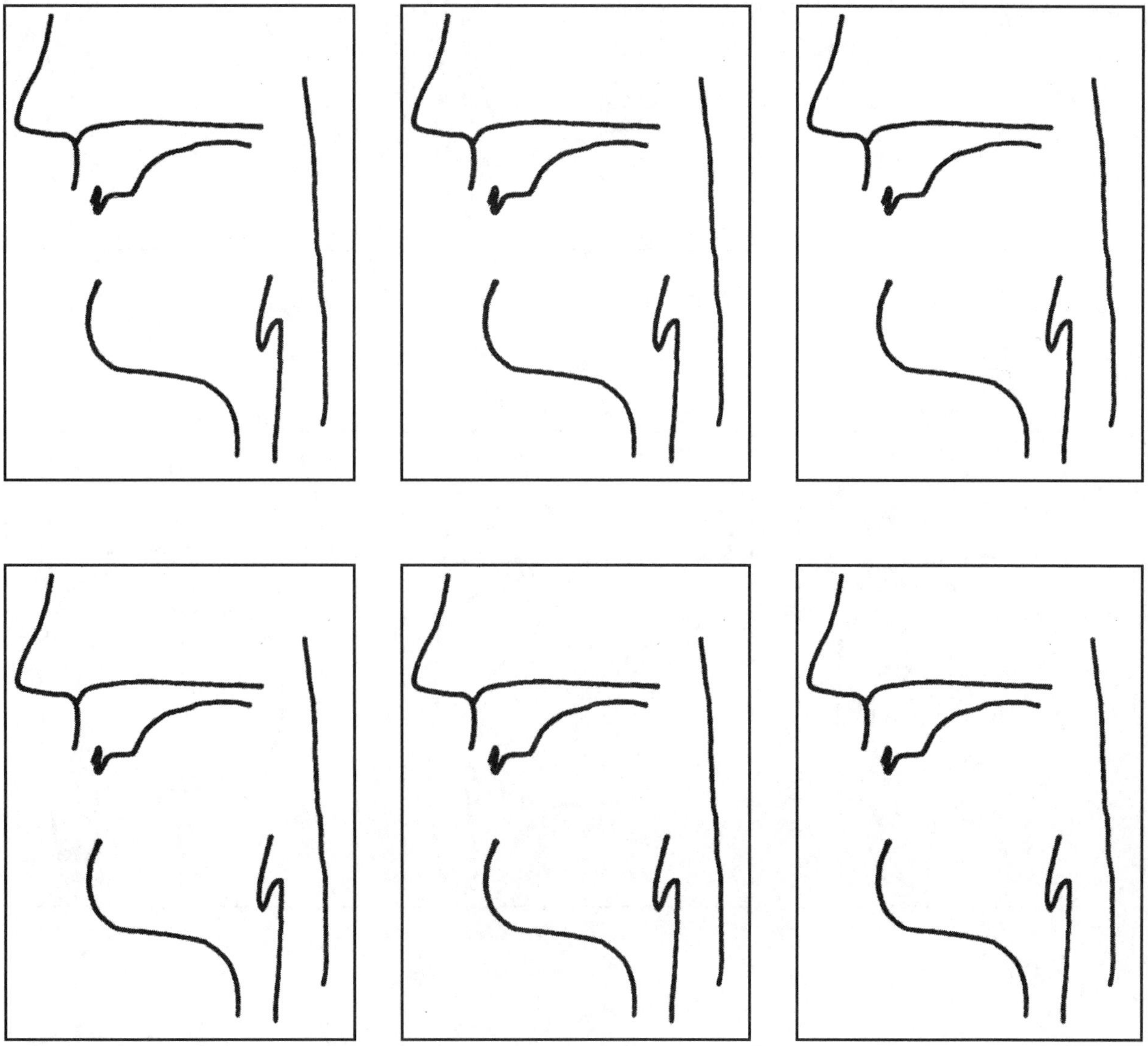

PRACTICE 2.7: Reading facial diagrams

For each of the following drawings, there is only one sound that could be produced by the vocal tract position. Figure out which consonant sound is represented, and write the phonetic symbol for that sound between the brackets below the drawing.

Make sure that you pay attention to voicing, to place and manner of articulation, and to the position of the velum.

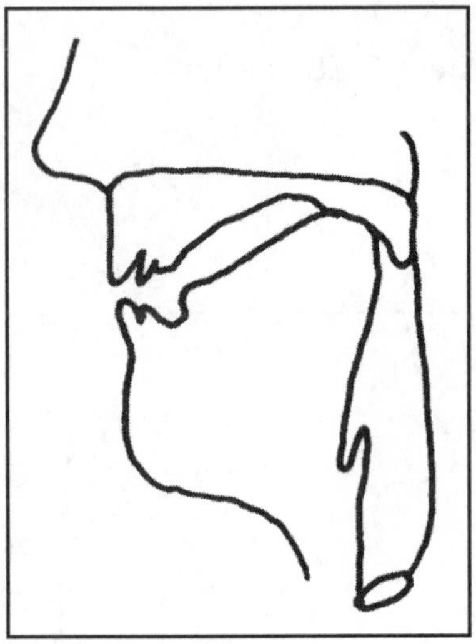

1. [ ]

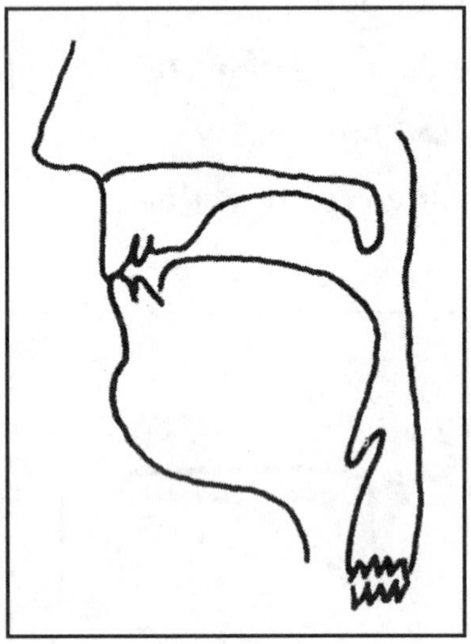

2. [ ]

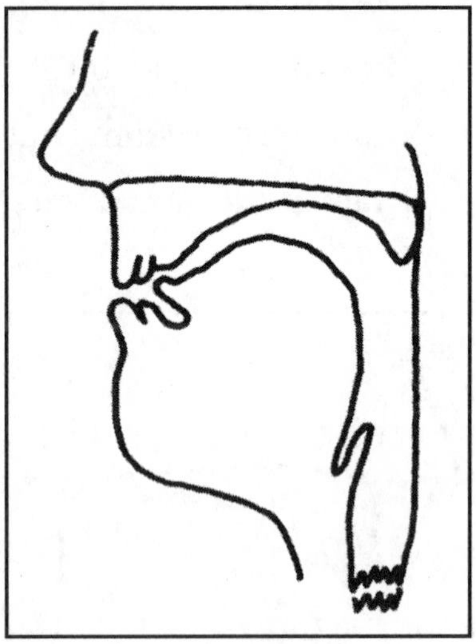

3. [ ]

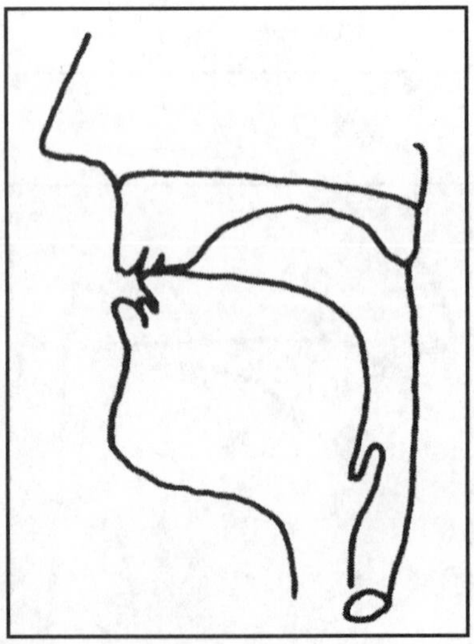

4. [ ]

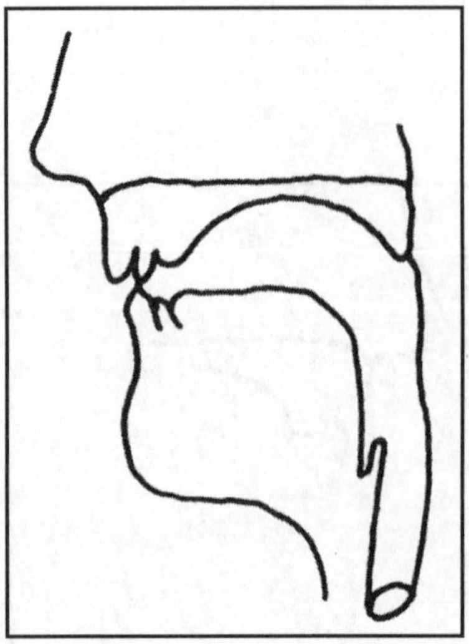

5. [ ]

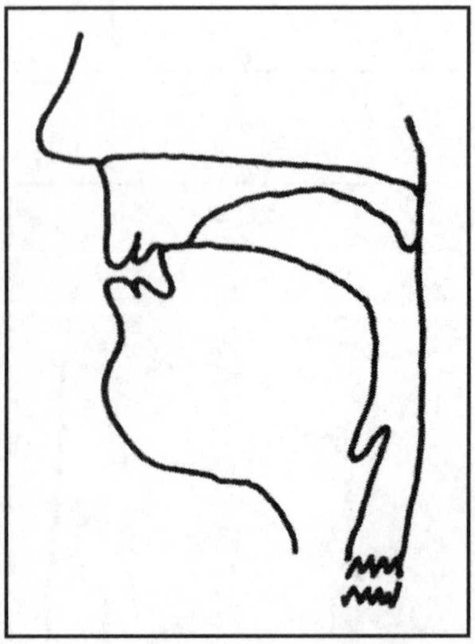

6. [ ]

American English Vowel Chart (Sections 6.2–6.3, pp. 33–35)

Vowels are classified according to:

- tongue height:
  high vs. mid vs. low
- tongue position:
  front vs. (central vs.) back
- lip position:
  rounded vs. unrounded
- tenseness:
  tense vs. lax

PRACTICE 2.8: Vowels (Figure 2.9, p. 34)

Fill in the following chart with the phonetic symbols corresponding to the vowel sounds of American English. In the blanks, indicate tongue position and height. Label the group of rounded vowels. Circle tense vowels.

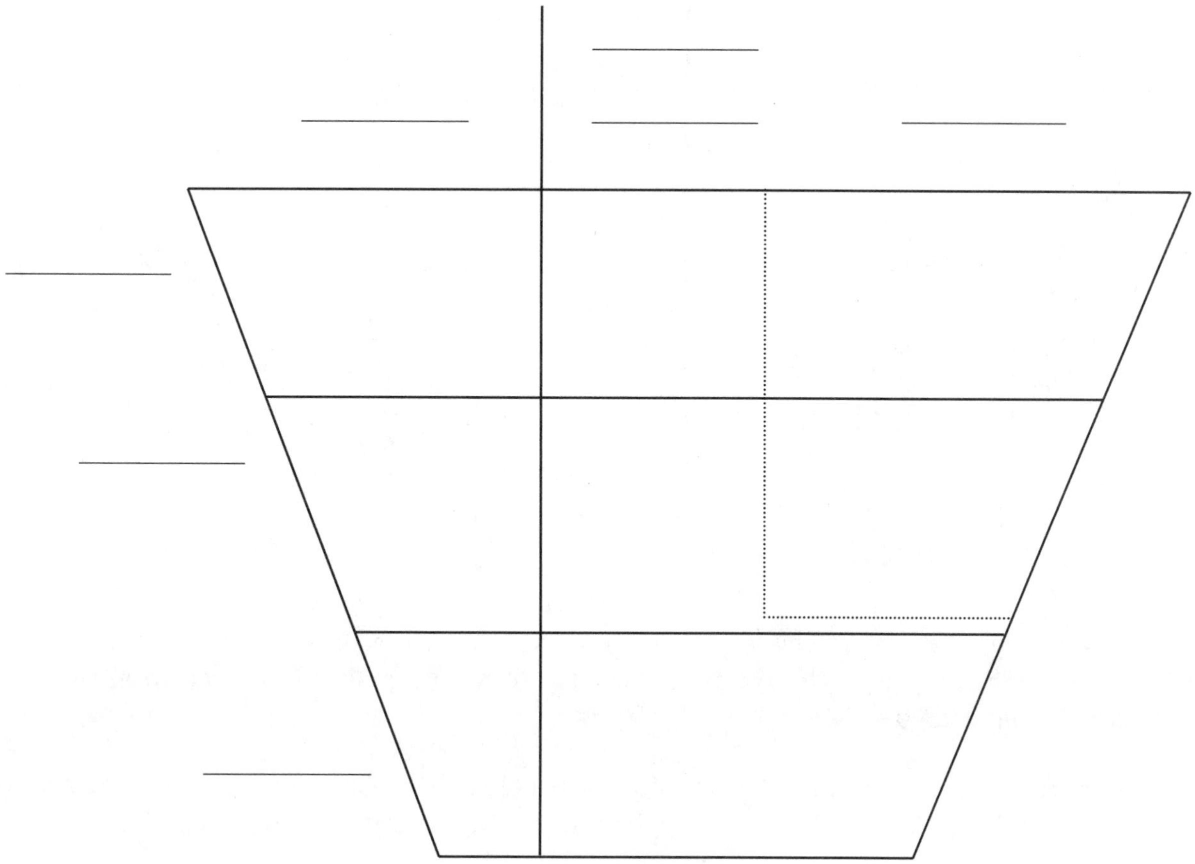

Facial Diagrams for Vowels

The following characteristics will help you read facial diagrams for vowels:

Tongue placement. The height (high, mid, or low) and position of the tongue (front, central, or back) determine the particular vowel being depicted:

Front vowels: The tongue body is raised more toward the hard palate, as in [i], [ɪ], and [æ].

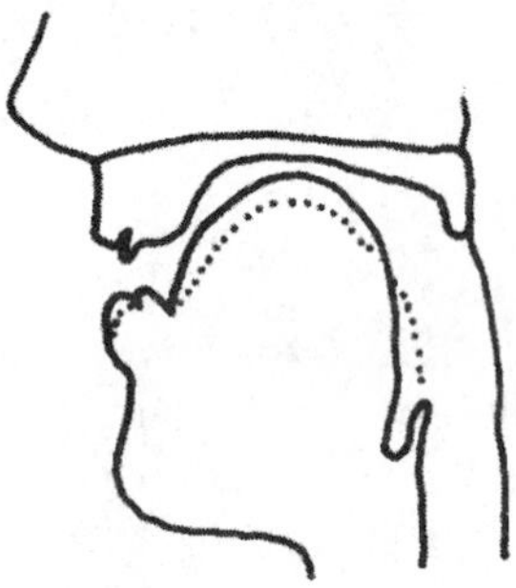

[i] — [ɪ] ····

Back vowels: The tongue body is raised more toward the velum, as in [u], [ʊ], and [ɑ].

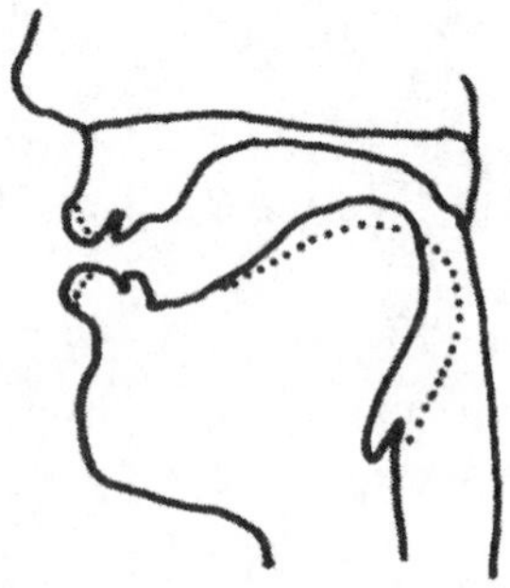

[u] — [ʊ] ····

High vowels: The tongue body is raised fairly high, as for [i], [ɪ], [u], and [ʊ].

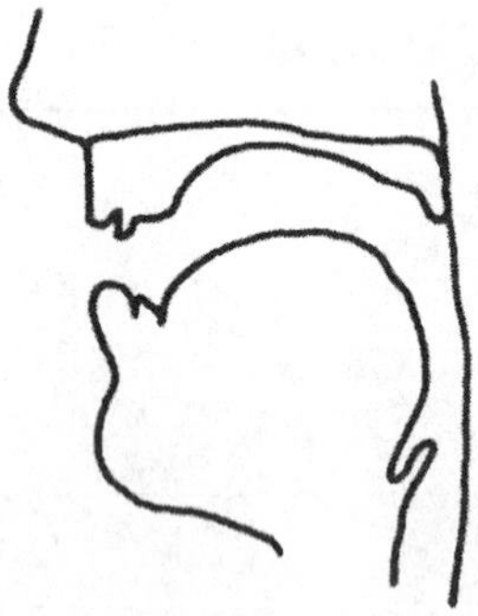

[æ] —

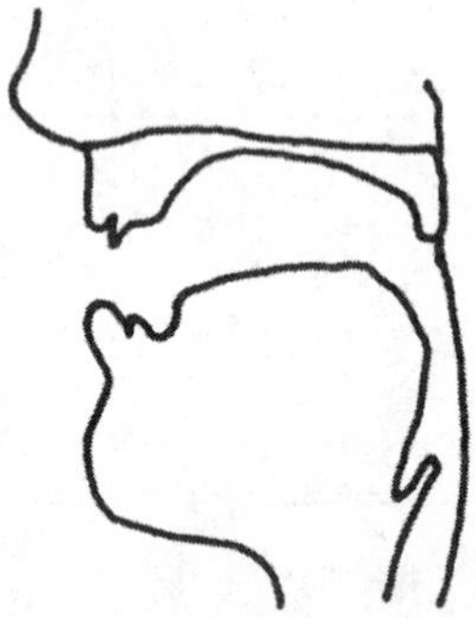

[ɑ] —

Low vowels: The tongue body is raised only slightly, as for [æ] and [ɑ].

Nasal passage. For oral vowels, the nasel passage is closed by the raised velum, as shown for all the English vowels here. For nasal vowels, the velum is lowered to allow air to flow through the nasal cavity.

Lip position. For rounded vowels, the lips protrude slightly. Compare the rounded vowels [u] and [ʊ] with the unrounded vowels [i] and [ɪ]. Also, the lips are closer together for high vowels and farther apart for low vowels.

These diagrams do not show the larnyx, but remember that vowels are voiced.

Practice 2.9

For each facial diagram, choose which vowel is being represented. Remember to look at the tongue height and position, the nasal passage, and the lip position.

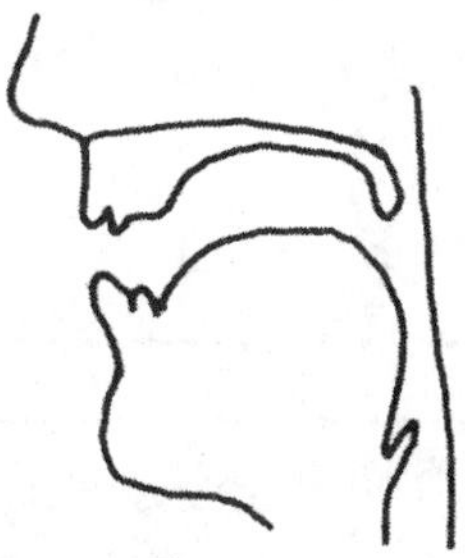

1. [i] [æ̃] [ʊ̃] [ɑ]

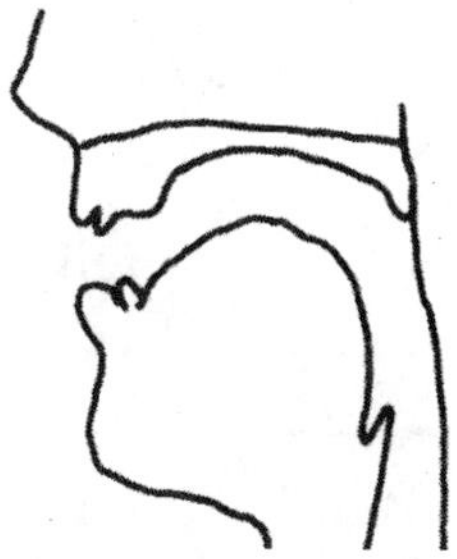

2. [ɪ̃] [ɛ] [u] [ɑ̃]

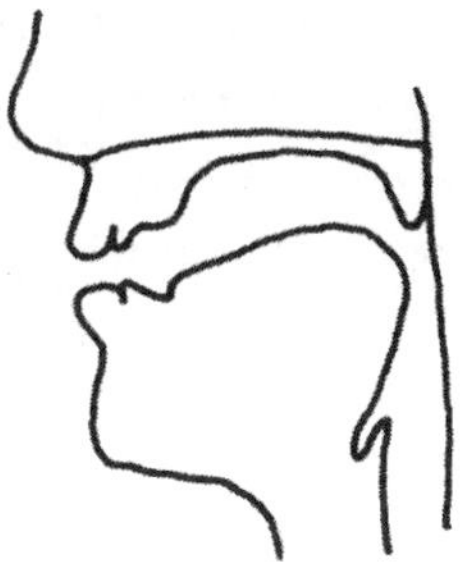

3. [ɪ̃] [æ̃] [u] [ɔ]

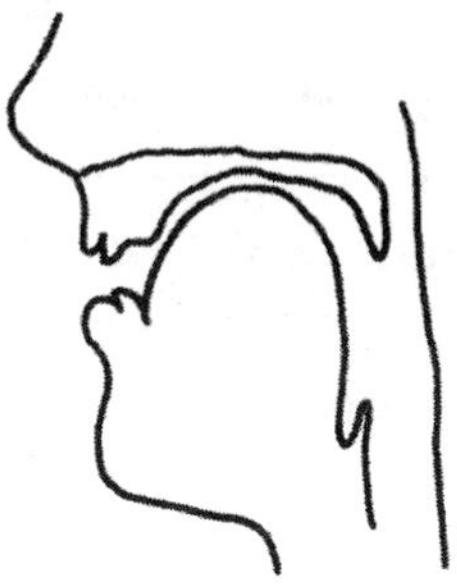

4. [ɪ̃] [ej] [o͠w] [ə]

Segments (Section 1, pp. 17–18)

To transcribe words successfully, you need to be able to identify individual sounds. An individual speech sound (or phone) is called a segment, and each segment is represented by a symbol in the phonetic alphabet. Words typically consist of a number of different speech sounds. To transcribe, you need to determine not only the number of speech sounds in a word but also what those speech sounds are. But don't be fooled by spelling. Each of the following boxes illustrates a reason why we can't rely on spelling to determine the number of speech sounds in an English word.

Some letters or combinations of letters have more than one speech sound associated with them. In each of the following example sets, determine if the underlined letter(s) are pronounced the same way for all the words presented.

1.	'o'	as in	hot	echo	woman
2.	'c'	as in	careful	century	cello
3.	'ou'	as in	should	tough	sound

Sometimes one speech sound can be represented using different letters or combinations of letters. In each of the following example sets, determine if the underlined letter(s) have the same or different speech sounds.

1.	through	clue	shoe	too
2.	real	see	sorry	Sheila
3.	straw	talk	fought	lost

Many words in English contain double letters. Double letters do not necessarily mean that there are two speech sounds. Say each of the following words and determine if the doubled letter is pronounced twice.

street book mitten killer

Finally, many words in English contain silent letters. These are letters that are not pronounced and that therefore do not correspond to a speech sound. Say each of the following words and determine if all of the letters are pronounced.

knife leave pneumonia catch

The lesson is: When you are transcribing words, you need to forget about spelling.

PRACTICE 2.10: Segments and phonetic symbols

To get ready for transcription, try the following exercises.

1. Determine the number of speech sounds in each of the following words. Count diphthongs as single sounds.

   a. thing ____________________ d. phosphate ____________________

   b. comb ____________________ e. scene ____________________

   c. psychic ____________________ f. fright ____________________

2. Give the phonetic symbol for the first sound in each of the following words.

   a. Thomas ____________________ d. knee ____________________

   b. unemployed ____________________ e. choice ____________________

   c. committee ____________________ f. ease ____________________

3. Give the phonetic symbol for the last sound in each of the following words.

   a. laugh ______________________ d. lamb ______________________

   b. sang ______________________ e. use ______________________

   c. bow ______________________ f. choice ______________________

[tɹænskɹɪpʃn̩ tajm] (Section 7, pp. 35–37)

Syllabic Consonants

r	[ɹ]	for the *r* sound at the beginning of a syllable, e.g., *real, right;* for the *r* sound at the end of a syllable, e.g., *more, car*
	[ɾ]	for the *d*-like sound in *butter, writer, atom, duty*
	[ɹ̩]	for the syllabic *r* in *burr* [bɹ̩], *earth* [ɹ̩θ], *perceive* [pɹ̩siv]; for the syllabic *r* in an unstressed syllable at the end of a word after a consonant, e.g., *ladder, tailor, longer, laser*
l	[l]	for the *l* sound in *light, pill, please*
	[l̩]	for the syllabic *l* in an unstressed syllable at the end of a word after a consonant, e.g., *babble, poodle, little, couple, Russell, panel*
m	[m̩]	for the syllabic *m* in an unstressed syllable at the end of a word after a stop or fricative, e.g., *chasm, communism*
	[m]	for all other *m* sounds
n	[n̩]	for the syllabic *n* in an unstressed syllable at the end of a word after a stop, affricate, or fricative, e.g., *button, seven, brazen*
	[n]	for all other *n* sounds

Vowels

The mid tense vowels have an off-glide in phonetic transcription only:

phonetic transcription:	[ej], [ow]
phonemic transcription:	/e/, /o/

Vowels before [ɹ]: There is a good deal of dialectal variation in the pronunciation of vowels before *r*. Some alternatives are given here.

[biɹ] or [bɪɹ]	beer	[buɹ]	boor
[bejɹ] or [bɛɹ]	bear	[boɹ] or [bɔɹ]	bore
[bæɹi] or [bɛɹi]	Barry	[bɑɹ]	bar

Schwa and Wedge

Schwa [ə]	Wedge [ʌ]
• used for unstressed vowels [əbawt] about • used for the words *the* and *a*	• used when there is some degree of stress on the vowel [sʌ́pɹ̩] supper • is not found before [ɹ] in the same syllable

Aspiration

p, t, k	Use [pʰ, tʰ, kʰ] for any 'p', 't', 'k' sound that occurs at the beginning of a syllable followed by a vowel that receives some degree of stress. [pʰæt] pat, [tʰɔt] taught, [kʰejk] cake [əpʰíɹ] appear, [ətʰǽk] attack
	Use [p, t, k] for any other 'p', 't', 'k' sound. [splæt] splat, [stɑp] stop, [skejt] skate

Canadian Raising

Most dialects in the United States do not have Canadian raising, although some do.

Phonetic Transcription: [aj] and [aw] before voiced consonants or when not followed by any consonant [bajd], [laj] bide and lie, [lawd], [baw] loud and bough [ʌy] and [ʌw] before voiceless consonants [bʌjt] bite, [lʌwt] lout
Phonemic Transcription: /aj/ and /aw/ in all environments

REMINDER

There are many dialectical differences in the pronunciation of vowels and syllabic consonants. For more details, go to **bedfordstmartins.com/linguistics/phonetics** and click on **American dialects.**

Practice 2.11: [tɹænskɹɪpʃn̩ ɛksɹ̩sajzəz]

Transcribe the following words as you would say them in normal everyday speech. Remember to include brackets, and remember to forget spelling. Watch out for syllabic consonants.

1. craft ________
2. sigh ________
3. health ________
4. beige ________
5. frog ________
6. paddle ________
7. angel ________
8. rich ________
9. tape ________
10. vague ________
11. rooster ________
12. instead ________
13. bottom ________
14. church ________
15. thought ________
16. had ________
17. exit ________
18. sugar ________
19. unit ________
20. question ________

Practice 2.12: Transcribing vowels

Remember that the tense mid vowels have an off-glide in phonetic transcription.

1. key ________
2. due ________
3. loaf ________
4. made ________
5. cheese ________
6. ate ________
7. wheeze ________
8. through ________
9. bone ________
10. east ________
11. baby ________
12. throw ________

Practice 2.13: Transcribing vowels before [ɹ]

This time watch out for vowels before [ɹ] sounds.

1. cheer ________
2. car ________
3. sir ________
4. oar ________
5. heart ________
6. sharp ________
7. there ________
8. star ________
9. her ________
10. horse ________
11. hard ________
12. shirt ________
13. chair ________
14. score ________
15. floor ________
16. course ________
17. harm ________
18. thwart ________

Practice 2.14: Diphthongs

Transcribe the following words as you would in normal everyday speech. Watch out for those diphthongs.

1. voice ________
2. hour ________
3. eyes ________
4. sight ________
5. prowl ________
6. knifed ________
7. trial ________
8. oily ________
9. prize ________
10. sigh ________
11. counter ________
12. down ________
13. bicycle ________
14. price ________
15. embroider ________
16. sighed ________
17. ice ________
18. joint ________

Remember: Transcription takes a lot of practice.

Practice 2.15: Schwa, wedge, and syllabic consonants

For this group, pay close attention to the schwa, wedge, and syllabic consonant sounds. You might want to determine which vowel gets primary stress to help you out. Remember to use syllabic consonants where necessary.

1. sludge ________
2. quality ________
3. luck ________
4. notice ________
5. thunder ________
6. behave ________
7. emphasis ________
8. announce ________
9. hung ________
10. oven ________
11. stuff ________
12. understand ________

Practice 2.16: Reading transcription

Give the correctly spelled English word for each of the following transcriptions.

1. [liʒɹ̩] ________
2. [æks] ________
3. [wɹ̩ði] ________
4. [wʌns] ________
5. [ʃejd] ________
6. [ʃaj] ________
7. [swit] ________
8. [t^{h}ub] ________
9. [ʧɔjs] ________
10. [mʌtn̩] ________
11. [p^{h}ajp] ________
12. [sɔfn̩] ________
13. [fowni] ________
14. [stæʧu] ________
15. [skwɛɹ] ________

Shared Phonetic Properties

Sounds are distinguished by their phonetic properties, but they can also share phonetic properties. Phonetic properties include such things as voice, place of articulation, manner of articulation, tongue height, and lip position.

PRACTICE 2.17: Shared phonetic properties

Each of the following groups of sounds contains at least one shared phonetic property. For each group of sounds, state the phonetic properties that the sounds have in common. Include as many as possible. The first is done for you.

1. [b, d, g] voiced (oral) stops
2. [v, d, m] ______________________
3. [s, ʧ, ʒ] ______________________
4. [j, ɹ, n] ______________________
5. [ɑ, o, ʊ] ______________________
6. [æ, ɪ, ɛ] ______________________

Groups of sounds that share phonetic properties are called **natural classes.**

Suprasegmentals (Section 8, pp. 37–43)

Suprasegmentals are inherent properties that are part of all sounds regardless of their place or manner of articulation. The three main suprasegmentals are **pitch**, **length**, and **stress**. Pitch is further divided into tone and intonation.

- Pitch: **Tone languages** are languages in which pitch movement is used to signal differences in meaning. Mandarin Chinese is a good example. Tone languages may use register and/or contour tones. A **register tone** is a level pitch, while a **contour tone** is a moving pitch.

  Intonation is pitch movement that is not related to differences in word meaning. For example, rising pitch is often used to signal a question or an incomplete utterance, and falling intonation a statement or a complete utterance.
- Length: Long vowels and consonants are sounds whose articulation simply takes longer relative to other vowels and consonants. Length is indicated with a [ː]. German is an example of a language having long and short vowels. Italian is an example of a language having long and short consonants.
- Stress: Stress is associated with vowels. Stressed vowels are vowels that are perceived as more prominent than other vowels. The most prominent vowel receives **primary stress**. Primary stress is usually indicated with a [´] placed over the vowel.

Articulatory Processes (Sections 9.2–9.3, pp. 43–48)

Articulatory processes describe articulatory adjustments that occur during speech. Processes typically function to make words easier to articulate. Processes also occur to make speech easier to perceive. The main types of processes are:

- Assimilation
- Dissimilation
- Deletion
- Epenthesis
- Metathesis
- Vowel reduction

The following boxes define and illustrate the different processes found in language.

Assimilation

Assimilation involves sounds changing to become more like nearby sounds. While there are many different kinds of assimilation, in general, assimilation can be divided into three main types:

1. Assimilation for voice:
   A sound takes on the same voice as a nearby sound.
   Includes: **voicing**, **devoicing**.

2. Assimilation for place of articulation:
   A sound takes on the same place of articulation as a nearby sound.
   Includes: palatalization, homorganic nasal assimilation, and more.

3. Assimilation for manner of articulation:
   A sound takes on the same manner of articulation as a nearby sound.
   Includes: **nasalization**, **flapping** (tapping), and more.

Note: Some types of assimilation, such as nasalization, can be either regressive or progressive. In **regressive assimilation**, a segment takes on some characteristic of the following segment. That is, a sound is influenced by what comes after it. In **progressive assimilation**, a segment takes on some characteristic of the preceding segment. That is, a sound is influenced by what comes before it.

Dissimilation

A sound changes to become less like a nearby sound so that the resulting sequence of sounds is easier to pronounce, e.g., *fifths* [fɪfθs] → [fɪfts].

Deletion

The process of deletion simply removes a sound from a phonetic context. Deletion frequently occurs in rapid speech, e.g., *fifths* [fɪfθs] → [fɪfs].

Epenthesis

The process of epenthesis adds a segment to a phonetic context. Epenthesis is common in casual speech, e.g., *warmth* [wɔɹmθ] → [wɔɹmpθ]

Metathesis

Metathesis is a process that changes the order of segments. Metathesis is common in the speech of young children, e.g., *coat* [kowt] → [towk].

Vowel Reduction

In vowel reduction, vowels move to a more central position when they are in unstressed syllables. That is, a vowel is pronounced as a full vowel when in a stressed syllable, and as a **schwa** when in an unstressed syllable.

Identifying processes: To identify processes, you need to look for differences between the starting and the ending pronunciation.

- If a sound is missing, **deletion** has occurred.
- If a sound has been added, **epenthesis** has occurred.
- If the order of sounds has changed, **metathesis** has occurred.
- If a sound has changed, you need to determine if either **assimilation** or **dissimilation** has occurred. To do this, follow these four steps:
  1. Determine the phonetic property that has changed (voice, place of articulation, or manner of articulation).
  2. Compare this phonetic property with the phonetic properties of the nearby sounds.
  3. If the changed phonetic property matches a phonetic property of a nearby sound, then **assimilation** has occurred. The phonetic property that matches will tell you the specific type of assimilation that has occurred.
  4. If the phonetic properties do not match, then **dissimilation** has occurred.

Remember: For assimilation, you also need to be able to identify when processes such as nasalization or place of articulation are regressive and when they are progressive. To determine this, you need to look at whether the influencing sound comes before (progressive) or after (regressive) the sound that is undergoing the change.

Consider the following example.

prince: [pɹɪns] → [pɹɪ̃nts]

In the above example, [t] occurs in the final pronunciation but not the starting; therefore, epenthesis has occurred. As well, [ɪ] has changed to [ɪ̃]. Remember that [˜] indicates a nasalized sound. The vowel has therefore changed from an oral to a nasal sound, and since the following sound is a nasal, assimilation—in particular, nasalization—has occurred. The influencing sound is the following nasal, meaning that the nasalization is regressive. So, the change in the pronunciation of the word *prince* from [pɹɪns] to [pɹɪ̃nts] involves two processes: epenthesis and regressive nasalization.

Practice 2.18: Identifying processes

Identify the process(es) at work in each of the following:

1. asterisk: [æstəɹɪsk] → [æstəɹɪks] ______
2. Peter: [pʰitɹ̩] → [pʰiɾɹ̩] ______
3. collards: [kɑlɹ̩dz] → [kɑljɹ̩dz] ______
4. good-bye: [gʊdbaj] → [gʊ̃mbaj] ______
5. sixths: [sɪksθs] → [sɪksts] ______

Review Exercises

1. For each part of the vocal tract, give its corresponding role in speech production.
   a. lungs ______
   b. larynx ______
   c. velum ______
2. Give the articulatory term describing sounds made at each of the following places of articulation.
   a. lips ______
   b. hard palate ______

c. uvula ______________________________

d. larynx ______________________________

3. Give the phonetic symbol for each of the following articulatory descriptions.

   a. [   ] voiceless glottal stop

   b. [   ] high front unrounded tense vowel

   c. [   ] voiced bilabial nasal

   d. [   ] voiceless labiodental fricative

4. Give the articulatory description that corresponds to each of the following phonetic symbols.

   a. [æ] ______________________________

   b. [v] ______________________________

   c. [j] ______________________________

   d. [ʌ] ______________________________

5. Give the phonetic symbol for the vowel sound in each of the following English words.

   a. stool ______________ d. pot ______________

   b. sight ______________ e. sit ______________

   c. meet ______________ f. put ______________

6. Transcribe the following words as you would say them in normal everyday speech. Mark primary stress.

   a. scorned ______________ f. duplicate ______________

   b. discover ______________ g. dictate ______________

   c. explosion ______________ h. occupied ______________

   d. genius ______________ i. informative ______________

   e. macaroni ______________ j. idolatry ______________

7. Transcribe the following words as you would say them in normal everyday speech. Pay special attention to vowels. Watch out; they get harder.

1. days	________	11. agitate	________	21. gnome	________
2. Xerox	________	12. roast	________	22. sixths	________
3. guess	________	13. thumb	________	23. masculine	________
4. yellow	________	14. bargain	________	24. precious	________
5. metal	________	15. machine	________	25. formula	________
6. unicycle	________	16. surrounded	________	26. comedy	________
7. extinguish	________	17. costume	________	27. graduate	________
8. popular	________	18. writer	________	28. irrigate	________
9. isolate	________	19. timetable	________	29. unforgivable	________
10. frighten	________	20. euphemism	________	30. called	________

8. For each of the following groups of sounds, circle the sound that does not belong and state a phonetic property that the remaining sounds share. There may be more than one possible answer.

   a. [f ð v m] ______________________________

   b. [d t n g] ______________________________

   c. [ɑ o ɪ u] ______________________________

9. Identify all the processes at work in each of the following:

   a. wash: [wɔʃ] → [wɔɹʃ] ______________________________

   b. winter: [wɪntɹ̩] → [wɪ̃nɹ̩] ______________________________

   c. clear: [kl̥iɹ] → [kəliɹ] ______________________________

   d. sandwich: [sændwɪʧ] → [sæ̃mwɪʧ] ______________________________

   e. animal: [ænɪml̩] → [æmɪ̃nl̩] ______________________________

☑ RECAP

Make sure you know the following material. (See also the Key Terms on pp. 50–51 of the main text.)

- the different parts of the vocal tract
- the difference between voiced and voiceless sounds
- the difference between nasal and oral sounds
- the characteristics of consonants, glides, and vowels
- the places and manners of articulation for consonant sounds
- the different tongue placements required to describe vowels
- the difference between tense and lax, and rounded and unrounded vowels
- the symbols and articulatory descriptions for English consonants
- the strident fricatives and affricates
- the symbols and articulatory descriptions for English vowels
- when and why aspiration occurs
- how to complete and decipher facial diagrams
- how to identify natural classes
- how to identify articulatory processes
- the suprasegmentals of tone, intonation, length, and stress
- transcription

Questions? Problems?

three

Phonology: The Function and Patterning of Sounds

Phonology is the study of how sounds vary and pattern in language. Following are some of the important topics and concepts covered in this chapter. Make sure you are familiar with them.

- Contrast
- Minimal pairs and near-minimal pairs
- Complementary distribution
- Phonemes and allophones
- Phonology problems
- Phonetic arid phonemic transcription
- Features
- Syllables
- Rules and statements
- Derivations and rule ordering

Since we will be dealing with many languages besides English, you will come across some phonetic symbols that have not yet been discussed. Articulatory descriptions will be provided for these unfamiliar sounds.

Contrast (Section 1, pp. 59–62)

Segments are said to **contrast** when their presence alone is responsible for forms having different meanings. Both consonant and vowel segments may contrast with each other. Which segments contrast with each other varies from language to language, as the following examples show.

	Language	Segments	Forms
Consonants	English	[kʰ] [g]	[kʰæp] 'cap' vs. [gæp] 'gap'
	Khmer	[kʰ] [k]	[kʰat] 'to polish' vs. [kat] 'to cut'
Vowels	English	[i] [æ]	[bit] 'beet' vs. [bæt] 'bat'
		[ow] [u]	[kʰowd] 'code' vs. [kʰud] 'cooed'
	Japanese	[i] [iː]	[toɽi] 'bird' vs. [toɽiː] 'shrine gate'
		[o] [oː]	[kibo] 'scale' vs. [kiboː] 'hope'

Determining which segments contrast is a first step in phonological analysis.

Minimal Pairs (Sections 1.1–1.2, pp. 59–62)

Minimal pairs are defined as two phonetic forms that differ by one segment that is in the same position in both forms, which causes the forms to have different meanings. Minimal pairs tell us that sounds contrast.

PRACTICE 3.1: Recognizing minimal pairs

For each of the following, answer Yes if the paired words constitute a minimal pair and No if they do not. Make sure you pay attention to the meanings given in single quotation marks.

1.	[bækt]	'towel'	and	[pækd]	'cloth'	________________
2.	[ʧogʊr]	'necklace'	and	[ʧogʊl]	'bracelet'	________________
3.	[telʌm]	'book'	and	[tɛlʌm]	'book'	________________
4.	[kətɑge]	'letter'	and	[kətage]	'paper'	________________

PRACTICE 3.2: Minimal pairs in English

For each of the following pairs of English consonant phonemes, find two minimal pairs. Wherever possible, one pair should show one contrast in initial position and the other pair in final position. The first pair is done for you. Don't be fooled by spelling.

1.	/ p : b /	paste : baste	rope : robe
2.	/ t : d /	________________	________________
3.	/ k : g /	________________	________________
4.	/ f : v /	________________	________________
5.	/ s : z /	________________	________________
6.	/ m : n /	________________	________________
7.	/ ɹ : l /	________________	________________
8.	/ t : θ /	________________	________________
9.	/ ʧ : ʤ /	________________	________________
10.	/ p : f /	________________	________________

Complementary Distribution (Section 2.1, pp. 62–63)

Not all segments found in a language contrast with each other. Some segments are in **complementary distribution**. Two phonetically similar segments are in complementary distribution when they never occur in the same phonetic **environment**. The term *environment* refers to the phonetic context in which the segments occur.

The following example will help illustrate the nature of complementary distribution.

Environment:		Before Nasals	After Nasals	Before Oral Sounds
English	Nasal Vowels	YES	NO	NO
	Oral Vowels	NO	YES	YES
Scots Gaelic	Nasal Vowels	YES	YES	NO
	Oral Vowels	NO	NO	YES

In English, nasal and oral vowels are in complementary distribution. Nasal vowels only occur before nasal consonants, while oral vowels occur after nasal consonants and also before oral sounds. Oral vowels are designated as occurring elsewhere, since there are always more oral sounds than nasal sounds in a language.

In Scots Gaelic, nasal and oral vowels are also in complementary distribution, but this distribution is different from what is found in English. In Scots Gaelic, nasal vowels occur both before and after nasal consonants, and oral vowels occur before oral sounds. However, nasal vowels may occur before oral sounds, but only if they are preceded by a nasal consonant.

As you can see, the occurrence of nasal and oral vowels in both English and Scots Gaelic is predictable.

Native speakers of a language think of segments that are in complementary distribution as instances of the same sound. Linguists say that these segments are phonetically different, since they have different articulations. However, for native speakers, since the segments do not contrast and since they occur in predictable environments, they are phonologically the same segment.

Practice 3.3: Complementary distribution in English

1. The English phoneme /p/ has (at least) three phonetic variants: [p] — unaspirated
   [p^h] — aspirated
   [p˺] — unreleased

   The following lists of words give examples of each phonetic variant.

[p]	[pʰ]	[p̚]
sport spirit operate nippy happening	pick poetry appear repair	collapse apt flipped ape mop clap

On the following chart, put a check in the box if the phonetic variant can occur in that environment. Explanations of the different environments are given below.

	#_____	_____#	s_____	_____C	V́_____V	V_____V́
[p]						
[pʰ]						
[p̚]						

Explanations of environments:

#_____ word-initial position

_____# word-final position

s_____ after [s]

_____C before a consonant

V́_____V between vowels, where the first vowel is stressed.

V_____V́ between vowels, where the second vowel is stressed.

2. The English phoneme /l/ has (at least) three phonetic variants: [l] — alveolar l
[ɫ] — velarized l
[l̩] — syllabic l

The following lists of words give examples of each phonetic variant.

[l]	[ɫ]	[l̩]
lip love allow malign slip slide	swallow silly salt ilk pull meal	paddle obstacle twinkle hassle bushel hurdle

On the following chart, put a check in the box if the phonetic variant can occur in that environment. Explanations of the different environments are given below.

	#___	C___V	V___#	C___#	___C	V́___V	V___V́
[l]							
[ɫ]							
[l̥]							

Explanations of environments:

#_____	word-initial position
C_____V	between a consonant and a vowel
V_____#	word-final after a vowel
C_____#	word-final after a consonant
_____C	before a consonant
V́_____V	between vowels, where the first vowel is stressed
V_____V́	between vowels, where the second vowel is stressed

PRACTICE 3.4: Complementary distribution in other languages

1. **Oneida:** Examine the following data from Oneida. Using the following chart, determine if the sounds [s] and [z] are or are not in complementary distribution. Note that [sh] represents [s] and [h], not [ʃ].

[s]		[z]	
[lashet]	'let him count'	[kawenezuzeʔ]	'long words'
[laʔsluni]	'white men'	[khaiize]	'I'm taking it along'
[loteswatu]	'he's been playing'	[lazel]	'let him drag it'
[skahnehtat]	'one pine tree'	[tahazehteʔ]	'he dropped it'
[thiskate]	'a different one'	[tuzahatiteni]	'they changed it'
[sninuhe]	'you buy'	[wezake]	'she saw you'
[wahsnestakeʔ]	'you ate corn'		

	#_____	_____C	C_____	V_____V
[s]				
[z]				

2. **Oneida:** Now determine if the sounds [s] and [ʃ] are or are not in complementary distribution. Again, [sh] represents [s] and [h], not [ʃ]. Hint: Look at specific vowels or consonants in the environment.

[s]		[ʃ]	
[lashet]	'let him count'	[ʃjatuheʔ]	'you write'
[laʔsluni]	'white men'	[tehʃjaʔk]	'let you break'
[loteswatu]	'he's been playing'	[jaʔteʃjatekhahʃjahteʔ]	'they would suddenly separate again'
[skahnehtat]	'one pine tree'		
[thiskate]	'a different one'		
[sninuhe]	'you buy'		
[wahsnestakeʔ]	'you ate corn'		

3. **Japanese:** Examine the following data from Japanese, and determine if the sounds [t], [ʦ], and [ʧ] are or are not in complementary distribution. Set up a chart to help you. Hint: You may want to look at specific vowels in the linguistic environment.

The symbol [ʦ] is a single segment representing a voiceless alveolar affricate.

1.	[taijoː]	'the sun'	10.	[ʧigai]	'difference'
2.	[tatami]	'mat'	11.	[ʧiɽi]	'dust'
3.	[tambo]	'rice paddy'	12.	[iʧigo]	'strawberry'
4.	[buta]	'pig'	13.	[deguʧi]	'exit'
5.	[gaitoː]	'cloak, overcoat'	14.	[iɽiguθi]	'entrance'
6.	[koto]	'fact'	15.	[ʦunami]	'tidal wave'
7.	[tegami]	'letter'	16.	[ʦukue]	'desk'
8.	[totemo]	'very'	17.	[doːbuʦu]	'animal'
9.	[ʧiɲɲi]	'truly'	18.	[zaʦuzi]	'chores'

Phonemes and Allophones (Section 2.2, pp. 63–64)

Phonemes and allophones are two units of representation used in phonology. These are used to capture native-speaker knowledge about how sounds behave in that language.

Phoneme refers to:

- the way in which the sounds are stored in the mind
- all "members" of the language's sound system
- underlying representation

Allophone refers to:

- the way in which the sounds are pronounced
- the individual members of the language's sound system
- surface representation

REMINDER

Don't forget that phonemes are indicated with / / slashes and allophones with [ ] brackets.

Solving Phonology Problems (Appendix, pp. 99–101)

The basic goal in solving a phonology problem is to determine if the sounds being examined belong to one phoneme or to separate phonemes.

When allophones belong to separate phonemes, they are:

1. Contrastive/distinctive
2. In unpredictable distribution
3. Easily perceived as different by native speakers
4. Not necessarily phonetically similar

When allophones belong to the same phoneme, they are:

1. Noncontrastive/rule-governed
2. In predictable distribution
3. Not easily perceived as different by native speakers
4. Always phonetically similar

Problem-Solving Flowchart

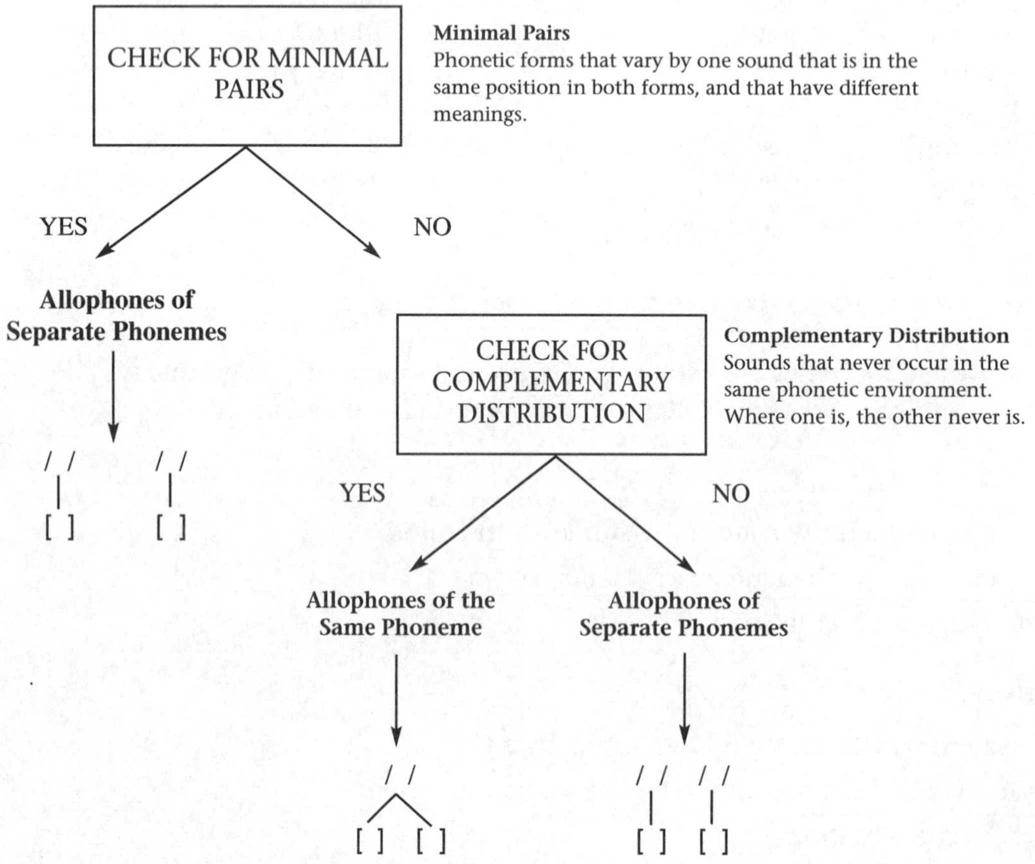

Repeat the above for each pair of sounds you are investigating.

Practice 3.5: Distinguishing phonemes and allophones

1. **Arabic:** [h] and [ʔ]

1. [ʔuruːb]	'wars'	5. [huruːb]	'flight'
2. [fahm]	'understanding'	6. [faʔm]	'coal'
3. [habba]	'gust, squall'	7. [ʔabba]	'grain, seed'
4. [haːl]	'cardamom'	8. [ʔaːl]	'condition'

2. **Biblical Hebrew:** [d] and [ð]
[ɣ] represents a voiced velar fricative.
[ʕ] represents a voiced pharyngeal fricative.
[x] represents a voiceless velar fricative.

1. [gaðol]	'great'	6. [ʕɛvɛð]	'servant'
2. [damim]	'blood'	7. [daɣeʃ]	'piercing'
3. [bɛɣɛð]	'garment'	8. [jəhuða]	'Judah'
4. [ʔaðam]	'man'	9. [xɛsɛð]	'steadfast love'
5. [davar]	'word'	10. [dawið]	'David'

3. **German:** [ç] and [χ]
[ç] represents a voiceless palatal fricative.
[χ] represents a voiceless uvular fricative.
[ʁ] represents a voiced uvular fricative.

1. [naχ]	'to, after'	6. [dɔχ]	'yet'
2. [çemi]	'chemistry'	7. [kɪʁçə]	'church'
3. [dɪç]	'you'	8. [aχaːt]	'agate'
4. [maχt]	'power'	9. [ʁɛçnən]	'to count'
5. [ʁɛçt]	'right'	10. [nɔχ]	'still, yet'

4. **Zinacantec Tzotzil:** [p] and [p'], [k] and [k']
Zinacantec Tzotzil is a Mayan language of Mexico.
[p'] represents a glottalized sound, made with simultaneous closure of the glottis and constriction of the throat.
[k'] represents a glottalized sound, made with simultaneous closure of the glottis and constriction of the throat.

1. [pim]	'thick'	7. [p'in]	'pot'
2. [bikil]	'intestines'	8. [bik'it]	'small'
3. [ka]	'particle'	9. [kok]	'my leg'
4. [nopol]	'nearby'	10. [p'ol]	'to multiply'
5. [p'us]	'hunchback'	11. [k'ok']	'fire'
6. [k'a]	'horse'	12. [pus]	'jail'

PRACTICE 3.6: More practice with phonemes and allophones

The following pages contain data sets from a number of different languages (some of the data may have been regularized). Each data set contains sufficient data to make valid conclusions about the sounds under consideration. For each data set:

- state your conclusion (i.e., allophones of the same phoneme or of separate phonemes)
- provide evidence to support your conclusion
- provide a representation of the phoneme(s)

1. **English: Long and short vowels**

   [Vː] When a colon-like symbol follows a vowel, it means that the vowel is long. This means that we take a longer time saying the vowel; do not confuse this use of the term *long vowel* with what you may have learned in elementary school (where the term referred to a vowel that sounds like the name of the letter).

1.	[gɪft]	'gift'
2.	[ɹɑːbd]	'robbed'
3.	[lʌk]	'luck'
4.	[moːwd]	'mowed'
5.	[slæpt]	'slapped'
6.	[mejs]	'mace'
7.	[hʌːg]	'hug'
8.	[nowt]	'note'
9.	[gɪːv]	'give'
10.	[sliːz]	'sleaze'
11.	[pɑt]	'pot'
12.	[kɹæːb]	'crab'

You could treat each vowel individually. However, it will be more efficient if you treat long vowels as a class. Assume that English has either short and corresponding long vowels as separate phonemes, or short and corresponding long vowels as allophones of the same phonemes.

2. **Korean:** [l] and [ɾ]

   [ʉ] represents a high central rounded vowel.

1.	[kal]	'dog'	10.	[onelppam]	'tonight'
2.	[kenel]	'shade'	11.	[silkwa]	'fruit'
3.	[iɾumi]	'name'	12.	[mul]	'water'
4.	[kiɾi]	'road'	13.	[seul]	'Seoul'
5.	[juŋutʃʉm]	'receipt'	14.	[kəɾiɾo]	'to the street'
6.	[pal]	'leg'	15.	[saɾam]	'person'
7.	[ilkop]	'seven'	16.	[tatʉl]	'all of them'
8.	[ipalsa]	'barber'	17.	[vəɾʉm]	'summer'
9.	[uɾi]	'we'			

3. **Inuktitut:** [k] and [q]
   [q] represents a voiceless uvular stop.
   (Note: Assume a relatively broad transcription as far as vowels are concerned.)

1. [qisik]	'sealskin'	7. [imaq]	'water'
2. [kamik]	'sealskin boots'	8. [tuvaq]	'sea ice'
3. [gimmik]	'dog, Huskie'	9. [savik]	'snow knife'
4. [iqaluk]	'fish'	10. [qukiut]	'gun, rifle'
5. [amaruq]	'Arctic wolf'	11. [nukaq]	'younger sibling'
6. [tasiq]	'lake'	12. [saku]	'harpoon head'

(To hear audio files of these words, go to **shindale.com/inuktitut**.)

4. **English:** [g], [g^j] and [g^w]

   [g^j] represents a fronted [g], made with the back of the tongue at or near the hard palate.
   [g^w] represents a rounded [g], made with simultaneous lip rounding.

1. [gɔn]	'gone'	7. [g^{j}ik]	'geek'
2. [g^{w}ufi]	'goofy'	8. [igɹ̩]	'eager'
3. [gli]	'glee'	9. [gejm]	'game'
4. [slʌg]	'slug'	10. [gowfɹ̩]	'gopher'
5. [gɹin]	'green'	11. [gæʤət]	'gadget'
6. [ɹæg^{w}u]	'Ragu'	12. [g^{j}is]	'geese'

5. **Yakut:** [i], [ɨ], [y] and [u]
   Yakut is a Turkic language of northeastern Siberia.
   [ɨ] represents a high central unrounded vowel.
   [y] represents a high front rounded vowel.

   For these sounds to be allophones of separate phonemes, you must find a minimal pair for:

   - [i] and [ɨ]
   - [i] and [y]
   - [i] and [u]
   - [ɨ] and [y]
   - [ɨ] and [u]
   - [y] and [u]

   You may use the same data item in more than one pair.

1. [bit]	'mark'	8. [ɨt]	'shoot'
2. [il]	'peace'	9. [tys]	'descend'
3. [sil]	'saliva'	10. [byt]	'end'
4. [kir]	'nibble'	11. [sur]	'gray'
5. [tɨs]	'paw'	12. [kur]	'belt'
6. [ɨk]	'wring'	13. [uk]	'insert'
7. [sɨl]	'year'	14. [tus]	'directly'

Phonetic and Phonemic Transcription (Section 3, pp. 69–72)

As we learned in the last chapter, phonetic transcription is a **phonetic representation** of normal, everyday speech. That is, it is a representation of pronunciation. Phonetic transcription is always indicated with [ ] brackets. In this chapter, we have been learning about phonemes, which represent the knowledge a native speaker has about how sounds pattern in his or her language. We can represent this knowledge using **phonemic transcription**. Phonemic transcription, as the name suggests, contains the phonemes of the language and is always indicated with / / slashes.

Since there are two levels of representation (phonetic and phonemic), a language will have two inventories of sounds. The phonetic inventory contains the allophones of the language, while the phonemic inventory contains the phonemes of the language. Allophones are used to transcribe phonetically, and phonemes are used to transcribe phonemically.

To understand the difference between phonetic and phonemic transcription, let's reconsider the English problem concerning allophones of /g/ on p. 45. Remember that in English, [g], [gʷ], and [gʲ] are allophones of the same phoneme, with [gʲ] occurring before front vowels, [gʷ] occurring before back vowels, and [g] occurring elsewhere. Given this information, we can convert English phonetic transcription into English phonemic transcription:

Phonetic	Phonemic	
[gʷufi]	/gufi/	'goofy'
[gʲik]	/gik/	'geek'
[slʌg]	/slʌg/	'slug'

Notice that in the phonemic transcription, only the phoneme /g/ has been used, while in the phonetic transcription, the allophones [gʲ] and [gʷ] have both been used, along with [g]. Also notice that in the phonetic transcription, [gʲ] occurs only before front vowels, and [gʷ] occurs only before back vowels, while in phonemic transcription, /g/ occurs in all environments.

Remember: The main difference between phonetic and phonemic transcription is that

- phonetic transcription includes both predictable and unpredictable phonetic information, while
- phonemic transcription includes only the unpredictable information. Anything that is predictable is excluded.

Practice 3.7: Phonemic transcription

To practice phonemic transcription, return to the phonology problems in Practice 3.6, and wherever allophones of the same phoneme were found, convert the first few words in the data set from the phonetic transcription provided into phonemic transcription. Identify the predictable phonetic property that is missing from the phonemic transcription.

Features (Section 4, pp. 72–83)

Features represent individual properties of a sound. Features are usually divided into four groups as follows:

- Major class features
  [+/–consonantal], [+/–syllabic], [+/–sonorant]
- Manner features
  [+/–continuant], [+/–delayed release (DR)], [+/–nasal], [+/–lateral]
- Laryngeal features
  [+/–voice], [+/–spread glottis (SG)], [+/–constricted glottis (CG)]
- Place features
  [LABIAL], [+/–round]
  [CORONAL], [+/–anterior], [+/–strident]
  [DORSAL], [+/–high], [+/–low], [+/–back], [+/–tense], [+/–reduced]

Since features represent articulation, they are always enclosed in phonetic (i.e., [ ]) brackets.

Except for [LABIAL], [CORONAL], and [DORSAL], all features are binary and are specified as either plus or minus. [LABIAL], [CORONAL], and [DORSAL] are used to represent the articulator that is active in executing the articulation:

- [LABIAL] for the lips;
- [CORONAL] for the tongue tip or blade; and
- [DORSAL] for the body of the tongue.

All other place features have plus and minus specifications. These features are used to represent place of articulation features specific to the active articulator. That is, labial sounds are [+/–round]; coronal sounds are [+/–anterior] and [+/–strident]; and dorsal sounds are [+/–high], [+/–low], [+/–back], [+/–tense] and [+/–reduced].

Features are used:

- **To represent sounds.** Features represent phonetic properties, and sounds are simply a number of phonetic properties executed simultaneously. Sounds, therefore, are composed of features. Features can be used to describe both vowels and consonants. See Tables 3.25 and 3.26 on pages 76–83 in the text for how to determine the features making up a sound, as well as pages 82–83 for feature charts of English vowels and consonants. To see an interactive chart with features, go to **bedfordstmartins.com/linguistics/phonology** and click on **IPA vowels and consonants**.

- **To capture natural classes. Natural classes** are groups of sounds that share a feature or features, or that pattern together in a sound system. For example, voiceless stops can be considered a natural class, as can rounded vowels.

- **To understand the nature of allophonic variation.** For example, voiceless sounds often change and become voiced when near other voiced sounds. This can be captured with a single feature.

PRACTICE 3.8: Features

1. State the feature that distinguishes each of the following pairs of sounds. (There may be more than one correct answer.) The first one is done for you.

   a. [θ] / [ð] ______[+/–voice]______

   b. [p] / [f] ____________

   c. [s] / [θ] ____________

   d. [b] / [m] ____________

   e. [ʧ] / [ʃ] ____________

2. Each of the following sets contains three sounds that belong to the same natural class. Add one other segment to each set, making sure that the natural class is preserved. Indicate the feature (including its value) that distinguishes the natural class. The first one is done for you.

	Segment Added	Distinctive Feature
a. [l̩ ə n̩]	[o]	[+ syllabic]
b. [θ s f]	[ ]	____________
c. [p m k]	[ ]	____________
d. [j ɹ n]	[ ]	____________
e. [ð f s]	[ ]	____________

3. Name the natural class that each of the following phonetic matrices describes.

   a. [–consonantal, –syllabic]

   b. [+consonantal, –syllabic, –sonorant, +continuant, +voice]

4. In each of the following sets, all the sounds except one belong to the same natural class. Draw a circle around the sound that does not belong, and state the feature that the remaining sounds share.

a. [t g v ʤ] ______________________

b. [j m ʒ w] ______________________

c. [m g d ɹ] ______________________

d. [ʧ m t ŋ] ______________________

5. In each of the following systems, some segments are boxed. Determine if the boxed segments constitute a natural class. If they do, state the feature(s) that make them a natural class.

a.

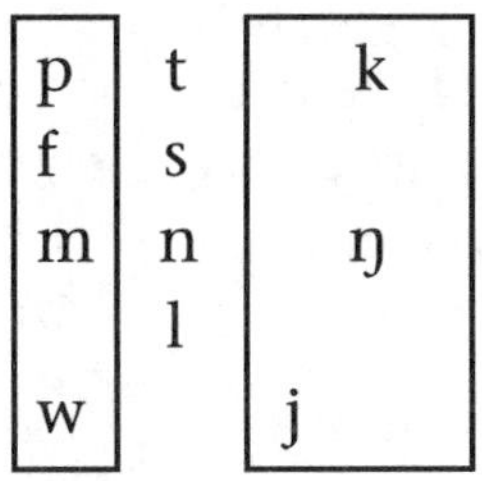

b.

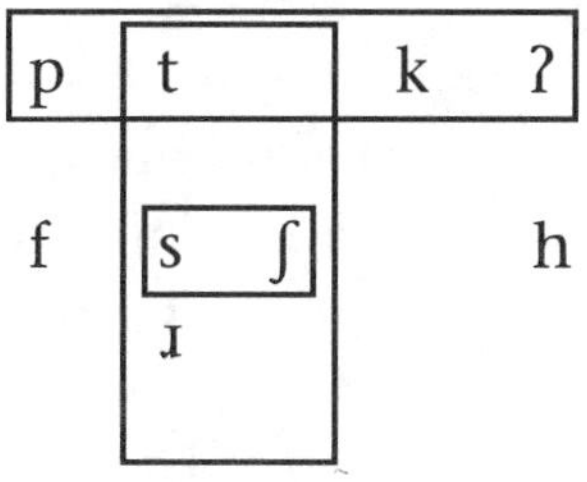

c.

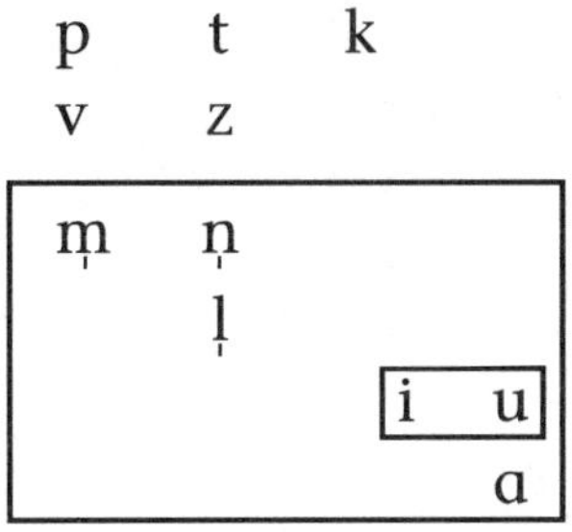

d.

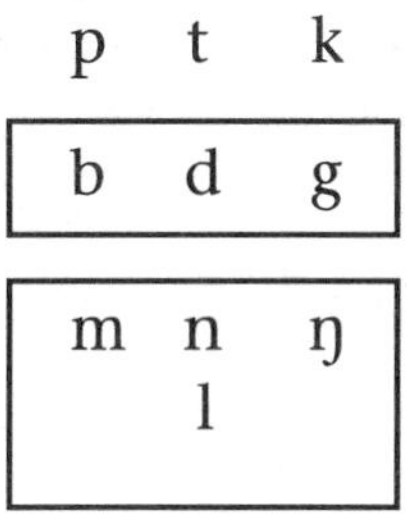

6. For each of the following groups of sounds, provide a feature matrix for features shared by the group. Then tell which feature or features distinguish individual sounds in the group from each other.

a. [ð θ f v]

b. [g ʤ]

c. [u o]

d. [i ɪ e ɛ æ]

Syllables (Section 5, pp. 83–91)

A **syllable** is a unit of representation consisting of one or more segments. There are four pieces of information crucial to understanding syllables, their structure, and their role in phonology. Make sure you know them.

- **Syllables** (Section 5.1, pp. 83–85). A syllable consists of a **sonorant** element (typically a vowel or syllabic consonant) and any associated less sonorous elements (typically consonants). Vowels usually form the core of the syllable, as they are the most sonorant type of sound. The core of a syllable is called the **nucleus**. **Onsets** are less sonorant segment(s) that occur before the nucleus, while **codas** are less sonorant segment(s) occurring after the nucleus.

- **Syllable Structure** (Section 5.1, pp. 83–85). Syllables have internal structure, which is represented above the individual segments making up the syllable. A syllable (σ) consists of an optional onset (O) and an obligatory **rhyme** (R). Rhymes consist of a nucleus (N) and an optional coda (Co).

- **Phonotactics** (Sections 5.2–5.3, pp. 85–87). Phonotactics is the set of constraints on which segments can occur together. For example, in English, [pl] is an acceptable onset, as in the word *please,* but [pn] is not an acceptable onset: words in English do not begin with this combination of sounds. Phonotactics can vary from language to language.

- **Syllable representations** (Section 5.4, pp. 87–89). When diagrammed, syllables are represented above the segments making them up. In this sense, they are **suprasegmental** units. There are three, and sometimes four, steps to putting together a representation of a syllable. These are illustrated below for the word *template.* Note that we are starting with phonemic transcription.

First: Assign the nucleus, the rhyme, and the syllable node. Vowels (including diphthongs) and syllabic consonants may occupy the nucleus position. Diphthongs are often diagrammed as a branching nucleus.

Second: Assign the onset. These are the segments to the left of the nucleus. Segments assigned to the onset are usually the largest sequence of sounds that can occur at the beginning of a syllable within a language.

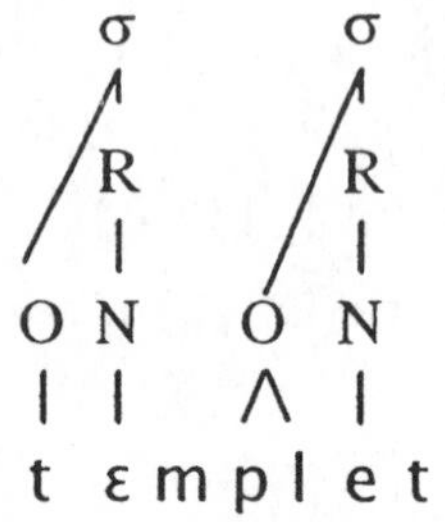

Third: Assign the coda. These are the segments to the right of the nucleus, which have not yet been syllabified into an onset.

Open syllables have no coda, while **closed syllables** have a coda.

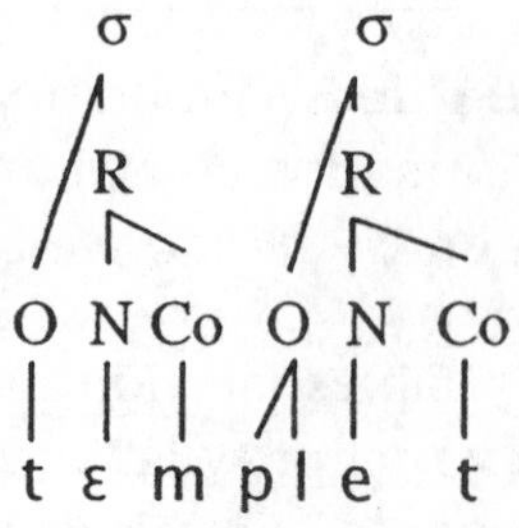

Fourth: As you can see from the representation being constructed, words can consist of a number of syllables. The last step in constructing syllabic representations simply involves combining syllables into words.

This step, however, is frequently omitted.

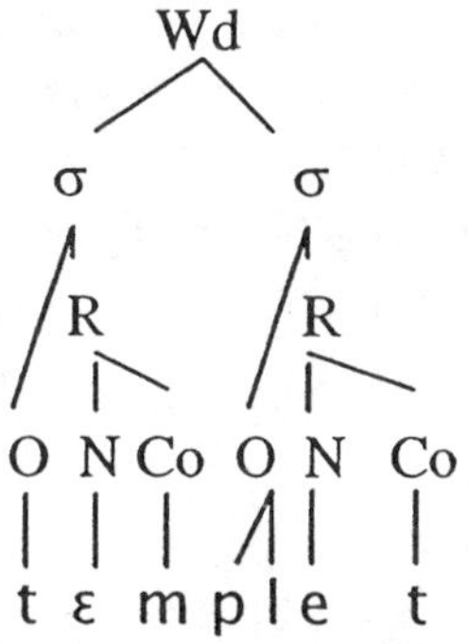

Practice 3.9: Syllables in English

Construct a syllable representation for each of the following English words. Remember to put them into phonemic transcription first. Underline all open syllables.

1. publish
2. downtown
3. banana
4. trombone
5. sprightly
6. beauty
7. lovely
8. satisfy
9. prompt

REMINDER

- Assign onsets before codas. This reflects a universal preference in language for onsets over codas.
- A syllable does not have to have either an onset or a coda. A syllable, however, must have a nucleus and therefore also a rhyme.

Variation in Syllable Structure: Syllable structure can vary from language to language, yet the process for building syllable representation, as outlined above, can still be used.

Practice 3.10: Syllable structure in other languages

In the following language data, all syllables have the structure CV(C). This means that all syllables begin with an onset, but they do not have to have a coda. That is, codas are optional. Construct syllable representations for the following words. The data are already in phonetic transcription.

1.	2.	3.
/z i ʧ n o/ 'chair'	/t a g k u/ 'shell'	/s e d n a k u/ 'sofa'

Syllables and Phonology: Syllables are often relevant to stating generalizations about the distribution of allophones. For example, English aspirated stops are found at the beginning of stressed syllables, and unaspirated stops are found elsewhere. Similarly, phonetic length is predictable in English: vowels are long when followed by a voiced **obstruent** in the coda position of the same syllable.

PRACTICE 3.11: Syllables and phonology

The following data are from the same language as above. In this language, stress is predictable and is marked by a [´] over a vowel. By making reference to syllable structure, determine where stress occurs.

Hint: You might want to first syllabify some of the words using the syllabification procedure from above.

1.	[fémba]	'foot'	8.	[póbzuʤi]	'lizard'
2.	[hagút]	'month'	9.	[gaʧótfobi]	'knee'
3.	[fezók]	'music'	10.	[talagubiták]	'cowboy'
4.	[waláp]	'mole'	11.	[páfzuliha]	'thin'
5.	[supóspa]	'gravy'	12.	[kéllaboga]	'arm'
6.	[tugábʧo]	'stone'			
7.	[jumajumáp]	'armadillo with cherry sauce'			

Rules and Statements (Section 6.1, pp. 92–95)

To understand and be able to put together rules and statements whenever your analysis uncovers allophones of the same phoneme, you need to remember that:

- Rules and statements capture the distribution of allophones that are in complementary distribution. Rules and statements convey the same information, the difference being that rules use phonological notation, while statements use articulatory descriptions. Since sound changes usually affect classes of sounds rather than individual sounds, we try to make our rules and statements as general as possible.
- Allophones in complementary distribution represent a predictable sound change. Such sound changes occur because segments are often affected by the phonetic characteristics of neighboring sounds. These changes are described using articulatory processes such as assimilation. Rules and statements, therefore, are also descriptions of these articulatory processes.

Rules and statements have three parts:

1. the phoneme
2. the allophone (what the change is)
3. the phonetic environment (where the change occurs)

PRACTICE 3.12: Rules and statements

1. Convert these statements into rules. Watch out for natural classes.

   a. Voiced oral stops become voiceless at the beginning of words.

   ____

   b. Alveopalatal affricates become fricatives between vowels.

   ____

   c. Vowels become nasalized before nasals.

   ____

   d. Schwa is deleted word-finally.

   ____

   e. A schwa is inserted between a voiceless bilabial stop and a voiced lateral liquid.

   ____

2. Convert the following rules into statements.

   a. $t \longrightarrow t^{ʔ} \quad / \quad ʔ\_\_\_$

   ____

   b. $\begin{Bmatrix} f \\ s \\ θ \\ ʃ \end{Bmatrix} \longrightarrow \begin{Bmatrix} v \\ z \\ ð \\ ʒ \end{Bmatrix} \quad / \quad V\_\_\_V$

   ____

   c. $\begin{Bmatrix} i \\ e \end{Bmatrix} \longrightarrow \begin{Bmatrix} ɪ \\ ɛ \end{Bmatrix} \quad / \quad \_\_\_\#$

   ____

d. $\begin{Bmatrix} p \\ t \\ k \end{Bmatrix} \longrightarrow \begin{Bmatrix} p^h \\ t^h \\ k^h \end{Bmatrix} \quad / \quad \#\_\_\_\acute{V}$

---

3. Go back over the rules given (not the statements you constructed) in exercise 2, and formulate them using feature matrices rather than phonetic symbols. Do the same for the rules you constructed (not the statements given) in exercise 1.

Practice 3.13: Discovering rules

For each of the following problems, decide what phonological process is in operation. Write a rule that captures the process.

1. **Polish: Voiced and voiceless stops**
   Voiced and voiceless stops are separate phonemes in Polish.

1. [klup]	'club'	7. [klubi]	'clubs'
2. [trup]	'corpse'	8. [trupi]	'corpses'
3. [trut]	'labor'	9. [trudi]	'labors'
4. [kot]	'cat'	10. [koti]	'cats'
5. [wuk]	'lye'	11. [wugi]	'lyes'
6. [sok]	'juice'	12. [soki]	'juices'

2. **South Midland and Southern American English:** [ɪ] and [ɛ]
   In some areas of the United States the phonemes [ɪ] and [ɛ] have merged in certain words. Write a rule to explain it.

1. [bɪn]	'Ben'	7. [sɪt]	'sit'
2. [pʰɪn]	'pin'	8. [sɪnt]	'cent'
3. [bɛt]	'bet'	9. [ɹɛk]	'wreck'
4. [bɪt]	'bit'	10. [hɪm]	'hem'
5. [pʰɪn]	'pen'	11. [hɛlow]	'hello'
6. [sɛt]	'set'	12. [hɪm]	'hymn'

REMINDER

When you find allophones of the same phoneme, there is a quick way to determine if your solution is in all likelihood correct. If your rule and statement describe an articulatory process such as assimilation, which is the result of neighboring sounds interacting with each other, then your solution is probably correct. If your rule and statement do not describe such a process, then you might want to rethink your analysis.

Derivations (Sections 6.2–6.3, pp. 95–97)

Derivations are a representation of how phonemes and allophones are related. Phonetic forms are derived from phonemic forms by applying rules. There are three parts to a derivation. These parts are very similar to the components of a **phonological rule**.

- **Underlying representation (UR).** The underlying representation is a representation of native speaker knowledge and therefore is always in phonemic transcription.
- **Rules.** Remember that phonemes and allophones are linked by a rule. The rule applies to change the phoneme into the allophone. This, of course, only occurs when the structural description (environment) specified in the rule is found in the underlying representation.
- **Phonetic representation (PR).** The phonetic representation is also called the **surface representation**. Since the surface representation always represents pronunciation, it is in phonetic transcription.

Recall from discussions that in English, liquids become voiceless after a voiceless stop at the beginning of a syllable. This is an example of devoicing, and it can be captured with a rule such as:

Liquid devoicing:

$$\begin{bmatrix} -\text{syllabic} \\ +\text{consonantal} \\ +\text{sonorant} \\ +\text{voice} \\ -\text{nasal} \end{bmatrix} \rightarrow [-\text{voice}] \;/\; \sigma \begin{bmatrix} -\text{syllabic} \\ +\text{consonantal} \\ -\text{sonorant} \\ -\text{continuant} \\ -\text{voice} \\ -\text{delayed release} \end{bmatrix} \underline{\qquad\qquad}$$

The first feature **matrix** captures the class of liquids. The second part of the rule captures the change in voicing that occurs. The third part of the rule captures that the rule only applies after a voiceless stop at the beginning of a syllable. Recall that σ is used to indicate a syllable.

The following derivation captures the relationship between English voiced and voiceless liquids as shown by the above rule.

UR	# pliz #	'please'	# læf #	'laugh'
Liquid devoicing	# pl̥iz #		____	
PR	[pl̥iz]		[læf]	

In the word *please,* liquid devoicing applies because [l] occurs after a voiceless consonant (i.e., [p]). The structural description of the rule has been met. Notice that after the rule has applied, [l] has become voiceless (i.e., [l̥]). The rule does not apply to the word *laugh,* as indicated by the line, since the structural description necessary for the rule to apply was not met: [l] occurs at the beginning of the word and not after a voiceless consonant. The phonetic form, therefore, remains the same as the underlying form.

Rule Ordering (Section 6.3, pp. 96–97)

More than one rule can apply during the derivation of a particular form. Sometimes the order in which rules apply is crucial to deriving the appropriate phonetic form. That is, one rule must apply before another because the application of one rule creates the environment for the second. A good example of this relationship involves the rule of liquid devoicing (from p. 93) and the rule of schwa deletion presented below.

Schwa deletion: $[ə] \rightarrow \emptyset \; / \; C_{\emptyset} \_\_\_ \; \sigma \; C_{\emptyset} \; \underset{[+\text{stress}]}{V}$

The first and second parts of the rule refer to the deletion of schwa. The third part of the rule captures that this occurs only when schwa is in an open syllable followed by a stressed syllable. The first $C_{\emptyset}$ represents any number of successive onset consonants from zero up that may occur before schwa. σ represents the syllable boundary, and the second $C_{\emptyset}$ again represents any onset consonants that may occur before the stressed vowel of the next syllable.

The Incorrect Order: Schwa deletion must apply before liquid devoicing. If liquid devoicing is applied before schwa deletion, then liquids incorrectly remain voiced in the phonetic form. This is shown in the following derivation of the word *collapse.*

UR	# kəlǽps #	'collapse'
Liquid devoicing	———	
Schwa deletion	# klǽps #	
PR	[klǽps]	

(Note: It is assumed that stress placement has already occurred. Normally, stress would not be present in the underlying form because it is predictable in English, and therefore it would be applied using a stress rule.)

The Correct Order: Since liquids in English are produced without voice following a voiceless stop, schwa deletion must occur first so that in the resulting output, liquids occur after voiceless stops, creating the necessary environment for liquid devoicing to apply.

UR	# kəlǽps #	'collapse'
Schwa deletion	# klǽps #	
Liquid devoicing	# kl̥ǽps #	
PR	[kl̥ǽps]	

As shown in the above derivation, the phonetic form now contains, as it should in English, a voiceless liquid.

> **REMINDER**
>
> Underlying representations capture the phonological knowledge speakers have about the contrastive sounds of their language. Therefore, these representations are always in phonemic transcription, which does not contain any predictable phonetic information.
>
> Since surface representations capture actual phonetic outputs, they are always in phonetic transcription. That is, they contain all of the predictable phonetic information not found in the underlying representation.
>
> Articulatory processes, in the form of rules, apply to add predictable phonetic information to the underlying representation, thereby creating the surface representation.

Practice 3.14: Rules and derivations

1. **Tamil:** [p] and [b], [k] and [g], [ʈ] and [ɖ], [t̪] and [d̪]
   [ʈ], [ɖ] are retroflex.
   [̪] means that a sound is dental.
   [ɨ] represents a high central unrounded vowel.

   Remember: When looking for complementary distribution, you must record the immediate surrounding phonetic environment around each occurrence of a sound.

1. [pal]	'tooth'	11. [id̪ɨ]	'this'
2. [abayam]	'refuge'	12. [ad̪ɨ]	'that'
3. [kappal]	'ship'	13. [kat̪t̪i]	'knife'
4. [saabam]	'curse'	14. [kud̪i]	'jump'
5. [kaakkaaj]	'crow'	15. [pat̪t̪i]	'ten'
6. [mugil]	'cloud'	16. [paad̪am]	'foot'
7. [t̪ugil]	'veil'	17. [iɖam]	'place'
8. [t̪aʈʈɨ]	'plate'	18. [kaaʈpaaɖi]	'name of a town'
9. [padɨ]	'lie down'	19. [paʈʈɨ]	'silk'
10. [t̪uukkɨ]	'carry'		

- Are the pairs of sounds separate phonemes or allophones of the same phoneme? What is the evidence for your answer?
- If these are allophones of the same phoneme, identify the articulatory process at work. Provide a statement and write a rule using feature notation. Make your rule as general as possible. Watch out for natural classes.
- Provide a derivation for 3, 6, and 14.

2. **Standard Spanish and Andalusian Spanish**

	Spelling	Standard	Andalusian	Gloss
1.	doy	[doj]	[doj]	'I give'
2.	lado	[laðo]	[laːo]	'side'
3.	robledo	[roβleðo]	[roβleːo]	'oak grove'
4.	lindo	[lindo]	[lindo]	'pretty'
5.	verdad	[berðað]	[beːðaː]	'truth'
6.	arder	[arðer]	[aːðeː]	'to burn (intransitive)'
7.	verde	[berðe]	[beːðe]	'green'
8.	pecado	[pekaðo]	[pekaːo]	'sin'
9.	anda	[anda]	[anda]	'he/she walks'
10.	virtud	[birtuð]	[biːtuː]	'virtue'
11.	donde	[donde]	[donde]	'where'
12.	florido	[floriðo]	[floriːo]	'florid, robust'
13.	conde	[konde]	[konde]	'count (aristocratic title)'
14.	mercado	[merkaðo]	[meːkaːo]	'market'

a. When does [d] become [ð] in Standard Spanish? Write a rule using features.

b. When does [d] become [ð] in Andalusian Spanish? Write a rule using features.

c. When is Standard Spanish [r] deleted in Andalusian Spanish?

d. When is Standard Spanish [ð] deleted in Andalusian Spanish?

e. Some of the rules that derive the Andalusian Spanish phonetic form must be ordered. Write derivations for *verdad* and *mercado*.

REMINDER

To solve a phonology problem, you must have a firm grasp on minimal pairs, near-minimal pairs, and complementary distribution. If you don't, then you need to get some help.

Review Exercise

Determine whether the sounds under consideration are allophones of the same phoneme or are separate phonemes. Provide evidence to support your conclusion. If the sounds are allophones of the same phoneme in complementary distribution, provide a phonological rule.

1. **Passamaquoddy:** [p] and [b]
Passamaquoddy (Maliseet) is a Native American language spoken in Maine and Canada.

1. [aptʃədʒ]	'good-bye'	5. [əptan]	'coat'
2. [wiphun]	'feather'	6. [əbu]	'he sits'
3. [aptʃ]	'again'	7. [wibid]	'his tooth'
4. [zipsiz]	'bird'	8. [wabeju]	'white'

2. **Kpelle:** Nasalized and oral vowels

Kpelle is a tone language spoken in Liberia and Sierra Leone. Tones have been omitted in the data here. A tilde [˜] over a vowel indicates that it is nasalized.

1. [sĩi]	'spider'	6. [kpẽla]	'water chevrotain'*
2. [nsũa]	'my nose'	7. [pɔ̃ja]	'a design, mark'
3. [nũui]	'the person'	8. [mẽla]	'its horn'
4. [mela]	'split it'	9. [ntɛɛ]	'send me'
5. [ntĩa]	'my taboo'	10. [nsoŋ]	'catch me'

* A water chevrotain is a hornless ruminant, also called a mouse deer.

3. **Hausa:** [r] and [ɽ]

Hausa is a language spoken in northern Nigeria. Tones are not shown here.

[r] represents a trill.

[ɽ] represents a retroflex flap.

[ɓ] represents a voiced bilabial implosive, in which the larynx moves downward, sucking air in.

1. [ʃaːɽaː]	'sweeping'	6. [rubuːtuː]	'writing'
2. [ʃahararreː]	'famous'	7. [barɡoː]	'blanket'
3. [ɓaɽɡoː]	'marrow'	8. [ʃaːɽaɽɽeː]	'swept'
4. [ɽuɓeːwaː]	'rotting'	9. [kʷoːɽaː]	'ringworm'
5. [baraː]	'begging'	10. [ɡʷoːro]	'kola nut'

4. **Bemba:** [s] and [ʃ]

Bemba is a Bantu language spoken in Zambia and elsewhere in East Africa.
Tones are not shown here.

1. [ukuʃika]	'to be deep'	8. [insa]	'clock, hour'
2. [amakalaʃi]	'glasses'	9. [isabi]	'fish'
3. [umuʃikaːle]	'soldier'	10. [fuseːke]	'go away!'
4. [ameːnʃi]	'water'	11. [ukusela]	'to move'
5. [umwaːnakaʃi]	'woman'	12. [akasuba]	'sun'
6. [insoːkoʃi]	'socks'	13. [soma]	'read!'
7. [nʃi]	'what'	14. [pasoːpo]	'beware!'

5. **Syrian Arabic:** [s] and [sˤ], [z] and [zˤ]

[sˤ] and [zˤ] are pharyngealized; they are formed with a secondary articulation involving a constriction in the pharynx.

[ħ] represents a voiceless pharyngeal fricative.

1. [nəsˤsˤ]	'half'	9. [sˤeːf]	'summer'
2. [buːzˤa]	'ice cream'	10. [nəsər]	'eagle'
3. [sˤadˤme]	'shock'	11. [naːs]	'people'
4. [seːf]	'sword'	12. [wəsˤex]	'dirty'
5. [nizˤaːm]	'discipline'	13. [sahəl]	'easy'
6. [zahər]	'flower'	14. [buːz]	'muzzle'
7. [sˤəhər]	'sister's husband'	15. [ħəzer]	'careful'
8. [fazˤzˤ]	'crude'	16. [zˤaːher]	'apparent'

☑ RECAP

Make sure you know how to do the following. (See also the Key Terms on pp. 98–99 of the main text.)

- spot minimal and near-minimal pairs
- determine complementary distribution
- define phonemes and allophones
- use phonemic and phonetic transcription
- identify consonantal and vowel features
- put together feature matrices
- construct syllable representations
- spot open and closed syllables
- put together rules and statements
- put together rules using feature notation
- construct derivations
- solve phonology problems

Questions? Problems?

four

Morphology: The Analysis of Word Structure

Morphology is the study of words and how they are formed and interpreted. Following are some of the important topics and concepts covered in this chapter. Make sure you are familiar with them.

Morphological terminology
Identifying morphemes
Identifying lexical categories
Analyzing word structure
Derivation
Form vs. function
Compounding
Inflection
Other morphological phenomena
Morphology problems
Morphophonemics

Morphological Terminology

The following terms are crucial to understanding morphology. You should know them. (Remember also to review the Key Terms on pages 139–140 in Chapter 4 in the main text.)

TERM	DEFINITION
Word	Words are the smallest free forms found in language. **Free forms** are elements that can appear in isolation, or whose position is not fixed. Words can be **simple** or **complex**.
Morpheme	A morpheme is the smallest meaning or functional unit found in language. Morphemes can be **free** or **bound**.
Allomorphs	Allomorphs are the different forms of a morpheme.
Affixes	Affixes are different types of bound morphemes. There are three types of affixes found in language: **prefixes**, **suffixes**, and **infixes**.
Root	A root is the core of a word. It is the portion of the word that carries most of the word's meaning.
Base	A base is any form to which an affix is added.
Stem	A stem is a base to which an inflectional affix is added.

Identifying Morphemes (Section 1.1, pp. 113–114)

Morphemes are the building blocks of words. A word may contain only one morpheme, making it a simple word, or a word may contain more than one morpheme, making it a complex word. Below are some hints for determining the number of morphemes that a word contains.

- A morpheme can carry information about meaning or function. For example, the word *haunt* cannot be divided into the morphemes *h* and *aunt,* since only *aunt* has meaning. However, the word *bats* has two morphemes, since both *bat* and *-s* have meaning. The *-s,* of course, means that there is more than one.

- The meanings of individual morphemes should contribute to the overall meaning of the word. For example, *pumpkin* cannot be divided into *pump* and *kin,* since the meaning of *pumpkin* has nothing to do with the meaning of either *pump* or *kin.*

- A morpheme is not the same as a syllable. Morphemes do not have to be a syllable, or morphemes can consist of one or more syllables. For example, the morpheme *treat* has one syllable, the morpheme *dracula* has three syllables, but the morpheme *-s* (meaning 'plural') is not a syllable.

- Often during word formation, changes in pronunciation and/or spelling occur. These do not affect a morpheme's status as a morpheme. For example, when *-y* is attached to the word *scare,* it becomes *scary,* and when *-er* is attached to *scary,* it becomes *scarier.* The root, however, is still *scare,* not *scar.*

Practice 4.1: Identifying morphemes

Identify the number of morphemes in each of the following words.

1. desert	______________	7. supply	______________
2. memory	______________	8. supplies	______________
3. format	______________	9. supplier	______________
4. flowchart	______________	10. faster	______________
5. bug	______________	11. power	______________
6. debug	______________	12. processor	______________

Free and Bound Morphemes (Section 1.1, pp. 113–114)

A free morpheme can stand on its own as a word (e.g., *scare, treat, dracula*). A bound morpheme must be attached to another element and cannot be a word by itself (e.g., scar*y*, treat*ed*, pumpkin*s*).

Practice 4.2: Free and bound morphemes

For each of the following words, fill in the number of morphemes and write the free and bound morphemes in the appropriate blanks. The first one is done for you.

WORD	# OF MORPHEMES	FREE	BOUND
1. eraser	2	erase	-er
2. wicked	____	____________	____________
3. invalid (A)	____	____________	____________
4. invalid (N)	____	____________	____________
5. Jack's	____	____________	____________
6. optionality	____	____________	____________
7. refurnish	____	____________	____________
8. inabilities	____	____________	____________
9. denationalize	____	____________	____________
10. deride	____	____________	____________
11. activation	____	____________	____________

Identifying Lexical Categories (Section 1.2, pp. 114–118)

In morphology, we are concerned with four **lexical categories**: nouns, verbs, adjectives, and prepositions. Nouns typically refer to concrete and abstract objects; verbs typically denote actions or states; adjectives typically refer to properties of nouns; and prepositions typically indicate relations in space or time.

PRACTICE 4.3: Lexical categories

For each of the following words, fill in the number of morphemes, and identify the root, the lexical category of the root, and the lexical category of the entire word. Be careful: the root's lexical category and the word's lexical category may or may not be the same. The first one is done for you.

WORD	# OF MORPHEMES	ROOT	ROOT CATEGORY	WORD CATEGORY
1. kindnesses	3	kind	adjective	noun
2. amazement	____	________	________	________
3. reusable	____	________	________	________
4. dishonest	____	________	________	________
5. Baltimore	____	________	________	________
6. lovelier	____	________	________	________
7. historical	____	________	________	________
8. uncontrolled	____	________	________	________
9. impersonal	____	________	________	________
10. trees	____	________	________	________
11. faster	____	________	________	________
12. rereads	____	________	________	________
13. beautiful	____	________	________	________
14. child	____	________	________	________

Word Structure (Section 1.2, pp. 114–118)

A word **tree** is a representation of a word's internal structure. To put together a word tree, you need to be able to determine the number of morphemes in a word, identify roots and affixes, and assign lexical categories.

Remember: Prefixes are attached to the front of a base, while suffixes are attached to the end of a base. Infixes are a type of affix that occurs inside another morpheme. Infixes are generally not found in English.

Below are some examples of how to draw a word tree.

1. Words with a single affix.

a.

1. Identify the root and determine its lexical category.

2. Attach the suffix and determine the lexical category of the resulting word. This may or may not be the same as the lexical category of the root.

b.

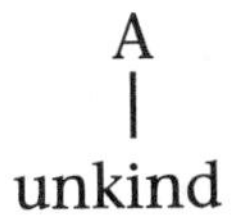

1. Identify the root and determine its lexical category.

2. Attach the prefix and determine the lexical category of the resulting word. This is typically the same as the lexical category of the root.

2. Words with multiple suffixes.

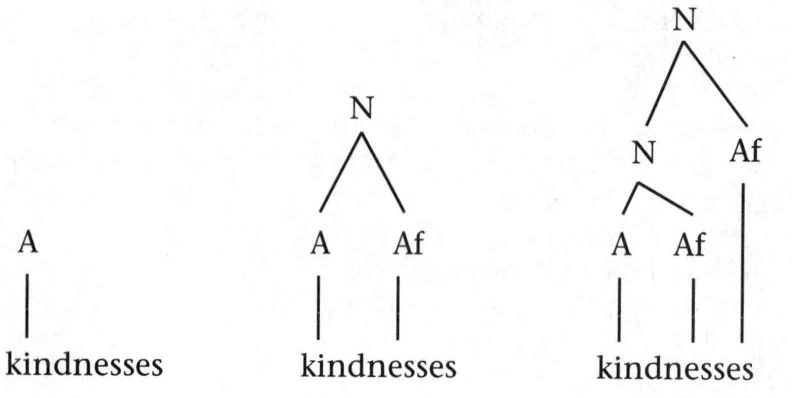

1. Identify the root and determine its lexical category.
2. Attach the first affix and determine the lexical category of the resulting word.
3. Attach the next affix and determine the lexical category of the resulting word.

3. Words with both a prefix and a suffix.

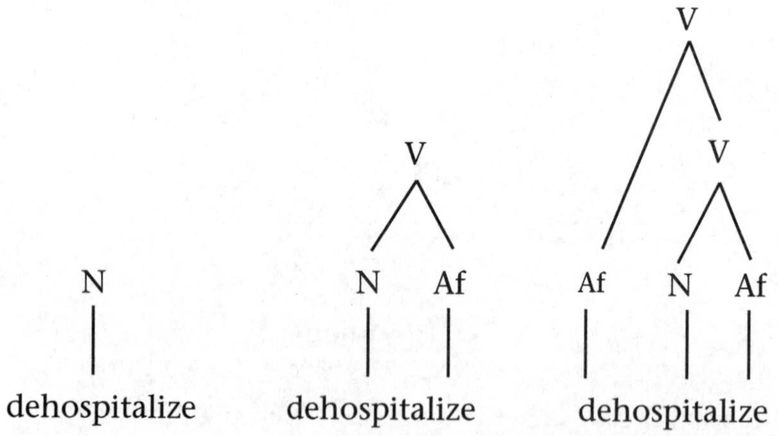

1. Identify the root and determine its lexical category.
2. Attach the first affix and determine the lexical category of the resulting word.
3. Attach the next affix and determine the lexical category of the resulting word.

4. Words that are structurally ambiguous.

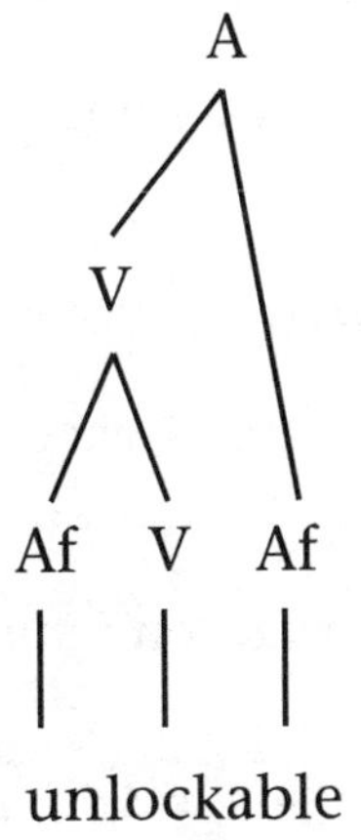

The prefix *un-* is first attached to create the verb *unlock.* The suffix *-able* is then attached to create the adjective *unlockable.*

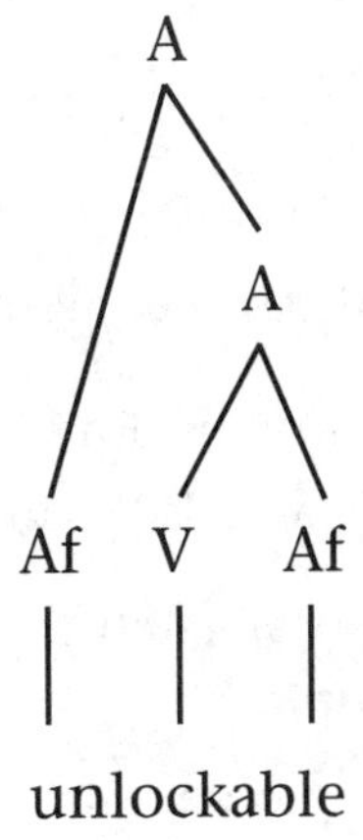

The suffix *-able* is first attached to create the adjective *lockable.* The prefix *un-* is then attached to create the adjective *unlockable.*

Practice 4.4: Drawing word trees

To practice, draw word trees for the following words:

1. trees
2. lovelier
3. dishonest
4. beautiful
5. amazement
6. reusable
7. impersonal
8. Baltimore

REMINDER
To be able to draw word trees correctly, you need to be able to identify nouns, verbs, adjectives, and prepositions. If you are having difficulty with these, get some help.

Derivation (Section 2, pp. 118–122)

Derivation is a process of affixation. Affixation is a morphological process that adds affixes to words. Derivational affixes are affixes that:

- build a word having a different (but usually related) semantic content than that of its base,
- usually change the lexical category of a word,
- are restricted in the class of bases to which they can attach.

English has many derivational affixes. English derivational suffixes have all of the characteristics of derivation just described. For example:

- *-ity* combines with an adjective such as *stupid* to create the noun *stupidity,* meaning the state or quality of being stupid.
- *-ful* combines with a noun such as *faith* to create the adjective *faithful,* meaning having faith.
- *-ment* combines with a verb such as *adjourn* to create the noun *adjournment,* meaning the state or action of adjourning.

English also has many derivational prefixes; however, these do not change the lexical category of the base. Despite this, English prefixes are still considered derivational. This is because of the semantic change that occurs when they are used to build words. For example:

- *re-* combines with a verb such as *do* to create the verb *redo,* meaning to do again.
- *anti-* combines with a noun such as *toxin* to create the noun *antitoxin,* meaning something against a toxin.

For more examples of English derivational prefixes and suffixes, see Table 4.6 on page 119 in the textbook.

Derivational affixes are often subject to restrictions. For example:

- Derivational affixes combine with bases of particular lexical categories.
  e.g., *-ize* must be attached to a noun; *-er* must be attached to a verb
- Derivational affixes combine with bases having certain phonological properties.
  e.g., *-en* must be attached to a base having one syllable and ending in an obstruent
- Derivational affixes combine with bases of specific origin.
  e.g., *-ant* must be attached to a base of Latin origin

Some derivational affixes cause a phonological change in the base. For example:

- *-ity* and *-(a)tion* change the stress of a word.
  e.g., módern → modérnity, módernize → modernizátion

The affixes that cause phonological change in the base are **Class I affixes**. **Class II affixes** do not cause phonological change in the base.

PRACTICE 4.5: Derivational affixes

1. Draw trees for the following words. Remember that a word can contain more than one derivational affix.

a. disappear	d. unbreakable
b. homeless	e. institutional
c. electricity	f. lodger

Now go back and identify which words have a Class I affix.

2. For each word below, write the affix and how the affix changes the lexical category of the word. Some words may have more than one affix. The first one is done for you.

Word	Affix	Change
1. affordable	-able	V → A
2. racial	________	________
3. kindness	________	________
4. disconnect	________	________
5. organization	________	________
6. combative	________	________
7. humorous	________	________
8. morality	________	________
9. remarry	________	________
10. Brazilian	________	________
11. demonize	________	________
12. validate	________	________
13. lighten	________	________
14. unpleasant	________	________
15 unbend	________	________

Compounding (Section 3, pp. 123–127)

Compounding is another technique for building words. Compounding involves the combination of two or more words into a new word. There are four important properties of English compounds:

- **Headedness.** The **head** of a compound is the morpheme that determines the category of the entire compound. Most English compounds are right-headed. That is, the category of the entire compound is the same as the category of the last member of the compound. For example, the compound *blackboard* is a noun, since the last member, *board,* is a noun.

- **Stress patterns.** Even though compounds can be spelled as one word, as two words, or with a hyphen separating the morphemes, a generalization can be made about the stress patterns found on them. Stress tends to be more prominent on the first member of the compound rather than the second: for example, *greénhouse* (a garden center) versus *green hoúse* (a house that is green).

- **Tense/Plural.** Tense and plural markers are usually added to the compound as a whole and not to the first member of the compound. For example, the plural of *fire engine* is *fire engines* and not *fires engine.* Similarly, the past tense of *drop kick* is *drop kicked* and not *dropped kick.*

- **Semantic patterns.** Compounds are used to express a wide range of meaning relationships. Many compounds are endocentric. In an **endocentric compound**, the entire compound denotes a subtype of the head. For example, a *teacup* is a type of *cup*, and a *lunchroom* is a type of *room.* Some compounds are exocentric. In an **exocentric compound**, the meaning of the compound does not come from the head. For example, a *redneck* is not a type of *neck*, but a type of person.

Incorporation. Another type of compounding is called **incorporation**. Incorporation usually involves combining nouns with a verb to form a compound verb.

e.g.,	Without incorporation:	They are *cleaning* the *house.*
	With incorporation:	They are *housecleaning.*

Incorporation is not very common in English, but it can be found in many other languages.

Practice 4.6: Compounds

1. Compounding can be used in conjunction with derivation to build words. Draw trees for each of the following words.

   a. washer-dryer

   b. presidential election

   c. (an) undertaking

   d. baby blue

2. For each of the following compounds, identify the lexical categories making it up and give another example of that type of compound. Give a different example for each compound. The first one is done for you.

COMPOUND	LEXICAL CATEGORIES	EXAMPLE
1. bathroom	noun + noun	movie star
2. scarecrow	______________	______________
3. skin-deep	______________	______________
4. bittersweet	______________	______________
5. upstairs	______________	______________

Now go back and draw a word tree for each compound.

Inflection (Section 4.1, pp. 127–128)

Inflection is sometimes a process of affixation. As will be discussed further, inflection can also be a process of **internal change** as well as a process of **suppletion**. Affixation is a morphological process that adds affixes to words. Inflectional affixes are affixes that:

- function to provide grammatical information
- never change the lexical category of a word
- occur at the outer edges of a word (e.g., last)

English has eight inflectional affixes. They are found on nouns, verbs, and adjectives.

NOUNS

1. PLURAL:	*-s* dogs, cats, roses
2. POSSESSIVE:	*-'s* Mary's book, Pat's book, the judge's book

VERBS

1. THIRD-PERSON SINGULAR:	*-s* She likes jazz. He walks slowly. He hisses loudly.
2. PAST TENSE:	*-ed* She filled the gas tank. He wanted a dog.
3. PROGRESSIVE:	*-ing* I am sighing. You are singing. She is walking. We are talking. He was running. They were leaving.

4. PAST PARTICIPLE:	*-en / -ed* I have spoken. He has filled the gas tank.

ADJECTIVES

1. COMPARATIVE:	*-er* greener, louder, faster, softer
2. SUPERLATIVE:	*-est* greenest, loudest, fastest, softest

PRACTICE 4.7: Recognizing lexical categories and inflection

For each of the following words, identify the lexical category of the root and the type of inflectional information found (e.g., past tense, superlative, plural). The first one is done for you.

WORD	LEXICAL CATEGORY	INFLECTIONAL INFORMATION
1. watched	verb	past tense
2. runs	________	________
3. sorriest	________	________
4. lamps	________	________
5. playing	________	________
6. driven	________	________
7. lovelier	________	________

PRACTICE 4.8: Identifying affixes
(Section 1.2, pp. 114–118; Section 4.2, pp. 128–130)

For each of the following English words, state whether it is simple or complex. If it is complex, state whether the affix is inflectional or derivational. The first one is done for you.

WORD	SIMPLE / COMPLEX	INFL / DERIV
1. desks	complex	inflectional
2. fly	________	________
3. prettier	________	________

4. stringy ____________________ ____________________
5. delight ____________________ ____________________
6. reuse ____________________ ____________________
7. fastest ____________________ ____________________
8. mistreat ____________________ ____________________

Form vs. Function

Many affixes have the same form, but different functions. That is, affixes having the same form can be either inflectional or derivational, or they can be different inflectional affixes or derivational affixes. You need to be able to identify affixes according to their function rather than by their form. The following exercise should help.

PRACTICE 4.9: Form vs. function of affixes

In each of the following groups of words, two words have the same type of affix, one word has a different affix, and one word has no affix at all. Underline the affix in each word. Then, next to each word, write S (same), D (different), or N (none), based on the items in the set. You may want to use a dictionary. The first one is done for you.

1. ovens ___S___
   lens ___N___
   hens ___S___
   listens ___D___

2. greedy ________
   ivory ________
   jealousy ________
   dirty ________

3. leaven ________
   harden ________
   spoken ________
   thicken ________

4. rider ________
   colder ________
   silver ________
   actor ________

5. greener ________
   farmer ________
   colder ________
   water ________

6. friendly ________
   slowly ________
   intelligently ________
   early ________

7. intelligent	________	8. candied	________
inhale	________	shopped	________
incongruous	________	cleaned	________
inhuman	________	candid	________

Word Trees to Show Inflection, Derivation, and Compounding

(Section 1.2, pp. 114–118; Section 2.1, pp. 119–122; Section 3, pp. 123–124; Section 4.2, pp. 128–130)

Remember that more than one process can be used to build a single word. A word like *blackboards,* for example, is a compound noun (*black* + *board*) with an inflectional suffix *-s* for the plural. If you are in doubt about the lexical category of an entire word, you can look at the affixes; sentence context can also help you determine the lexical category.

For example, the tree for the word *workable* as in the sentence *I like the* *workable* *solution* might be diagrammed as follows:

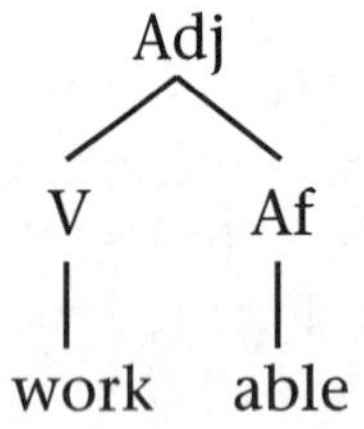

Derivation

Practice 4.10: Drawing word trees

Draw one tree diagram for each of the following words, and identify whether inflection, derivation, and/or compounding was used to build the word.

WORD	CONTEXT SENTENCE
1. taken	The baby has taken his first steps.
2. spoonfeeding	Mother is spoonfeeding the baby.
3. softest	The softest pillow has the
4. silkiest	silkiest cover.
5. introductions	Mary performed the introductions.
6. steps	John steps up the ladder.
7. steps	I hate those steep steps.
8. stringier	My hair is stringier than hers.

	WORD	CONTEXT SENTENCE
9.	skiers	The skiers were rich.
10.	father	My father lives in France.
11.	stone cold	Your french fries are stone cold.
12.	making	Jill is making candy.
13.	boxing	We watched the boxing on television.
14.	criticize	You criticize too much.
15.	creamy	Creamy chocolate is delicious.
16.	keepers	The keepers locked up for the night.
17.	blessing	Give me your blessing.
18.	blessing	She is blessing the bread.
19.	schoolteacher	My mother was a schoolteacher.
20.	clumsiness	I detest clumsiness.
21.	windmills	There are lots of windmills in Holland.
22.	hammered	John hammered on the door.
23.	thickeners	There are many different types of thickeners.
24.	unlocked	We unlocked the door.
25.	declaw	You should not declaw your cat.
26.	retry	She should retry the recipe.
27.	inside	The cat is inside the box.
28.	impure	Impure water is dangerous.
29.	sleepwalking	George is often found sleepwalking.
30.	defrosting	The steaks are defrosting.

REMINDER

Remember that all English prefixes are derivational even though they do not cause a lexical category change.

More on Inflection (Section 4.3, pp. 130–133)

In addition to affixation, inflection can be marked by using internal change, suppletion, **reduplication**, and tone placement.

PROCESS	DEFINITION
Internal Change	This process provides grammatical information by changing a portion of the morpheme. That is, the tense or number of a word is marked by changing a sound within the morpheme. e.g., *run* → *ran*
Suppletion	This process provides grammatical information by changing the entire morpheme. That is, the tense, number, etc., of a word is marked by replacing one morpheme with an entirely different morpheme. e.g., *go* → *went*
Reduplication	A process that copies all (full) or a portion (partial) of the base to mark a semantic or grammatical contrast. This process has only limited use in English. e.g., Turkish: [iji] 'well' → [iji iji] 'very well' Tagalog: [lakad] 'walk' → [lalakad] 'will walk'
Tone Placement	This process is similar to stress placement in that a difference in tone can be used to create different words, or to mark a change in tense or number. This process is found in tone languages. e.g., Mono-Bili: Past (high tone) Future (low tone) *dá* 'spanked' *dà* 'will spank' *wó* 'killed' *wò* 'will kill'

PRACTICE 4.11: More inflection

Each of the following words has been inflected. For each, identify the type of inflectional process that has been used to mark the grammatical contrast. The first has been done for you.

WORD	TYPE OF INFLECTION
1. drove	internal change
2. was	______________
3. (is) jumping	______________

4. kitsji 'small'
   kitsji kitsji 'very small'
   (from Fa d'Ambu) ________________________________

5. better ________________________________

6. lovelier ________________________________

7. George's ________________________________

8. gavu 'good'
   gagavu 'very good'
   (from Fa d'Ambu) ________________________________

9. mice ________________________________

REMINDER

Many more inflectional phenomena, including case and agreement, are widely used in language. For more information on these, go to

bedford/stmartins.com/linguistics/morphology and click on **inflection**.
bedford/stmartins.com/linguistics/syntax and click on **case**.

Other Morphological Phenomena (Section 5, pp. 133–138)

In addition to derivation and compounding, other common word-building processes include:

PROCESS	DEFINITION
Cliticization	Clitics are morphemes that behave like words in terms of meaning and function. Clitics differ, though, in that they cannot stand alone as a word. Cliticization attaches these elements to either the beginning of a following word or the end of a preceding word. e.g., *re* from *are* is attached to *they* as in *they're*
Conversion	A process that assigns an existing word to a different lexical category. e.g., *butter* (N) → *(to) butter* (V)
Clipping	A process that shortens a word by removing one or more syllables. e.g., *condominium* → *condo*
Blending	A process that creates a new word by combining portions of two existing words. e.g., *spiced* + *ham* → *spam*
Backformation	A process that creates a word by removing a supposed affix from an existing word. e.g., *donation* → *donate*
Acronym	A new word created by using the initial letters of the words in a phrase or title. e.g., *radar, UNICEF*
Onomatopoeia	Words that have been created to sound like the thing they name. e.g., *buzz, hiss, sizzle*
Coinage	A process that creates a totally new word. e.g., *Teflon* New words can also be created from names. e.g., *boycott*

PRACTICE 4.12: Word-formation processes

1. Identify the process responsible for the formation of each of the following English words. Choose from any of the morphological and word-formation processes in the preceding two tables as well as inflection, derivation, and compounding. The first one is done for you.

   1. Ebonics blending (**eb**ony + ph**onics**)
   2. (to) ship ________________
   3. geese ________________

4. support hose ______________________
5. splat ______________________
6. jumped ______________________
7. healthy ______________________
8. demo ______________________
9. sadness ______________________
10. he's ______________________
11. headline ______________________
12. beep ______________________
13. SARS ______________________

2. There are many examples of different word-formation processes in the following passage. Find all the examples of acronym, backformation, blending, clipping, coinage, compounding, conversion, and onomatopoeia.

> When Dave woke up, he should have been ready for brunch since he'd slept late. Despite the cheerful chirping of the birds outside and the annoying buzz of the infomercial coming from the TV at the foot of the bed, the external world held no charm. Dave had a headache hammering behind his right eyeball, his stomach hurt, and his nose was running. As he reached for a Kleenex, he reflected bitterly on his luck. Today was supposed to be his first scuba lesson, but instead he'd come down with the flu. As he fingered the blanket, he recalled that the last time he'd gone to the clinic had not inspired confidence. The med student who saw him enthused about his condition in a most off-putting way; he sent Dave for a CAT scan and a blood test, and even suggested hopefully that laser surgery might be in order. In Dave's present condition, this all seemed like too much effort. Maybe, Dave thought as he reached for the remote, he should just laze around for the day, drink Coke, and eat sandwiches while channel-surfing.

Introduction to Morphology Problems (See Appendix, pp. 140–142)

The goal in tackling morphology problems is to isolate and identify all the morphemes in the data given. To do this, you must identify recurring strings of sounds and match them with recurring meanings. It sounds harder than it really is. Here are a few easy ones to try.

PRACTICE 4.13: Easy morphology problems

All data are given in phonetic transcription.

1. **Mende** (Sierra Leone)

1. [pɛlɛ]	'house'	[pɛlɛi]	'the house'
2. [mɔm]	'glass'	[mɔmi]	'the glass'
3. [dɔmi]	'story'	[dɔmii]	'the story'
4. [kali]	'hoe'	[kalii]	'the hoe'
5. [hele]	'elephant'	[helei]	'the elephant'
6. [kaamɔ]	'teacher'	[kaamɔi]	'the teacher'
7. [navo]	'boy'	[navoi]	'the boy'
8. [numu]	'person'	[numui]	'the person'

a. What is the morpheme meaning 'the'? ______________________________

b. If [sale] means 'proverb', what is the form for 'the proverb'? ____________

c. If [kpindii] means 'the night', what does [kpindi] mean? ______________

2. **Ganda** (Uganda)

1. [omukazi]	'woman'	[abakazi]	'women'
2. [omusawo]	'doctor'	[abasawo]	'doctors'
3. [omusika]	'heir'	[abasika]	'heirs'
4. [omuwala]	'girl'	[abawala]	'girls'
5. [omulenzi]	'boy'	[abalenzi]	'boys'

a. What is the morpheme meaning SINGULAR? ______________________________

b. What is the morpheme meaning PLURAL? ______________________________

c. If [abalanga] means 'twins', what is the form for 'twin'? ______________

3. **Kanuri** (Nigeria)

1.	[gana]	'small'	[nəmgana]	'smallness'
2.	[kura]	'big'	[nəmkura]	'bigness'
3.	[kurugu]	'long'	[nəmkurugu]	'length'
4.	[karite]	'excellent'	[nəmkarite]	'excellence'
5.	[dibi]	'bad'	[nəmdibi]	'badness'

a. What type of affix is shown (i.e., prefix, suffix, infix)? ________________

b. What is the affix? ____

c. If [kəji] means 'sweet', what is the form for 'sweetness'? ________________

d. If [nəmgəla] means 'goodness', what is the form for 'good'? ______________

e. What morphological process was used to form the words in the second column? ____________________

f. Draw a word tree for [nəmkurugu] 'length'.

Practice 4.14: More morphology problems

The following pages contain somewhat more difficult problems based on data sets from different languages. These data sets are intended to give you practice in doing morphological analysis. Each contains sufficient data to make valid conclusions; however, the data may have been regularized somewhat. Data are in phonetic transcription unless otherwise noted.

1. **Toba Batak**
Toba Batak is a Malayo-Polynesian language of Sumatra. Although tones are marked, you may disregard them for this exercise.

1.	[deŋgán]	'good'	[duméŋgan]	'better'
2.	[tíbbo]	'tall'	[tumíbbo]	'taller'
3.	[rɔá]	'ugly'	[rumɔa]	'uglier'
4.	[gokan]	'full'	[gumokán]	'fuller'
5.	[rahis]	'steep'	[rumáhis]	'steeper'
6.	[holom]	'dark'	[humolom]	'darker'

a. What morpheme indicates the comparative? ____________________

b. What kind of affix is this morpheme? ____________________

c. If [datu] means 'wise', what is the form for 'wiser'? ________________

d. If [sɔmal] means 'usual', what is the form for 'more usual'? ______________

e. If [ʤumɛppɛk] means 'shorter', what is the form for 'short'? ______________

f. If [lumógo] means 'drier', what is the form for 'dry'? ________________

2. **Turkish**

[y] represents a high front rounded vowel.
[œ] represents a mid front rounded vowel.

1.	[ʃehiɾ]	'city'
2.	[ʃehiɾden]	'from the city'
3.	[el]	'hand'
4.	[elim]	'my hand'
5.	[elimde]	'in my hand'
6.	[kœpɾy]	'bridge'
7.	[kœpɾyleɾ]	'bridges'
8.	[kœpɾyleɾe]	'to the bridges'
9.	[kœpɾyde]	'on the bridge'
10.	[zilim]	'my bell'
11.	[zilleɾ]	'bells'
12.	[eve]	'to the house'
13.	[evde]	'in the house'
14.	[evden]	'from the house'
15.	[kœpɾyden]	'from the bridge'
16.	[elleɾinize]	'to your hands'
17.	[sesleɾiniz]	'your voices'
18.	[otobysleɾ]	'buses'

a. What morphemes mean:

1. city ______________
2. hand ______________
3. bridge ______________
4. bell ______________
5. house ______________
6. voice ______________
7. bus ______________
8. from ______________
9. to ______________
10. on, in ______________
11. my ______________
12. your ______________
13. PLURAL ______________

b. What is the order of morphemes?

Fill in the boxes with: PLURAL, POSSESSIVE, POSTPOSITION, ROOT

c. What do the following mean in English?

1. [ʃehiɾde] ______________
2. [elleɾiniz] ______________

d. How would you say 'to the buses' in Turkish? ______________

3. **Classical Nahuatl**

Nahuatl is an Aztecan language of Mexico.

1.	[tikʷiːka]	'you (SG) sing'	8.	[kikʷa]	'he eats it'
2.	[kʷiːka]	's/he sings'	9.	[kikʷaʔ]	'they eat it'
3.	[tikʷiːkaʔ]	'we sing'	10.	[aːltia]	'he bathes'
4.	[ankʷiːkaʔ]	'you (PL) sing'	11.	[aːltiaʔ]	'they bathe'
5.	[kʷiːkaʔ]	'they sing'	12.	[kikʷaːni]	'he customarily eats it'
6.	[kʷa]	'he eats'	13.	[aːltiaːni]	'he customarily bathes'
7.	[kʷaʔ]	'they eat'	14.	[tiaːltiaːni]	'you (SG) customarily bathe'

a. What are the morphemes for:

1. sing ________________
2. eat ________________
3. bathe ________________
4. you (SG) (subject) ________________
5. s/he (subject) ________________
6. it (object) ________________
7. we (subject) ________________
8. you (PL) (subject) ________________
9. they (subject) ________________

b. What is the suffix that marks a plural subject in the present? ______________

c. How is the customary present marked? ______________________________

REMINDERS

1. An affix is an infix only when it is inserted into a root.
2. Don't forget to use morphological boundary markers (i.e., hyphens) for all bound affixes (prefixes, suffixes, and affixes). Root words do not need morphological boundaries.

Morphophonemics (Section 6, pp. 138–139)

Morphemes do not always have the same form. Allomorphs are the different forms of a morpheme. Consider the following English example.

- **The Allomorphs:** The English plural morpheme *-s* has three different phonetic forms:

  [-s] in words like *cats*
  [-z] in words like *dogs*
  [-əz] in words like *dishes*

- **The Conditioning Environment:** Which phonetic form is realized depends on the phonological characteristics of the final segment in the preceding word:

  [-s] occurs after a base ending in a voiceless consonant that is not strident
  [-z] occurs after a base ending in a voiced segment that is not strident
  [-əz] occurs after a base ending in a strident consonant

  The specific environment in which the different allomorphs occur is often referred to as the distribution of the allomorphs. This interaction between morphology and phonology is called **morphophonemics**.

- **The Underlying Representation:** One allomorph is selected as the underlying representation of the morpheme. This is typically the allomorph that has the widest distribution.

  [-z] is selected as the underlying representation, since it occurs after the most sounds (voiced consonants and vowels, which are also voiced)

- **The Derivation:** Rules are required to derive the correct phonetic form from the underlying representation.

Coda epenthesis:	Insert a schwa whenever [-z] occurs after a base that ends in a strident sound.
Devoicing:	Devoice [-z] after a voiceless consonant in the same coda.

  These rules are often a reflection of the phonological processes at work in the pronunciation of the morphemes. And just like in phonology, rules must sometimes be ordered so that the correct phonetic form is derived. Coda epenthesis must occur before devoicing. If the devoicing rule occurs first, then [-z] becomes voiceless and epenthesis fails to apply.

Practice 4.15: Morphophonemics

Spot the allomorphs in the following exercises, and answer the questions that follow.

1. **English**

1. [ɪnɛdɪbl̩]	'inedible'	5. [ɪnsəpɔɹtəbl̩]	'insupportable'
2. [ɪmpɑsɪbl̩]	'impossible'	6. [ɪnəbɪləti]	'inability'
3. [ɪŋkejpəbl̩]	'incapable'	7. [ɪmɔɹl̩]	'immoral'
4. [ɪntɑləɹənt]	'intolerant'	8. [ɪŋkəmplit]	'incomplete'

a. What are the three different allomorphs of the morpheme meaning 'not'?

____

State the environment (in words) in which the allomorphs occur.

1. ____

2. ____

3. ____

b. Which allomorph would you choose as the underlying representation of the morpheme?

____

c. Give the underlying representation of the words *inedible, impossible,* and *incapable.*

____

d. What phonological process is at work in the data?

____

e. What are the rules you would need to derive the phonetic forms? Do these rules need to be ordered?

____

2. **Turkish**

Vowel harmony is a process that results in all vowels of a word sharing a certain feature or features. Morphophonemic rules of vowel harmony are found in many languages. Look at the data from Turkish, and answer the following questions.
[y] represents a high front rounded vowel.
[œ] represents a mid front rounded vowel.

1.	[gœz]	'eye'	[gœzleɾ]	'eyes'
2.	[mum]	'candle'	[mumlɑɾ]	'candles'
3.	[top]	'gun'	[toplɑɾ]	'guns'
4.	[ɑt]	'horse'	[ɑtlɑɾ]	'horses'
5.	[ip]	'thread'	[ipleɾ]	'threads'
6.	[gyl]	'rose'	[gylleɾ]	'roses'
7.	[mektup]	'letter'	[mektuplɑɾ]	'letters'
8.	[anne]	'mother'	[anneleɾ]	'mothers'
9.	[limɑn]	'harbor'	[limɑnlɑɾ]	'harbors'
10.	[ʃule]	'flame'	[ʃuleleɾ]	'flames'

a. What are the allomorphs of the plural morpheme? ____________ ____________

b. What phonological feature distinguishes the vowels of the allomorphs?

____

c. What feature of the last vowel in the root determines the choice of the plural allomorph? ______________________

3. **Dutch**

In Dutch, there are "strong verbs" and "weak verbs" depending on the form of the past tense and past participle (the past participle is the verb form used with *have* in English, e.g., *has* done). Examine the data from Dutch, which is in Dutch orthography, and answer the following questions.

WEAK VERBS

Root	Infinitive	Past Participle	
werk	werken	gewerkt	'work'
luister	luisteren	geluisterd	'listen'
poets	poetsen	gepoetst	'brush'
winkel	winkelen	gewinkeld	'go shopping'
regen	regenen	geregend	'rain'
fietst	fietsten	gefietst	'bike' (i.e., go by bicycle)
zag	zagen	gezagd	'saw, harp on something'

STRONG VERBS

Infinitive	Past Participle	
bijten	gebeten	'bite'
laten	gelaten	'let, leave off'
sterven	gestorven	'die from'
nemen	genomen	'take'

a. How is the infinitive formed for weak verbs in Dutch? ______________________

b. How is the past participle formed for weak verbs in Dutch? ______________________

What are the two forms of the past participle of the weak verb?

______________________ ______________________

Under what conditions is each form used?

______________________ ______________________

c. It is interesting that the two forms of the past participle of the weak verb in Dutch are pronounced the same. What do you think is the pronunciation, and what phonological process has occurred? ______________________

d. Strong verbs undergo internal change, which need not concern us here. What affix is added to form the past participle of strong verbs in Dutch? ______________________

e. *Iemand* heeft mijn auto gestolen means 'Someone has stolen my car.' Is *gestolen* a weak verb or a strong verb? How do you know? ______________________

Review Exercises

The following exercises will provide review in solving morphology problems.

1. **Ancient Egyptian**

   Ancient Egyptian was written in hieroglyphs (see Chapter 15 in the main text). We do not know how the vowels were pronounced, so it is transliterated without vowels. The following data have been transcribed with IPA symbols instead of the traditional orthography for ancient Egyptian.

   [t^j] represents a palatalized [t].

1.	sn	'brother'	snwj	'2 brothers'	snw	'brothers'
2.	snt	'sister'	sntj	'2 sisters'	snwt	'sisters'
3.	nt^{j}r	'god'	nt^{j}rwj	'2 gods'	nt^{j}rw	'gods'
4.	nt^{j}rt	'goddess'	nt^{j}rtj	'2 goddesses'	nt^{j}rwt	'goddesses'

   a. What morphemes mean:

      1. sibling ____________________
      2. deity ____________________
      3. FEMININE ____________________
      4. MASCULINE ____________________
      5. DUAL ____________________
      6. PLURAL ____________________

   b. What is the order of morphemes?
      Fill in the boxes with terms from this list: DUAL, FEMININE, PLURAL, ROOT

      1. M SG [ ]
      2. F SG [ ] [ ]
      3. M PL [ ] [ ]
      4. F PL [ ] [ ] [ ]
      5. M DU [ ] [ ] [ ]
      6. F DU [ ] [ ] [ ]

2. **Luganda**

Luganda is a Bantu language of eastern Africa.

1. [muntu]	'person'	11. [musege]	'wolf'
2. [kati]	'stick'	12. [bawala]	'girls'
3. [kitabo]	'book'	13. [kugulu]	'leg'
4. [bitabo]	'books'	14. [katiko]	'mushroom'
5. [magulu]	'legs'	15. [matu]	'ears'
6. [miti]	'trees'	16. [buti]	'sticks'
7. [muti]	'tree'	17. [bintu]	'things'
8. [kutu]	'ear'	18. [muwala]	'girl'
9. [butiko]	'mushrooms'	19. [misege]	'wolves'
10. [kintu]	'thing'	20. [bantu]	'people'

Five noun classes are represented here according to the forms for singular and plural. Fill in the following chart. In the boxes labeled "CLASS," give an arbitrary number to the class. For each class, in the box labeled "SG," write the morpheme for the singular. In the box labeled "PL," write the morpheme for the plural. In the box labeled "STEMS," write the stems (the morphemes without the singular or plural), and in the corresponding space in the box labeled "GLOSS," write the meaning of the stem between single quotes. Some of the data have been filled in for you.

CLASS	SG	PL	STEMS	GLOSS
1	mu-	ba-		

3. **Fore** (Papua New Guinea)

1.	[natuwi]	'I ate yesterday.'	8.	[natuni]	'We ate yesterday.'
2.	[nagasuwi]	'I ate today.'	9.	[nagasuni]	'We ate today.'
3.	[nakuwi]	'I will eat.'	10.	[nagasusi]	'We (DUAL) ate today.'
4.	[nata:ni]	'You ate yesterday.'	11.	[nakuni]	'We will eat.'
5.	[nata:naw]	'You ate yesterday?'	12.	[nakusi]	'We (DUAL) will eat.'
6.	[nakiyi]	'He will eat.'	13.	[nata:wi]	'They ate yesterday.'
7.	[nakiyaw]	'He will eat?'	14.	[nata:si]	'They (DUAL) ate yesterday.'

- Don't forget that what are inflectional affixes in many languages can be translated into separate words in English.
- 'Yesterday,' 'today,' and 'tomorrow' are translations of the English past, present, and future tenses (respectively).

a. Identify the Fore morphemes that correspond to the following English words:

1. I	______________	6. they (DUAL)	______________
2. he	______________	7. eat	______________
3. we	______________	8. yesterday	______________
4. they	______________	9. today	______________
5. we (DUAL)	______________	10. will	______________

b. What morphemes mark a: QUESTION? ______________

STATEMENT? ______________

c. Describe the order of the morphemes in terms of personal pronouns, question/statement markers, verbs, and adverbs.

d. Give the Fore words for the following:

1. He ate yesterday? ______________________________
2. They (DUAL) will eat? ______________________________
3. They ate today. ______________________________

☑ RECAP

Make sure you know how to do the following. (See also the Key Terms on pp. 139–140 of the main text.)

- define morphological terms
- divide a word into its morphemes
- assign lexical categories
- build word trees
- identify inflection and derivation
- construct compound words
- recognize endocentric and exocentric compounds
- recognize processes used to build words
- do morphological analysis
- identify morphological processes in unfamiliar languages
- find allomorphs

Questions? Problems?

five

Syntax: The Analysis of Sentence Structure

Syntax is the study of the system of rules and categories that underlies sentence formation. Following are some of the important topics and concepts covered in this chapter. Make sure you are familiar with them.

Syntactic categories
Phrases
Phrase structure tests
Phrase structure trees and the Merge operation
Simple sentences
Complement options
Sentences with complement clauses
Deep structure and transformations
Questions and the Move operation
Verb raising and *Do* insertion
Coordination, relative clauses, and passives

Syntactic Categories (Section 1.1, pp. 152–155)

There are two types of **syntactic categories**: **lexical** and **nonlexical**. Some of the major characteristics of each include:

Lexical:

- words that have meaning (semantic content)
- words that can be inflected
- includes **nouns**, **verbs**, **adjectives**, **adverbs**, and **prepositions**

Nonlexical:

- words whose meaning is harder to define
- words that have a **grammatical** function
- includes **determiners**, **auxiliary verbs**, **degree words**, and **conjunctions**

The lexical category to which a word belongs can be determined by examining (1) its meaning, (2) the type of inflectional affixes that it can take, and (3) the nonlexical category words with which it can co-occur.

Be careful: Some words can belong to more than one category.

PRACTICE 5.1: Syntactic categories

Each of the following sentences contains some underlined words. Identify the category of each underlined word. Note that the underlined word can be either lexical or nonlexical.

Words can often be assigned to more than one category, so pay close attention to how the word is being used in the sentence.

1. Pamela's heart beat fast and her hands trembled a lot as she listened to the intermittent knocking on the front door of her shanty, located near the railroad tracks beside a hobo jungle, and she thought, "That's a bum rap if I ever heard one."
2. "The leg, he is fractured," he said in broken English.
3. The Great Barrier Reef is 900 miles long, and Wilmer Chanti, the great explorer, says it could be circumnavigated in forty days.
4. When I turned the key to open my lab door, I thought it would be my usual dull day, until I noticed that my little cucaracha had flopped over on his back, frantically waving his little legs, and I realized that someone had bugged my bug.
5. It was a dark and stormy night, its green clarity diluted by my roommate who, as usual, was making cutting remarks as she drank my scotch.
6. "I hate pineapples," said Tom dolefully.
7. Here's how to make a fortune. Buy fifty male deer. Then you will have fifty bucks.

Phrases (Section 1.2, pp. 155–160)

A **phrase** is a unit of sentence structure between a word and a sentence. Although a phrase can consist of a single word, a phrase usually consists of two or more words. There are three important components to a phrase.

- **Heads.** A phrase must have a head. The **head** of a phrase is the obligatory core around which the phrase is built. Four categories usually function as the head of a phrase, thereby allowing for four types of phrases.

  1. NP (noun phrase)
  2. AP (adjective phrase)
  3. VP (verb phrase)
  4. PP (prepositional phrase)

  The head of a noun phrase is, of course, a noun; the head of an adjective phrase, an adjective; the head of a verb phrase, a verb; and the head of a prepositional phrase, a preposition.

- **Specifiers.** A phrase can optionally contain a specifier. **Specifiers** help to make the meaning of the head more precise. Specifiers mark phrasal boundaries. In English, specifiers occur before the head, thus marking the beginning of a phrase.

  1. Det (determiners) specify a noun
     e.g., *the, a, these, that*
  2. Adv (adverbs) specify a verb
     e.g., *always, often, never*
  3. Deg (degree words) specify an adjective or a preposition
     e.g., *very, quite, really*

- **Complements.** A phrase can also optionally contain a complement. **Complements** provide more information about entities that are implied by the head of the phrase. In English, complements come after the head, thus marking the end of a phrase. Complements are typically other phrases.

REMINDER

Specifiers can help determine the category to which a word belongs. This is because the type of specifier found in a phrase depends on the category of the head. So, if a word can occur with a determiner, it is a noun; if it occurs with an adverb, it is a verb; and if it occurs with a degree word, it is an adjective or preposition.

Following are some examples of the four different types of phrases.

1. Noun Phrase (NP)

a. *presidents* —contains only the head noun (*presidents*)

b. *the presidents* —contains a specifier (*the*) and the head noun (*presidents*)

c. *presidents of the USA* —contains the head noun (*presidents*) and a complement prepositional phrase (*of the USA*)

d. *the presidents of the USA* —contains a specifier (*the*), the head noun (*presidents*), and a complement prepositional phrase (*of the USA*)

The complement prepositional phrase *of the USA* consists of a head preposition (*of*) and a complement noun phrase (*the USA*). The noun phrase *the USA* then consists of a specifier (*the*) and a head noun (*USA*).

2. Adjective Phrase (AP)

a. *happy* —contains only the head adjective (*happy*)

b. *very happy* —contains a specifier (*very*) and the head adjective (*happy*)

c. *happy with the results* —contains the head adjective (*happy*) and a complement prepositional phrase (*with the results*)

d. *very happy with the results* —contains a specifier (*very*), the head adjective (*happy*), and a complement prepositional phrase (*with the results*)

The complement prepositional phrase *with the results* consists of a head preposition (*with*) and a complement noun phrase (*the results*). The noun phrase *the results* then consists of a specifier (*the*) and a head noun (*results*).

3. Verb Phrase (VP)

a. *sings* —contains only the head verb (*sings*)

b. *often sings* —contains a specifier (*often*) and the head verb (*sings*)

c. *sings a song* —contains the head verb (*sings*) and a complement noun phrase (*a song*)

d. *often sings a song* —contains a specifier (*often*), the head verb (*sings*), and a complement noun phrase (*a song*)

The complement noun phrase *a song* consists of a specifier (*a*) and a head noun (*song*).

4. Prepositional Phrase (PP)

a. *in the car* —contains the head preposition (*in*) and a complement noun phrase (*the car*)

b. *almost in the car* —contains a specifier (*almost*), the head preposition (*in*), and a complement noun phrase (*the car*)

The complement noun phrase *the car* contains a specifier (*the*) and a head noun (*car*).

REMINDER

Phrases have hierarchical structure.

Give an example of:

1. a noun phrase containing a specifier, a head noun, and a complement.
2. an adjective phrase containing a specifier and a head adjective.
3. a verb phrase containing a head verb and a complement.
4. a prepositional phrase containing a head preposition and a complement.

> **REMINDER**
>
> Prepositional phrases are different from the other three types of phrases in that prepositional phrases must almost always contain a complement, and that complement is usually a noun phrase.

PRACTICE 5.2: Heads, specifiers, and complements

For each of the following phrases, determine the head of the phrase, any specifiers, and any complements. Remember that every phrase must have a head, but not every phrase has a specifier and complement. The first one is done for you.

	HEAD	SPECIFIER	COMPLEMENT
1. the rat	rat	the	none
2. men			
3. in the barn			
4. really mean			
5. worked			
6. worked at the station			
7. extremely boring			
8. that destruction of the city			
9. never walks to the park			
10. very small			
11. in the room			
12. awfully cute			
13. seldom smiles			
14. swept the floor			
15. the poem about love			
16. pancakes			

Go back and determine the type of each phrase. Remember, the lexical category of the head determines the type of phrase.

Phrase Structure Tests (Section 1.4, pp. 161–162)

There are a number of tests that can be done to determine whether a group of words is or is not a syntactic unit (a constituent). Three frequently used tests are the **substitution test**, the **movement test**, and the **coordination test**. Be careful, though; not every test works for every phrase.

Substitution Test

The substitution test states that a group of words is a phrase if it can be substituted with a single expression, such as *they, do so,* or *there,* and still be grammatical. The expression used as a substitute tells you the type of phrase you have.

NP: A noun phrase can be substituted with a pronoun.
e.g., *The boys* played in the mud. *They* played in the mud.
(*they* = *the boys*)

VP: A verb phrase can be substituted with *do so.*
e.g., The girls will *play in the mud,* if the boys *do so.*
(*do so* = *play in the mud*)

PP: A prepositional phrase can sometimes be substituted with *there* or *then.*
e.g., The boys played *in the mud.* The boys played *there.*
(*there* = *in the mud*)

Movement Test

The movement test states that a group of words is a phrase if it can be moved to another position in the sentence and still be grammatical.

e.g., The children bought candy *at the store.* ⟶
At the store, the children bought candy.

Coordination Test

According to this test, a group of words is a phrase if it can be joined to another group of words using a conjunction (*and, but, or*) and still be grammatical.

e.g., The children *bought candy* and *left the store.*
(two verb phrases joined with the conjunction *and*)

Practice 5.3: Phrase structure tests

1. Apply the substitution test to determine which of the bracketed sequences in the following sentences are phrases.

    1. [Juanita and Juan] arrived [in San Juan] [on Epiphany].

2. The cabbage [rolls were] salty.
3. They moved [the desk with the wooden top].
4. Little Andrew swallowed [all the pills].
5. Mike is [writing a ballad about American soldiers in Iraq].

2. Apply the movement test to determine which of the bracketed sequences in the following sentences are phrases.

1. The [army was surrounded] by the enemy.
2. Leona likes [Viennese waltzes and Argentinean tangos].
3. Jean ate his lunch [in the revolving restaurant].
4. Eat, drink, and [be merry for] today will become yesterday.
5. The polar bears [were swimming among] the ice floes.

3. Use a conjunction (*and, but, or*) and join each of the following phrases with a phrase of the same type. Use the substitution test to determine the type of phrase.

1. the new desk
2. assembled the new desk
3. new
4. in a hole
5. rather huge
6. worked on a movie
7. beside the fence
8. really lovely
9. talked to the girls
10. a dentist

Phrase Structure Trees (Section 1.2, pp. 155–160)

Phrases are built using the **Merge** operation. Merge combines words using the **X'** (X-bar) **schema** in which X stands for any head.

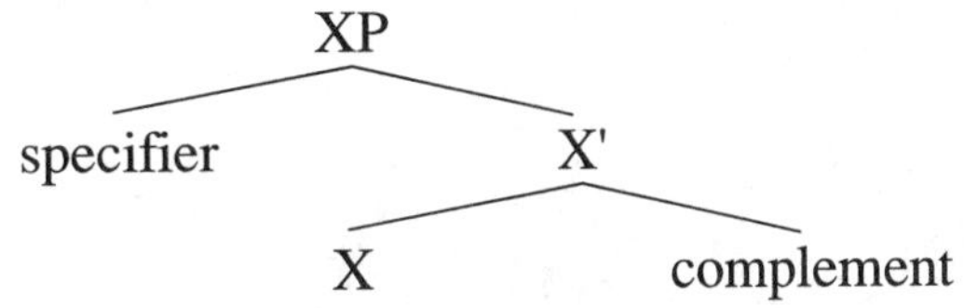

Specifiers attach to the phrasal, XP level, while complements attach to the intermediate X' level. Even though specifiers and complements are optional, X' is always present in the representation of a phrase, called a tree diagram.

Following is an example of a fully diagrammed tree for the noun phrase *a book on Shakespeare* which contains a head, a specifier, and a complement.

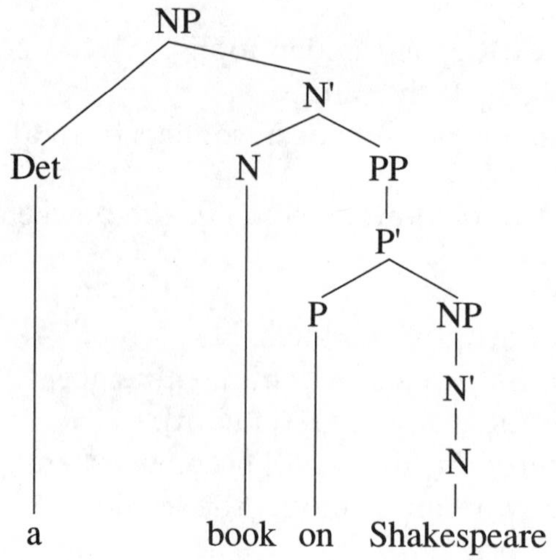

Merge created the above complex phrase by combining the noun phrase *Shakespeare* with the preposition *on* to create the prepositional phrase *on Shakespeare.* This phrase was then combined with the noun *book* and the specifier *a* to create the noun phrase *a book on Shakespeare.*

PRACTICE 5.4: Drawing phrase structure trees

Draw tree diagrams for each of the following phrases. Remember, specifiers come before the head, and complements come after the head.

1. the rat
2. men
3. in the barn
4. really mean
5. ran
6. ran into the shed
7. rather boring
8. hate those pancakes
9. the denial of the accusation
10. very small
11. right into the room
12. awfully cute
13. seldom smiles
14. swept the floor
15. fond of candy
16. silly
17. the poem about love
18. read the poem
19. jumped over the barn
20. usually eats lunch

REMINDER

Use the substitution test to help determine the type of phrase you are dealing with. The substitution test not only can tell you if a group of words is or is not a phrase, but also can tell you the type of phrase you have. So don't just guess.

Simple Sentences (Section 1.3, pp. 160–161)

A sentence is the largest unit of syntactic analysis. Like a phrase, a sentence consists of a specifier, a head, and a complement.

- **NP.** The noun phrase is typically referred to as the subject, and it can consist of any of the possibilities we saw during our discussion of phrases. The subject is the specifier of I.
- **I (Infl).** This is the head of the sentence, and it is used to refer to inflection. There are two possibilities for I: +Pst and –Pst. +Pst is used for sentences in the past tense, and –Pst is used for sentences in either the present or future.
- **VP.** The verb phrase is a part of what is typically referred to as the predicate. Like the subject NP, the VP can consist of any of the possibilities we saw during our discussion of phrases. The VP is often considered to function as the complement of I.

Sentences, like phrases, are built according to the X' schema. Since I is the head of a sentence, IP is used to represent this syntactic unit.

Below is an example of a fully diagrammed tree for the sentence *The children read a book.*

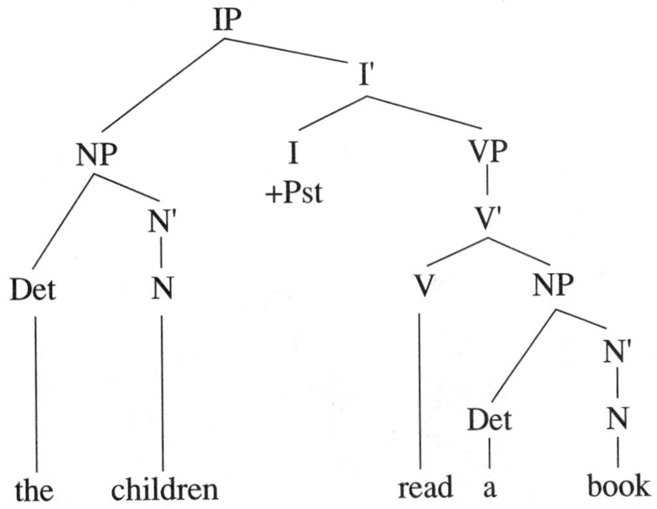

Auxiliary Verbs

A sentence may include an auxiliary verb. Auxiliary verbs can be either **modal** or **nonmodal**.

Modal auxiliary verbs	include *will, would, can, could, should, must, might, may* occupy the I position
Nonmodal auxiliary verbs	include *have, be* occupy a V position in VP take VP as a complement

Below is an example of a fully diagrammed tree for the sentence *The children will read a book,* which contains a modal auxiliary.

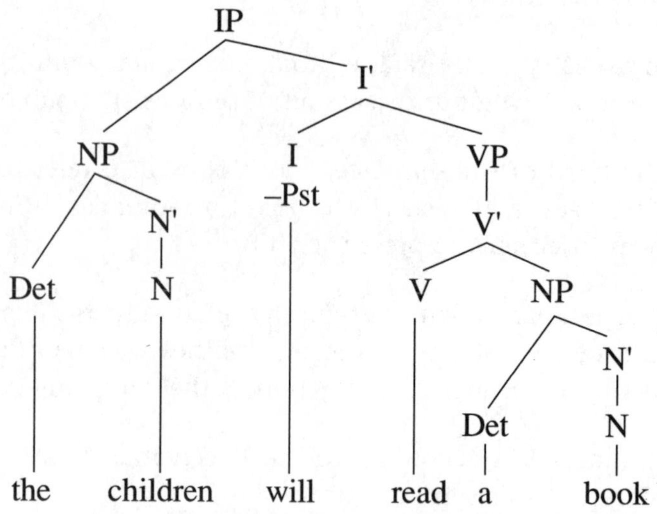

Below is an example of a fully diagrammed tree for the sentence *The children are reading a book,* which contains a nonmodal auxiliary.

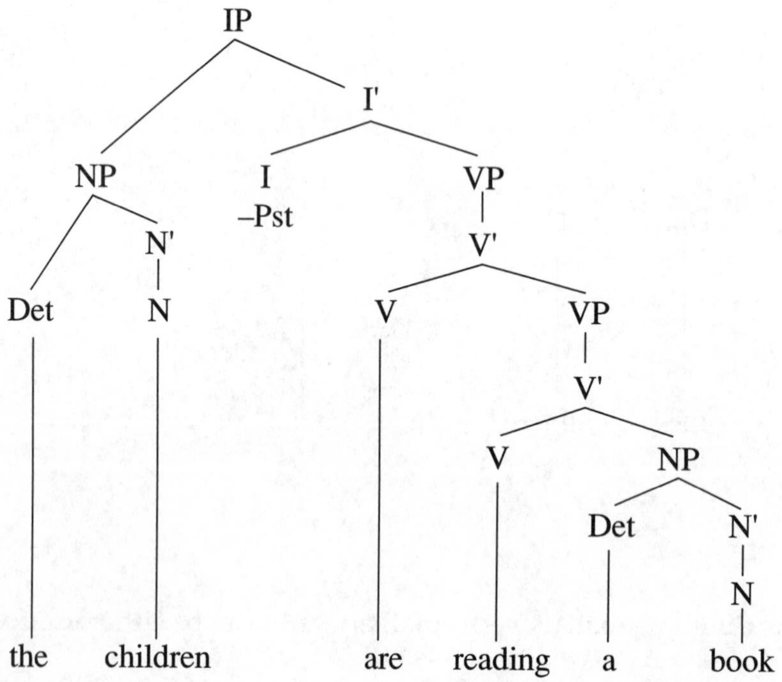

A sentence may contain both a modal and a nonmodal auxiliary verb. Consider the sentence *The children will be reading a book.* How would the tree for this sentence be different from the tree shown above? Try putting together a tree diagram for this sentence.

PRACTICE 5.5: Diagramming simple sentences

The following exercise will give you some practice with simple sentences. Draw a tree diagram for each of the following sentences.

1. Students often write exams.
2. A penguin walked into the room.
3. Dogs should always go for a walk.
4. Those monsters were hiding under the bed.
5. Abner concealed the document.
6. Marge usually watches the sunset.
7. The children are playing with a dinosaur.
8. That garbage smells.
9. Grandparents may live in condominiums.
10. Carl has drawn trees.

REMINDER

Construct your tree diagrams above the sentence, not below it.

Complement Options (Section 2, pp. 162–167)

To ensure that the Merge operation builds grammatical sentences, the individual words in a sentence must occur with complements of the right type. For example, many verbs (e.g., *throw*) require a complement noun phrase and must therefore appear in a structure containing a noun phrase in the complement position. If such a verb were entered into a structure without a noun phrase complement, the result would be an ungrammatical sentence. The complement(s) with which a word can occur are called its complement options. Merge, therefore, combines words into sentences in a manner consistent with both the X' schema and the complement options of the individual words.

Information on the complement options of words along with the meaning and pronunciation of words are found in a speaker's mental **lexicon**. Information about a word's complement options is often referred to as **subcategorization**.

PRACTICE 5.6: Complement Options

1. Determine the complement options that the verbs listed below require. Do this by thinking of grammatical and ungrammatical sentences containing the verb.

1. panic	4. write
2. watch	5. wonder
3. imagine	6. play

2. Nouns, adjectives, and prepositions also have restrictions on the types of complements with which they can and cannot occur. Determine the complement options required by the following lexical items.

1. pleasure	4. intelligent
2. with	5. at
3. contribution	6. upset

Sentences with Complement Clauses (Section 2.3, pp. 165–167)

Sentences themselves may also function as complements. That is, a sentence can occur in the complement position of a phrase. A sentence contained within a phrase is called a **complement clause (CP)**.

Like other syntactic units, a CP consists of a head, a specifier, and a complement. The head of a CP is a **complementizer (C)**. Complementizers include words such as *that, if,* and *whether.* The complement of a complementizer is an IP, a sentence. The specifier position within a CP functions as a landing site for phrases undergoing the **Move** operation.

Below is a tree diagram for a sentence containing a complement clause within the verb phrase.

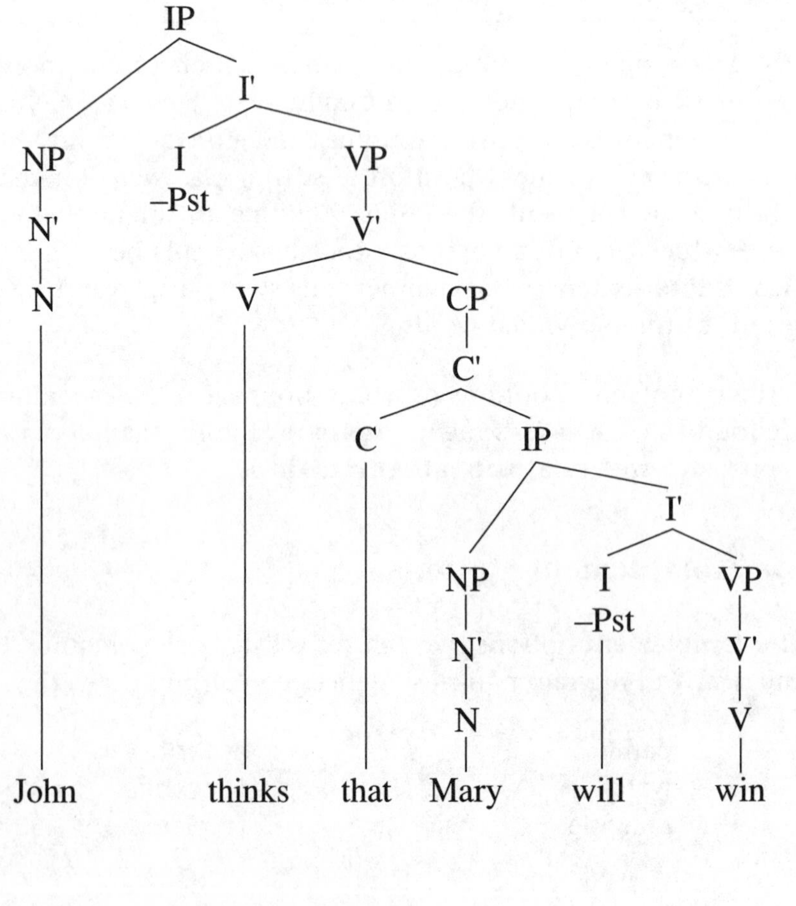

SOME HINTS FOR DRAWING PHRASE STRUCTURE TREES

1. Every sentence (IP) consists of an NP and an I'. I' consists of an I and a VP.

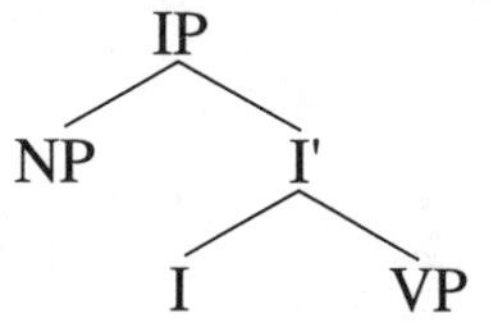

2. Identify the verb. Check if this verb has a specifier and/or a complement. Remember that the optional specifier, an adverb, marks the beginning of the phrase, and either the verb or the complement marks the end of the verb phrase.

3. Identify I. I can be either –Pst or +Pst. +Pst is only used if a sentence is in the past tense. Modal auxiliary verbs occur under I, but nonmodal auxiliaries occur under the V. Remember these take a VP as their complement.

4. Identify the subject NP. Remember that an optional determiner, the specifier, marks the beginning of this noun phrase, and either the noun or a complement marks the end of the noun phrase.

5. The complement of the verb can be a complement clause (CP).

   Since a CP contains an IP, you will also need to identify and diagram the NP and I', and the I and VP under I'.

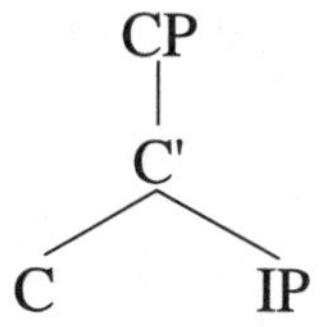

Practice 5.7: Diagramming sentences with complement clauses

Draw a tree diagram for each of the following sentences.

1. Stan hopes that Sean will become a pilot.
2. Nancy believes that aliens exist.
3. Sailors know that the ship could sink.
4. The realtor wonders whether Louise can sell the house.
5. The passengers fear that the plane will never land.

PRACTICE 5.8: More practice with phrase structure trees

The following exercise contains many examples of simple sentences as well as sentences with complement clauses. Draw a tree diagram for each. Watch out: they get harder.

1. The repairman fixed the watch.
2. Neighbors can be unfriendly.
3. Nurses never complain.
4. The train has left.
5. The assistant should be sending e-mails.
6. Children are very curious.
7. The flowers look quite attractive.
8. The driver of that car is speeding down the highway.
9. The salesman wonders if those customers will buy the car.
10. George hopes that Fred will win the race.
11. Kayleigh usually thinks that working on the car is fun.
12. The smugglers perhaps thought that the police were working on the case.
13. The tourists hope that whales will be swimming near the boat.

Questions (Section 3.1, pp. 167–171; Section 3.4, pp. 173–177)

Merge is responsible for building the structure of a sentence and operates in conjunction with both subcategorization information and the X' schema. However, Merge cannot create all the structures of a language. Some structures require a second operation. Move transforms an existing structure (e.g., a statement) into another type of structure (e.g., a question). Move does this by transporting elements from one position in a sentence to another.

There are three important consequences of Move.

- CP. Move transports elements to positions with a CP. Auxiliary verbs move to C, while *wh* phrases move to the specifier position of C. Every sentence must, therefore, include a CP. If a sentence contains an embedded CP, a complementizer can occur under the C. For all other CPs, information on whether the sentence is a question or a statement is found under the C: If C contains +Q, the structure is a question; and if C is empty, it is a statement.

- **Trace.** Moved elements leave behind a **trace** (t). A trace records (1) that a movement occurred, and (2) where in the structure the moved element originated.

- **Levels of Representation.** Two levels of representation result: **deep structure** and **surface structure**. Merge generates the deep structure. The surface structure is the result of applying any additional operations, such as Move. The surface structure is often called the final syntactic form. If no elements have moved, then the deep and surface structures are the same.

Move operates to create both ***yes-no*** and ***wh*** **questions**.

Yes-No Questions

Yes-No questions are so named because the response to such a question is usually "yes" or "no." *Yes-No* questions are formed by moving an auxiliary verb, either modal or nonmodal, from its position in I to the complementizer position within a CP. This is often called **Inversion**.

Inversion: Move I to C
e.g., Mary **will** leave → **Will** Mary **t** leave

After Merge:

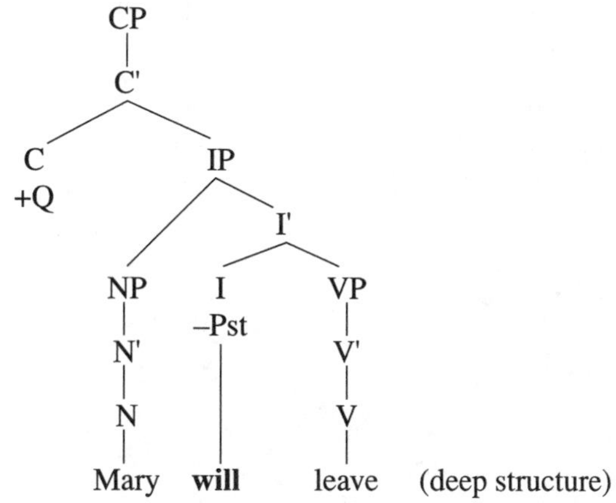

After Inversion:

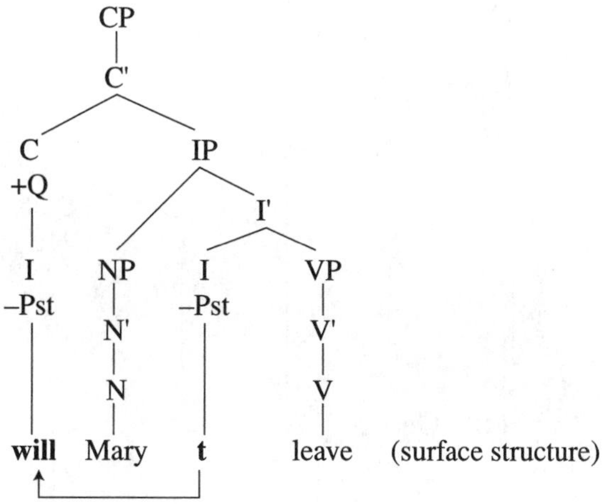

Wh Questions

Wh questions are so named because they begin with a *wh* word (e.g., *what, who*). *Wh* questions are the result of two applications of the Move operation: Inversion and *Wh* Movement.

***Wh* Movement:** Move a *wh* phrase to the specifier position under CP.

e.g., George **should** buy *what* → *What* **should** George **t** buy *t*

After Merge:

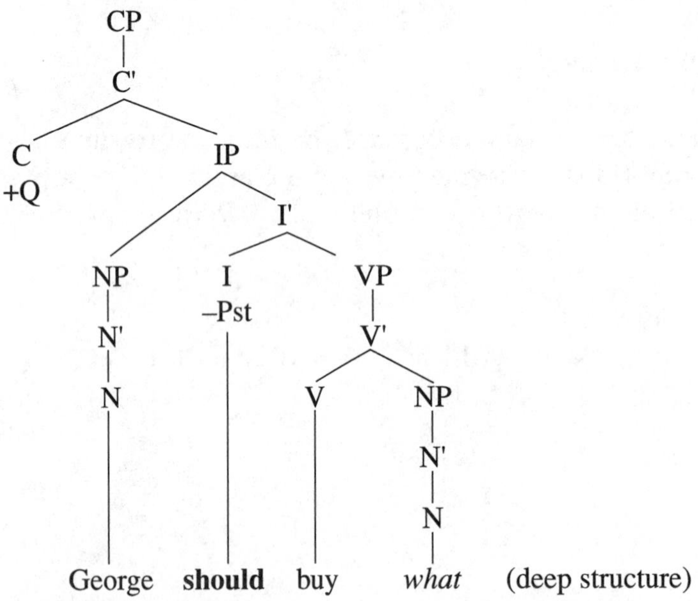

After Inversion and *Wh* Movement:

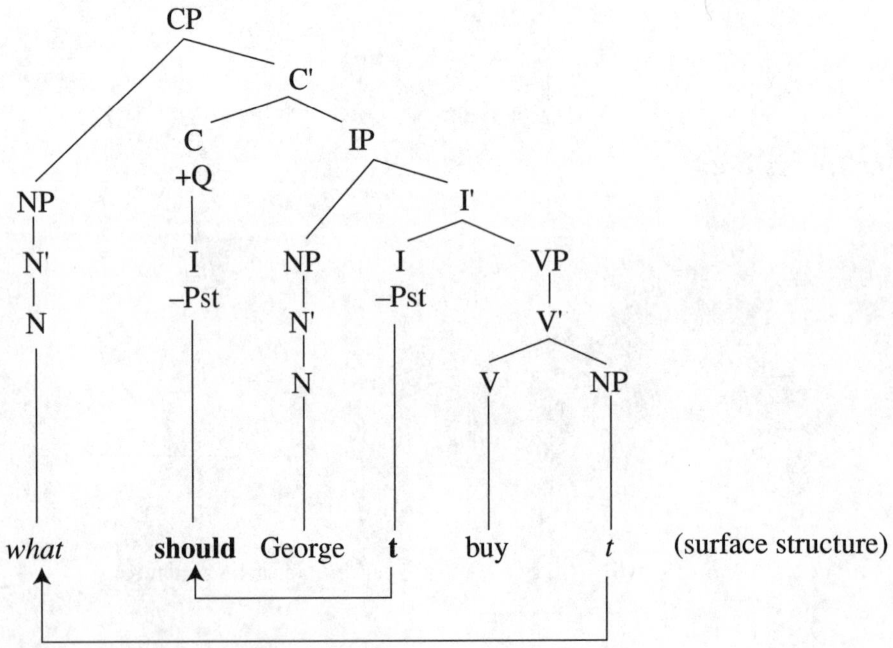

PRACTICE 5.9: Questions

For each of the following sentences, draw a tree diagram for both the deep and surface structures. On the surface structure, indicate with arrows the elements that have moved and where they have moved.

1. Can a dog bark?
2. Will the trip be enjoyable?
3. What must Megan do?
4. Whom should the teacher praise?
5. Which coat should Joan wear?
6. Who can see the shore?

REMINDER

1. Each movement leaves a trace in its original position. When you draw the surface structure tree, do not forget to include a *t* in the original position of a moved element.
2. *Wh* Movement moves an entire phrase.

Other Operations

Move can also transport a verb to a new position in the sentence. This is often called **Verb Raising**. As well, new elements can be added to a structure. One example of this operation is **Do** Insertion.

Verb Raising (Section 4.1, pp. 178–182)

Remember, there are two types of auxiliaries: modal and nonmodal. Modal auxiliaries occur in I and nonmodal auxiliaries occur in V. Both types of auxiliaries can be inverted to create a question. However, nonmodal auxiliaries must first be moved from V to I, since Inversion moves I to C. This is called Verb Raising.

Verb Raising: Move V to I

e.g., Mary is leaving → Mary is **t** leaving

After Merge:

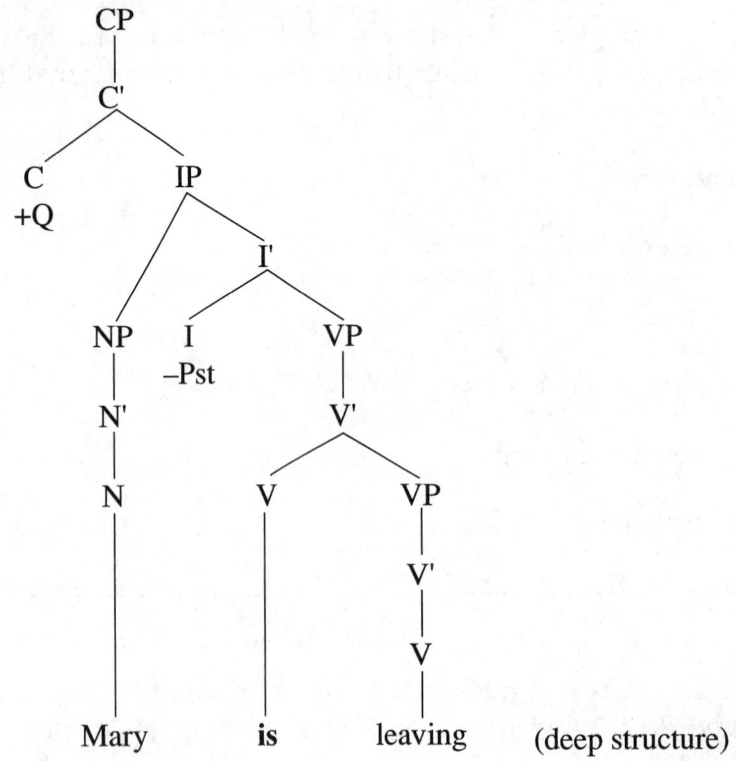

After Verb Raising:

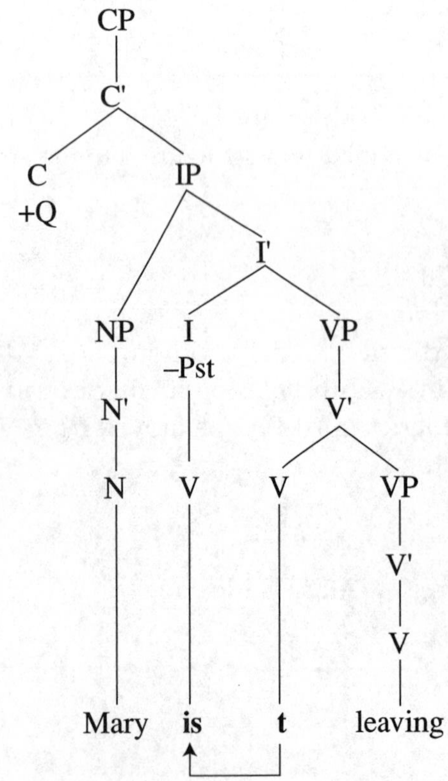

After Inversion:

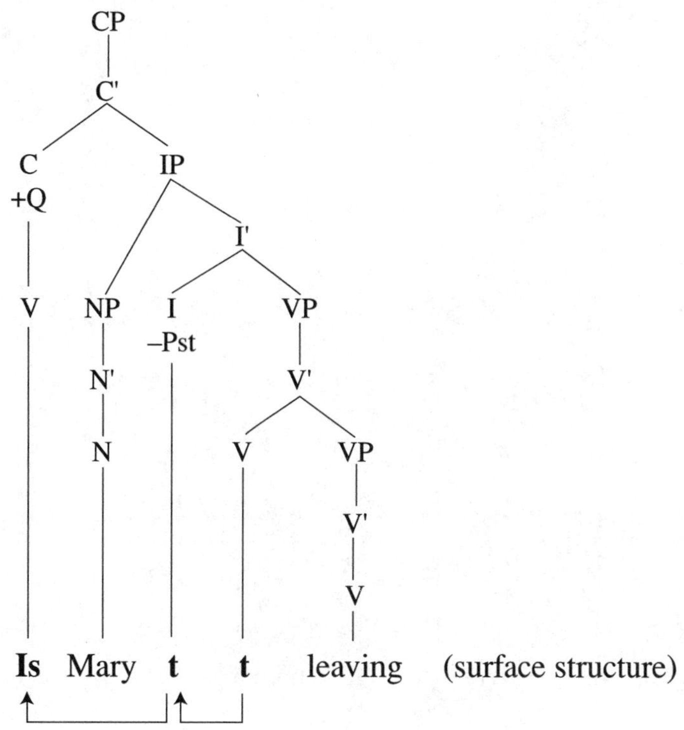

Verb Raising can also occur during the formation of *wh* questions.

e.g., What was Sylvia thinking?

Sylvia **was** thinking *what* → Sylvia **was t** thinking *what* → **was** Sylvia **t t** thinking *what* → *what* **was** Sylvia **t t** thinking *t*

Deep Structure:

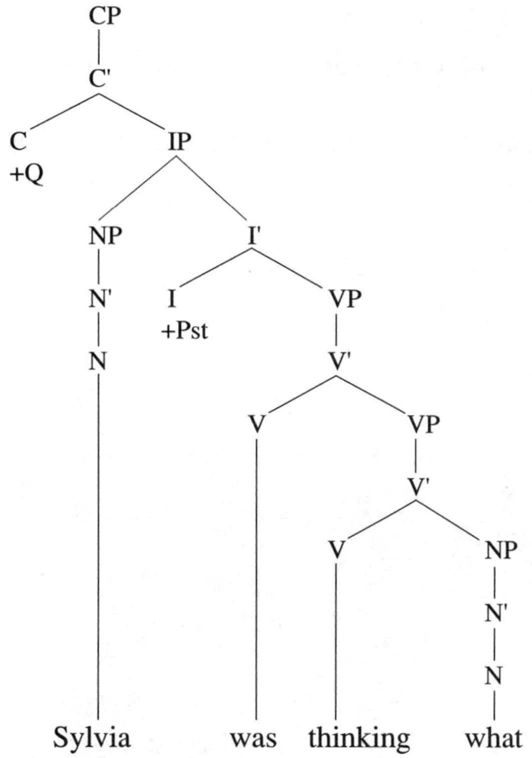

Surface Structure

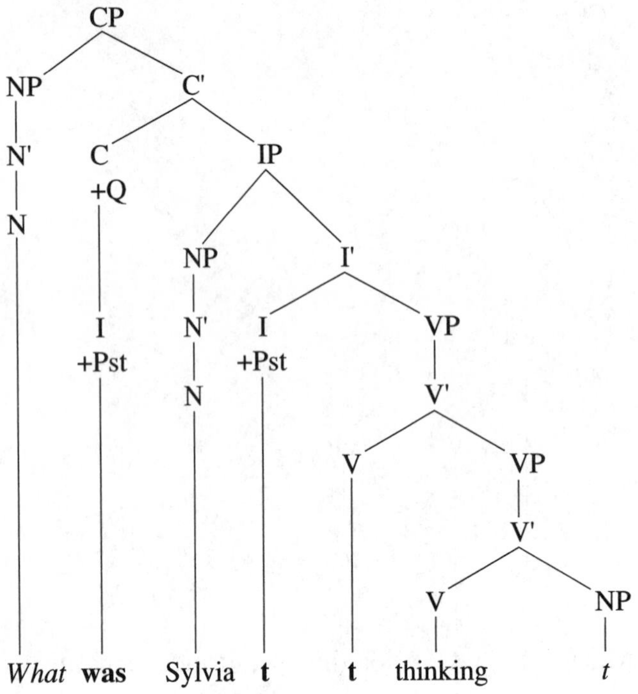

Do Insertion (Section 3.3, pp. 172–173)

Auxiliary verbs, whether modal or nonmodal, are optional in English. As a result, many English sentences will not contain auxiliary verbs. Yet, these sentences can still be changed into questions. This is done by inserting *do, did,* or *does* into the sentence.

***Do* Insertion:** Insert *do* into an empty I position.

e.g., Mary left → Mary **did** leave → **Did** Mary **t** leave

After Merge: Note that we assume that the verb after Merge is actually *leave* under V with +Past under I.

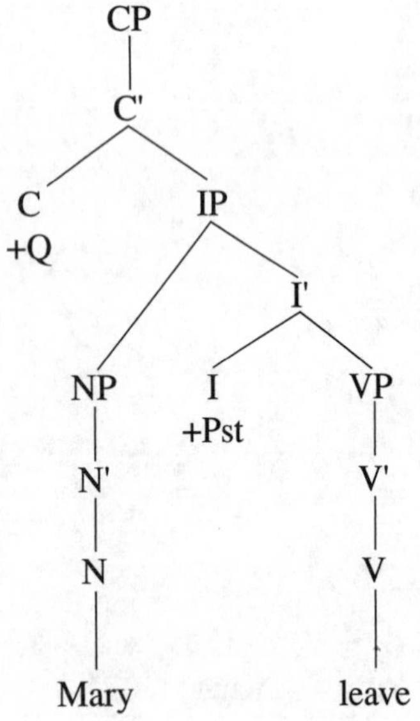

(deep structure)

After *Do* Insertion:

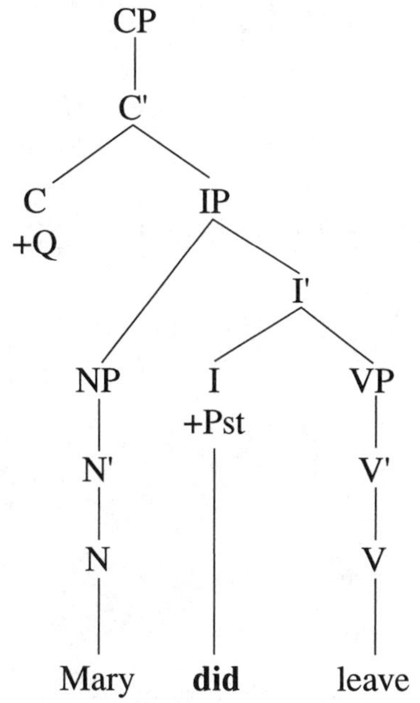

After Inversion:

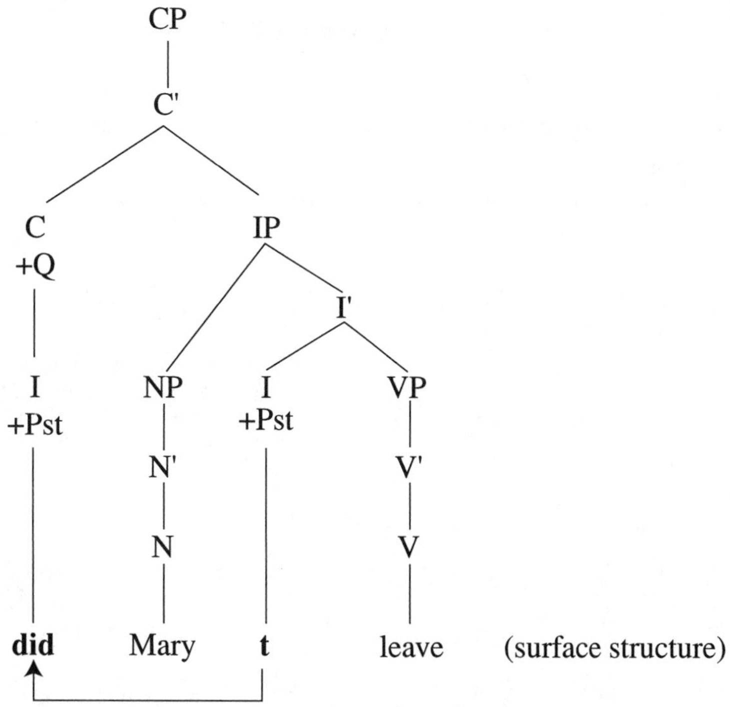

Remember: *Do* Insertion can also occur during the formation of *wh* questions.

e.g., *What* **did** George buy?

George buy (+Pst) *what* → George **did** buy *what* → **did** George **t** buy *what* → *what* **did** George **t** buy *t*

PRACTICE 5.10: Do Insertion and Verb Raising

1. Draw a tree diagram of both the deep structure and the surface structure for *What did George buy?* On the S-structure, draw arrows from the traces to the moved elements.

2. For each of the following sentences, draw a tree diagram of both the deep and surface structures.

   a. Does Gillian like fish?

   b. Who did Jessica invite?

   c. Did the elves sweep the floor?

   d. What did Sally paint?

   e. Have the boys seen the pictures?

   f. What book was the class reading?

REMINDER

In English, only the nonmodal auxiliary verbs can be raised from their position under V to under the I position. This is not true of all languages. For example, in French any type of verb can be moved to this position.

Identifying Deep Structure and Transformations

(Section 3, pp. 167–177)

You need to be able to determine the deep structure for any sentence you are given, and to do so you need to be able to identify any of the movements that have occurred. Remember, Inversion, *Wh* Movement, and Verb Raising are all applications of the Move operation. *Do* Insertion is also a syntactic operation. You may also have to construct a tree diagram of the deep and surface structures.

Here are some clues to help you identify which movements have occurred and put surface structure sentences back into deep structure:

YOU SEE:	YOU THINK:	YOU DO:
A modal auxiliary verb ahead of the subject.	Inversion has taken place.	Put the modal auxiliary back into its deep structure position in I.
A nonmodal auxiliary verb ahead of the subject.	Inversion has taken place. Verb Raising has taken place.	Put the nonmodal auxiliary back into its deep structure position under V.
A *wh* word or phrase.	*Wh* Movement has taken place.	Examine each verb in the sentence. Determine if a verb is missing either a subject or an object, and put the *wh* word or phrase into that position. Examine each preposition in the sentence. Determine if a preposition is missing its object. Put the *wh* word or phrase into that position.
Do, Does, or *Did* at the beginning of a sentence or after a *wh* phrase.	*Do* Insertion has taken place.	Remove *do, does,* or *did* from the sentence.

Practice 5.11: Practice with transformations (Sections 2–3, pp. 162–177)

Draw a tree diagram of each sentence. If movement has occurred, draw both the deep and surface structure, and list all transformations that have occurred to derive the surface structure.

1. Who does the jury blame?

2. Margo dreamed that Frances might fly to England.
3. Are those students using the library?
4. What was Sarah writing?
5. Could vandals have destroyed those billboards?
6. Josh thinks that girls never phone Bill.
7. Who will the children live with?
8. Who should be preparing the meal?
9. At which airport are the visitors arriving?
10. Would the winner claim the prize?
11. Dianne knew that Tom might like the meal.
12. Do children like cake?

REMINDER

1. You are trying to determine which elements have already moved; therefore, you must never move any additional words or phrases.
2. No movements may have occurred, only one movement may have occurred, or more than one movement may have occurred.
3. To find the deep structure, you need to:
   - find all instances of Move
   - determine if *Do* Insertion has occurred

Other Structures (Section 5, pp. 182–188)

Some other syntactic structures include **coordinate structures**, **relative clauses**, and **passives**. Each of these structures builds on the basic syntactic system (i.e., Merge and Move) for forming sentences.

Coordination (Section 5.1, pp. 182–184)

Coordination joins structures together using a conjunction such as *and, but,* or *or.* Any level of structure (X, X', or XP) can be joined. Only structures of the same type can be joined together. That is, a NP must be conjoined with another NP. If structures of different types are joined, the result is an ungrammatical structure. Finally, conjoining structures results in a larger structure of the same type. So, joining two NPs together results in a larger NP.

e.g., Vs: $[\text{draw}]_V$ and $[\text{color}]_V$ those pictures
N's: that $[\text{car}]_{N'}$ and $[\text{truck}]_{N'}$
PPs: $[\text{up the stairs}]_{PP}$ and $[\text{into the hallway}]_{PP}$

Relative Clauses (Section 5.2, pp. 184–186)

A relative clause is a type of complement clause (CP) that provides information about a preceding noun. Relative clauses can modify either subjects or objects. Relative clauses are similar to *wh* questions: both begin with a *wh* word and both involve *Wh* Movement. And as in *wh* questions, *Wh* Movement can move a *wh* word or phrase from either the subject or the **direct object** position.

e.g., The girl [**who t** lives across the street]$_{CP}$ came for a visit.
- modifies the noun *girl*
- *wh* word moved from subject position

Norm brought the flowers [**which** Sue has **t**]$_{CP}$.
- modifies the noun *flowers*
- *wh* word moved from object position

Passives (Section 5.3, pp. 186–188)

A sentence may be either **active** or **passive**. In an active sentence, the agent or doer of the action occurs in the subject position. In a passive sentence, this agent may be either absent or present within the VP as the object of a preposition. The direct object of an active sentence becomes the subject of a passive sentence. Passive sentences are formed using **NP Movement**, another type of Move. NP Movement transports an object from its deep structure position as a complement of the verb to an empty subject position.

e.g., **Active:** The chef prepared the meal.

Passive: The meal was prepared. / The meal was prepared by the chef.

Practice 5.12: Identifying other structures

The following exercises will give you some practice with identifying coordinate structures, relative clauses, and passives.

1. For each of the following coordinate structures, determine the category of the structures that have been joined together.

   a. Stephen watched television but Gloria listened to the radio.
   b. Terry drove the Ninja-Turtle and the Monster-Mutt.
   c. Bill believes that the world is round and that the sun is hot.
   d. Andrea usually eats dinner and goes to bed.

2. Each of the following sentences contains a relative clause. Put brackets around this clause. Remember: A relative clause is a CP.

   a. The movie which Henry likes is really awful.
   b. Sarah was talking to the cyclist who won the race.
   c. The building which Winston designed may be demolished.

3. Decide if each of the following sentences is active or passive. Remember: A passive sentence does not necessarily include an agent.

   a. That lamp could be fixed.
   b. Those tigers were trained by a professional.
   c. The company should make a donation.
   d. The winner was given a prize.

Review Exercise

Draw a tree diagram for each of the following sentences. You will need to use what you have learned about simple sentences, sentences with complement clauses, and various types of movement. If movement has occurred, draw arrows from the trace to the moved element, and list the transformations.

1. Sally lives right in the middle of Chicago.
2. The unicorn might be eating the lilies.
3. The rabbit was hiding under the bridge.
4. The castle fell into the sea.
5. The media have reported that the candidate won the election.
6. Did Bill write that check?
7. Does William think that Harry can succeed in business?
8. The jury believed that the prisoner was guilty.
9. Can the clown amuse that boy?
10. What does Mary want?
11. Who did Carol talk to?
12. Which color has Jamie chosen?

☑ RECAP

If you can do the following, then you've conquered syntax. (See also the Key Terms on pp. 188–189 of the main text.)

- describe the differences between lexical and nonlexical categories
- assign words to their syntactic category
- determine whether a group of words is a phrase
- identify and diagram phrases
- diagram simple sentences and complement clause structures
- determine complement options
- understand how the Merge operation builds sentences
- find the deep structure of a sentence
- understand Move operations
- draw tree diagrams to show Inversion, *Wh* Movement, Verb Raising, and *Do* Insertion
- recognize coordinate structures, relative clauses, and passives

Questions? Problems?

six

Semantics: The Analysis of Meaning

Semantics is the study of meaning in human language. **Meaning** refers, very generally, to the content of an utterance.

Important concepts and topics in this chapter include:

Semantic relations
Meaning
Concepts
Ambiguity
Thematic roles
Pragmatics
Conversation

Semantic Relations (Sections 1.1–1.2, pp. 202–205)

Determining the semantic relations that exist among words, phrases, and sentences constitutes one of the basic analytic tools available for evaluating meaning.

Relations between words:

- **Synonyms**—two words that have similar meanings
  e.g., filbert / hazelnut
- **Antonyms**—two words that have opposite meanings
  e.g., hot / cold
- **Polysems** (homonyms)—one word that has two or more related meanings
  e.g., bright (shining or intelligent)
- **Homophones**—two words with the same form (i.e., pronunciation) but two distinct meanings
  e.g., pen (a writing instrument or an enclosure)

Relations between sentences:

- **Paraphrases**—two sentences that have different forms but the same meaning
  e.g., The cat ate the mouse.
  The mouse was eaten by the cat.

- **Entailment**—two sentences in which the truth of the first implies the truth of the second, but the truth of the second does not necessarily imply the truth of the first
  e.g., George killed the spider.
  The spider is dead.
- **Contradiction**—two sentences such that if one is true, the second must be false
  e.g., The coelacanth is extinct.
  A fisherman has just caught a coelacanth.

Practice 6.1: Identifying semantic relations

For each of the following, identify the relation that exists between either the words or the sentences. The first one is done for you.

1. test
   exam ______synonyms______
2. Mary sang a solo.
   The solo was sung by Mary. ____________
3. bug (insect)
   bug (microphone) ____________
4. Sam is a widower.
   Sam's wife is alive. ____________
5. The shark bit a swimmer.
   The swimmer is injured. ____________
6. parent
   offspring ____________
7. George gave Sally the book.
   George gave a book to Sally. ____________
8. Pat just became an aunt.
   Pat is the father of three children. ____________
9. hungry
   famished ____________
10. steak (a piece of meat)
    stake (a sharp piece of wood) ____________

REMINDER

Polysems (homonyms) and homophones are not the same. Polysems have related meanings while homophones have unrelated meanings. Homophones need not have identical spelling.

Meaning (Section 1.3, pp. 206–209)

As native speakers of a language, we all know the meaning of a great many words in our language. And if we come across a word whose meaning is unknown to us, we can always look it up in a dictionary. But, to understand the dictionary definition, we need to understand the meanings of the words making up the definition. It is easier to determine the semantic relations between words than the precise meaning of a word. Examples of some theories of meaning are given below.

Connotation

This theory states that the meaning of a word is simply the set of associations that the word evokes. For example, a *desert* has associations of heat, dryness, and sand, even though some deserts do not have sand or are in cold areas.

Denotation

This theory states that the meaning of a word is not the set of associations it evokes, but rather the entity to which it refers—its denotation or referent in the real world. Accordingly then, the word *desert* would refer to that set of regions in the world characterized by barrenness and lack of rain.

Extension and Intension

This theory attempts to combine the first two. Extension refers to the set of referents of a word, and intension to the associations it evokes. Thus, the extension of *desert* would correspond to the set of barren, arid regions in the world, such as the Gobi, the Sahara, and the Kalahari. The intension would correspond to the concepts of barrenness and aridity, not necessarily to a specific existing desert. Thus, the meaning of a word includes both its extension and its intension.

Componential Analysis

This theory is based on the idea that meaning can be decomposed into smaller semantic units. For example, the semantic features [+living, +human, –adult] give us the category of children.

Componential analysis is useful for making generalizations, especially where verbs are concerned. For example, the verb *read* would typically have a human subject, and the verb *drink* would require an object that is a liquid.

Practice 6.2: Theories of meaning

1. For each of the following expressions, attempt to define its meaning according to the theories of connotation, denotation, and extension and intension discussed above.

   a. summer　　b. a linguistics instructor　　c. grass

2. Identify the types of phrases with which the verbs in A and B can occur. What difference in meaning between the verbs in A and the verbs in B determines the type of complement the verbs require?

A	**B**
sweep	crawl
kick	fell

3. Examine the following two groups of words and determine the semantic feature(s) each group has in common. What semantic feature(s) are different among members of each group? What about between the two groups?

   Group A: grandmother / mother / daughter / widow
   Group B: grandfather / father / son / widower

4. Now try doing a componential analysis for:
   - ewe and lamb
   - mare, filly, and colt

5. What difficulties do connotation, denotation, extension, intension, and componential analysis have in determining what meaning is?

Concepts (Section 2, pp. 209–217)

Linguists use the term *concepts* to refer to the system we use to identify, classify, and organize all elements of our many and varied experiences. Our conceptual system reveals how meaning is expressed through language.

Fuzzy Concepts

Fuzzy concepts are concepts that can differ from person to person. They have no clear-cut boundaries. Think about how much something has to cost before you would consider it expensive.

Graded Membership

Concepts have internal structure. Members of a concept can be graded according to how typical they are within that concept. The most typical member is selected as the **prototype**. Other members are arranged around the prototype. Members having more properties in common with the prototype occur closer to the prototype. Members sharing fewer properties occur farther away from the prototype.

Metaphor

The concepts expressed by language do not exist in isolation, but are interconnected and associated. Metaphors, the understanding of one concept in terms of another, can be used to make these connections. For example, emotions are often compared to spatial terms such as *up* or *down* (e.g., *George is feeling down today*). A number of metaphors attribute animal-like properties to people.

Lexicalization

Lexicalization refers to the process whereby concepts are encoded into the words of a language. How concepts combine for lexicalization varies from language to language. For example, in English, many verbs such as *roll, slide,* and *limp* contain both the idea of motion and the manner in which the motion occurs. Other languages (e.g., Spanish) cannot use one word to express both concepts, but require separate words for each. Spanish verbs of motion, though, express both the concept of motion and the direction of its path.

Grammaticization

Grammaticization refers to concepts that are expressed as affixes or nonlexical categories. Concepts such as tense, number, and negation are often grammaticized across languages. However, many other concepts can also be grammaticized. For example, statements in Hidatsa are accompanied by a morpheme that indicates the evidence for its truth (e.g. certainty, common knowledge, or unknown).

PRACTICE 6.3: Concepts

1. For each of the following concepts, determine whether they are fuzzy, are graded, or have been grammaticized.

   a. the comparative and superlative
   b. cats
   c. mountains
   d. time
   e. vegetables

   For any of the above that exhibit a graded membership, determine the member that is prototypical for you. How might this differ from person to person?

2. **Menomini.** Quite often, languages contain different forms of grammaticized affixes or functional categories whose use depends on some semantic characteristic of a stem or complement. Consider the data below from Menomini, a Native American language of Wisconsin. There are three different types of nouns depending on what forms they appear in. What are the three types of nouns, and what is the semantic basis for this?

	Unpossessed	'a person's—'	'my—'	Gloss
1.	o:s	_____	neto:s	'canoe'
2.	_____	mese:t	nese:t	'foot'
3.	_____	_____	neme:h	'elder sister'
4.	atu:hpwani:k	_____	neta:tu:hpwani:k	'tablecloth'

5.	_____	_____	nekiah	'mother'
6.	_____	mɛhkaːt	nɛhkaːt	'leg'
7.	_____	metɛːʔʧjak	netɛːʔʧjak	'soul'
8.	_____	_____	nekiːʔs	'son'
9.	toːwahkɛh	_____	netoːwahkɛh	'water drum'
10.	ahkɛːh	_____	netahkɛːh	'kettle'
11.	_____	_____	neniːh	'maternal aunt'
12.	_____	meːs	neːs	'head'

3. **Kiswahili.** The data below from Kiswahili (an African language) can be divided into three noun classes, as revealed in the inflection of singular and plural. There is a semantic basis for the three noun classes represented here. What are the three noun classes, and how is each inflected for singular and plural? What is the semantic basis that determines which class a noun belongs to?

	Singular	**Plural**	**Gloss**
1.	mtu	watu	'person'
2.	mlima	milima	'mountain'
3.	kiti	viti	'chair'
4.	mto	mito	'river'
5.	kitana	vitana	'comb'
6.	mgeni	wageni	'guest'
7.	kitanda	vitanda	'bed'
8.	mke	wake	'wife'
9.	kifungo	vifungo	'button'
10.	mti	miti	'tree'

4. **German.** In German, some prepositions assign either accusative or dative case, based on semantic grounds. In the data below, the article *das* marks the accusative case, while the article *dem* marks the dative case. What is the semantic basis for the case assignment shown here? What concept is contained in the German articles that is not found in English articles?

1.	Der Doktor geht in das Zimmer.	'The doctor goes into the room.'
	Der Doktor sitzt in dem Zimmer.	'The doctor sits in the room.'
2.	Das Auto fährt vor das Haus.	'The car drives to the front of the house.'
	Das Auto wartet vor dem Haus.	'The car waits in front of the house.'
3.	Sie setzt sich neben das Kind.	'She sits down near the child.'
	Sie sitzt neben dem Kind.	'She sits near the child.
4.	Sie legt die Feder unter das Buch.	'She puts the pen under the book.'
	Die Feder ist unter dem Buch.	'The pen is under the book.'

Ambiguity (Section 1.1, pp. 203–204; Section 3.2, pp. 219–220)

A sentence is ambiguous when it has more than one meaning. There are two main types of ambiguity.

- **Lexical ambiguity.** This type of ambiguity results from one word in the sentence having more than one meaning. Polysemy and homophony give us lexical ambiguity. For example, the sentence *The glasses are on the table* has two meanings: (1) the drinking glasses are on the table, and (2) the eyeglasses are on the table. The ambiguity arises because the word *glasses* has two possible meanings.

- **Structural ambiguity.** This type of ambiguity results from a phrase in the sentence having more than one possible structure. Each possible structure is associated with a different interpretation (or reading).

  Consider the ambiguous sentence *The surface was painted with red flowers and leaves.* In this sentence, the ambiguity is found within the noun phrase, which will, therefore, have two different syntactic structures.

  Reading One: Both the flowers and the leaves are red.

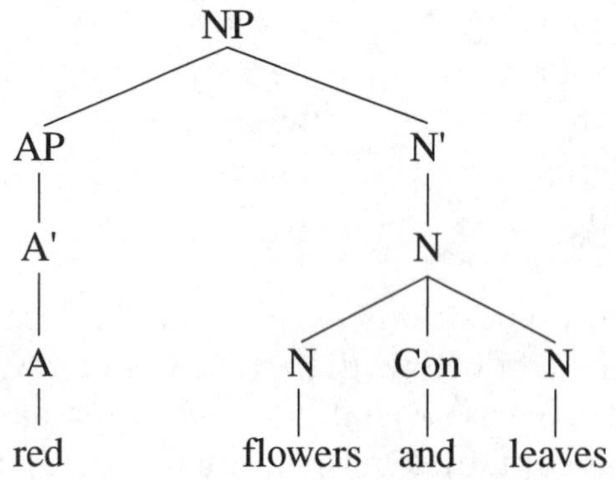

  Reading Two: Only the flowers are red.

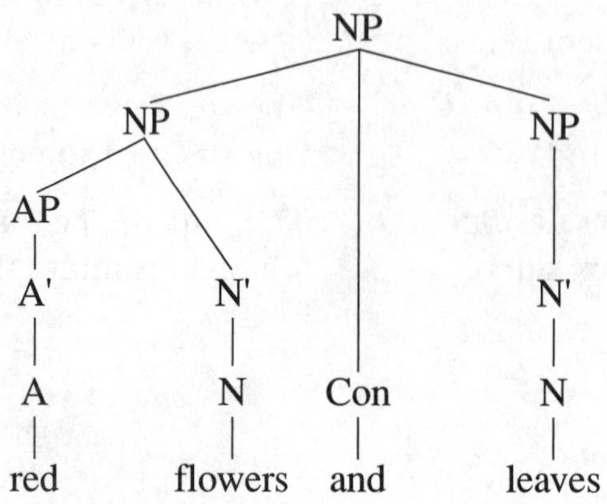

Ambiguity can also be found within the verb phrase. Consider the ambiguous sentence *Sam ate the cake in the kitchen.* In this example, the verb phrase has two different possible structures.

Reading One: Sam ate the cake that was in the kitchen.

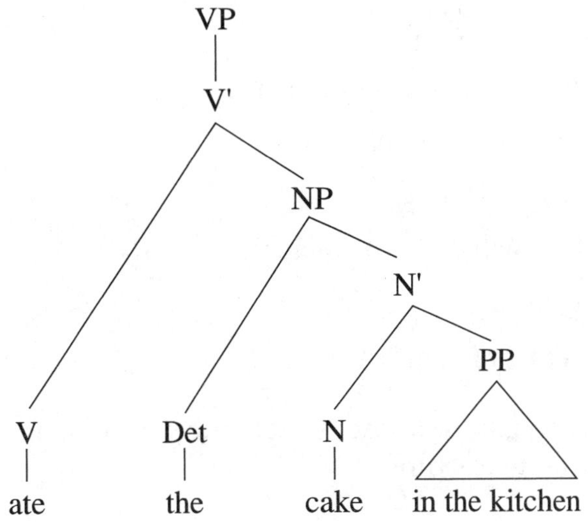

Reading Two: Sam was in the kitchen eating cake.

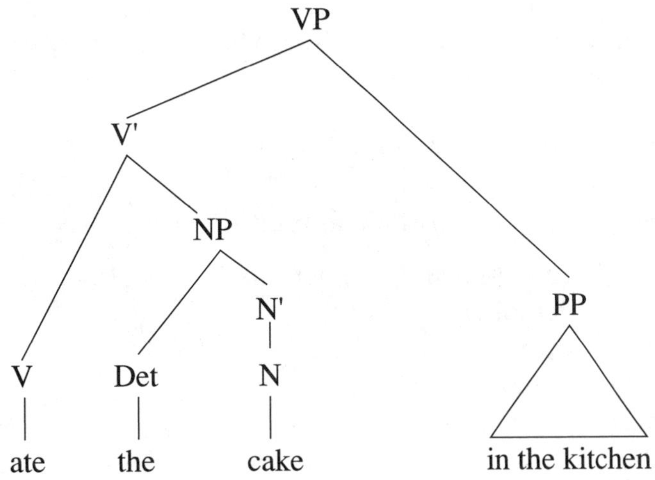

SOME HINTS FOR IDENTIFYING AMBIGUITY

1. Determine if the ambiguity is coming from one word in the sentence (lexical) or from more than one possible combination of the words in the sentence (structural).
2. For lexical ambiguity, identify the word that is ambiguous and determine the two (or more) possible meanings of the word.
3. For structural ambiguity, determine the phrase containing the ambiguity (usually noun or verb) and the possible meanings. Match each meaning with a different syntactic structure.

PRACTICE 6.4: Identifying ambiguity

Each of the following sentences is ambiguous. For each sentence, state whether the ambiguity is lexical or structural and provide an unambiguous phrase or sentence for each possible meaning.

1. Cool beer and wine are what we want.
2. I met the woman standing by the water cooler.
3. Congress passed a dangerous drug bill.
4. Businessmen like black and white ties.
5. George and Harry or Fred will draw the picture.
6. I want to look at the pictures in the attic.
7. The instructor left his key in the office.

Draw tree structures for ambiguous phrases in sentences 1, 3, 5, and 6. Remember that each meaning will have a different structure.

Thematic Roles (Section 3.3, pp. 221–225)

To interpret any sentence, we need to know who is doing the action, what is undergoing the action, the starting point of the action, etc. **Thematic**, or theta, **roles** capture the relation between a sentence and the event it describes.

There are three important properties of thematic roles.

- **Common thematic roles.** Some of the common thematic roles include:

  Agent (actor)—The entity performing an action.
  Theme—The entity undergoing an action.
  Source—The starting point of a movement.
  Goal—The end point of a movement.
  Location—The place where an action occurs.

- **Thematic role assignment.** Thematic roles are assigned to noun phrases based on their position within the sentence. Typically, verbs and prepositions assign thematic roles.

Verbs	Assign the agent role (if it has one) to its subject noun phrase Assign the theme role (if it has one) to its complement noun phrase
Prepositions	Assign a thematic role (the specific one depends on the preposition) to its complement noun phrase

  Knowledge of the thematic roles that verbs and prepositions assign is stored in our mental lexicon.

Thematic role assignment can be diagrammed as follows:

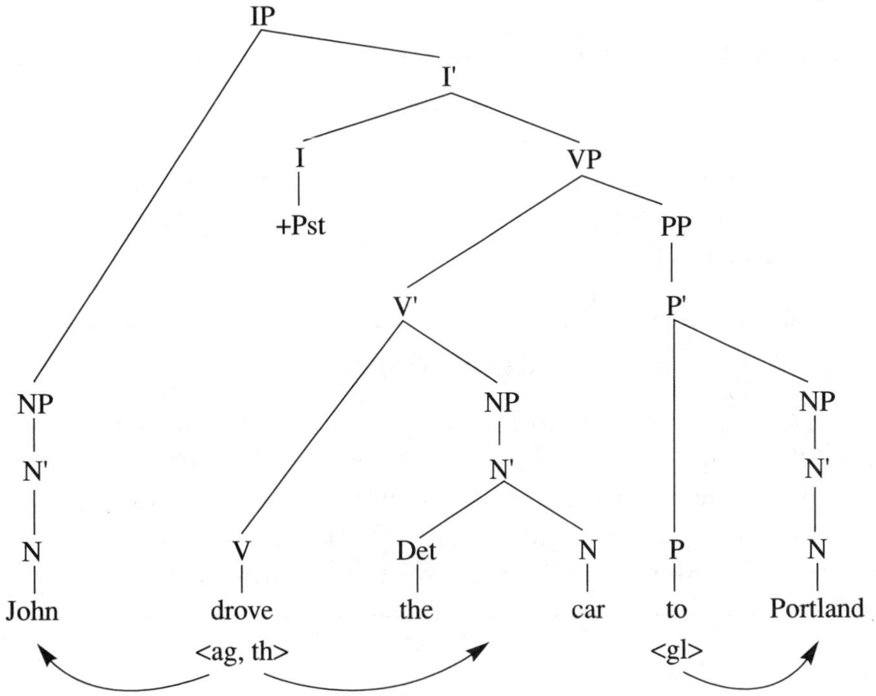

In the above sentence, the verb *drove* assigns the agent role <ag> to the noun phrase *John* and the theme role <th> to the noun phrase *the car,* while the preposition *to* assigns the goal role <gl> to the noun phrase *Portland.*

- **Thematic roles and deep structure.** Thematic roles are assigned at deep structure. A noun phrase's position in the syntactic representation that is the result of the Merge operation determines its thematic role. For example, the *wh* question *What did George lose?* has the deep structure *George lost what.* Accordingly, the verb *lost* assigns the agent role to *George* and the theme role to *what. What* retains this role even after the Move operation changes its position in the structure.

Practice 6.5: Identifying thematic roles

For each of the following sentences, identify all the noun phrases and the thematic role assigned to each noun phrase.

1. Sarah drove that bus from Indianapolis to Terre Haute.
2. The children are eating their ice cream in the kitchen.
3. Which shoes did you buy at the store?
4. The cat was chased around the garden by a large dog.
5. The boys walked to the park.
6. Sally mailed her nephew a parcel.

7. What did Bill leave at your house?
8. The letter was sent.
9. Ginger scribbled her address on the paper.
10. The minister in the pulpit was ordained recently.

Go back through each sentence and for each thematic role, determine the verb or preposition that assigned the role. Make sure you put any sentences in which a transformation has occurred into deep structure first.

REMINDER

The interpretation of a sentence involves many factors. Both the syntactic structure and the meaning of the words in that structure contribute to the meaning of a sentence. The construction in which words occur may also contribute to the meaning of the sentence. As well, the role each NP in a sentence plays must be interpreted. And, when words in a sentence can be combined in more than one way, ambiguity results.

Pragmatics (Sections 4.1–4.3, pp. 228–232)

Besides the structure of a sentence and the thematic roles assigned to the noun phrases within a sentence, there are many other factors involved in sentence interpretation. **Pragmatics** is the study of the role other necessary information has in sentence interpretation.

Beliefs and Attitudes

Nonlinguistic knowledge can be used to interpret elements within a sentence. For example, in the sentence *The city council denied the demonstrators a permit because they advocated violence,* we assume that the **pronoun** *they* refers to the demonstrators and not the council members because of our beliefs about demonstrators. If we change the verb from *advocate* to *abhor,* we now assume that *they* refers to the council and not the demonstrators. Again, this is based on our world beliefs.

Presupposition

Presupposition refers to the assumption or belief implied by the use of a particular word. For example, in the sentence *John admitted that the soccer team had cheated,* the use of the verb *admit* presupposes or implies that the team had actually cheated. A similar implication is not present in the sentence *John said that the soccer team had cheated.*

Setting/Deictics

The form and interpretation of some words depend on the location of the speaker and listener within a particular **setting**. These words are called **deictics**. Some examples of English deictics include *here/there* and *this/that. Here* and *this* are used to refer to items close to the speaker, while *there* and *that* are used to refer to words close to the listener.

Discourse / Topic

Many sentences can only be interpreted in reference to information contained in preceding sentences. **Discourse** is the term used to describe the connected series of utterances that are produced during a conversation, lecture, story, or other type of speech act. **Old (given) information** refers to knowledge that is known to the participants of the speech act, while **new information** refers to knowledge that is introduced into the speech act for the first time. The **topic** is what a sentence or discourse is all about. Often, the subject of a sentence corresponds to the topic. Some languages (e.g., Japanese) use a marker to indicate the topic of the discourse.

PRACTICE 6.6: Sentence interpretation

How do we interpret the following sentences based on the underlined expressions? How does the underlined expression influence our interpretation?

1. a. At the wedding, every friend of the bride cried when she walked down the aisle.
   b. At the wedding, every friend of the bride cried when she saw the couple together.
2. a. Karen was killed in a car wreck.
   b. Karen was murdered in a car wreck.
3. a. Kevin declared that the accusation was false.
   b. Kevin acknowledged that the accusation was false.
4. a. When I come back to China, I'll climb the Great Wall.
   b. When I go back to China, I'll climb the Great Wall.
5. a. A priest is at the hospital.
   b. The priest is at a hospital.

Conversation (Section 4.4, pp. 232–234)

We use words and sentences to convey messages. And we often do this by having a conversation with someone. Conversations have rules. These rules refer to our understanding of how language is used to convey messages. Our knowledge of these rules also contributes to our interpretation of utterances.

- **General principle.** The general principle guiding all conversational interactions is the Cooperative Principle:

  Cooperative Principle—Make your contribution appropriate to the conversation.

- **Specific maxims.** Conversations also have more specific guidelines (i.e., **maxims**). If we follow these maxims, then we have adhered to the Cooperative Principle. These maxims can be violated for specific purposes.

Maxim of Relevance—Make your contribution relevant to the conversation.

Maxim of Quality—Make your contribution truthful.

Maxim of Quantity—Make your contribution only as informative as required.

Maxim of Manner—Make your contribution unambiguous, clear, and logical.

- **Conversational implicature.** During the course of a conversation, we are often able to make inferences about what is meant but was not actually said. Consider, for example, the following interaction:

  Mike: How did you do on the last exam?
  Jim: Want to come with me to the Registrar's Office?

  In the above example, Jim violates the Maxim of Relevance, and even though he doesn't actually say how he did on the exam, it can be inferred from his response that he did rather badly.

PRACTICE 6.7: Violations of conversational maxims

You've just missed your bus and are standing at the bus stop waiting for the next one. The time is 2 P.M. and the next bus is due at 2:15 P.M., but you don't know that. You ask people at the bus stop when the next bus is due, and receive several replies. Each reply you receive may or may not violate one or more conversational maxims. For each reply, identify which maxim(s), if any, have been violated.

1. When's the next bus?
   At 2:30. (He's lying.)

   ____

2. When's the next bus?
   When I was little, I was obsessed with buses. I wanted to be a bus driver. I had hundreds of different kinds of buses. Little buses, big buses, red buses, blue buses, and even double-deckered buses. Did you know that in England, many buses are double-deckered? I have made a study of buses. I think the next bus will be here in 15 minutes. Did you know I wanted to be a bus driver? Did you know . . .

   ____

3. When's the next bus?
   Let me think! If the last bus was here at 1:50 and if they run every 20 minutes or so, then the next bus should be here at 2:10. (He has no idea.)

   ____

4. When's the next bus?
   At 2:15, but if we were in Denver that would be 3:15.

   ____

5. When's the next bus?
   I don't know.

   ____

Review Exercises

1. **Grammaticized concepts:** Look at the data from Burmese. What concept is grammaticized in Burmese that is usually not grammaticized in English? How is this concept indicated?

   [˳] below a sound indicates that it is voiceless.
   Tones are marked as diacritics above the vowels.

1.	mjô	'be floating'	m̥jô	'set afloat'
2.	nôu	'be awake'	n̥ôu	'waken'
3.	láʔ	'be bare'	l̥áʔ	'uncover'

2. **Thematic roles:** Write three sentences of your own, and label thematic roles for each NP. You should have at least one example of each of the following:

   agent
   theme
   source
   goal
   location

   ____

   ____

   ____

   ____

   ____

   ____

3. **Pragmatics and sentence interpretation:** Look at each snippet of conversation, and answer the questions that follow.

    a. Prosecution lawyer to defense witness: *Have you stopped taking drugs? Just answer with a simple yes or no.*

    If the witness has never taken drugs, can she answer the question? Why or why not?

    b. Doctor to patient with bursitis: *Can you reach the top shelf?*
    Short student to tall student in the library: *Can you reach the top shelf?*

    Is the implicature the same for both questions? Why or why not?

    c. A letter of recommendation for a student applying to graduate school: *I am writing to recommend Joe Blow for graduate study. He was my advisee, and I have always found him unfailingly polite and punctual. Also, he dresses extremely well. Sincerely . . .*

    What maxims are being violated? What is the implicature of the letter?

RECAP

Make sure you know how to do the following. (See also the Key Terms on pp. 235–236 of the main text.)

- identify the semantic relations between words
- identify the semantic relations between sentences
- define connotation, denotation, extension, and intension
- do componential analysis
- recognize fuzzy concepts, grammaticized concepts, and lexicalized concepts
- recognize the semantic basis for different word classes
- recognize lexical ambiguity
- recognize and represent structural ambiguity
- identify noun phrases and their thematic roles
- identify the effect of world knowledge in sentence interpretation
- identify when presupposition occurs in sentence interpretation
- recognize the different forms of deictic terms
- identify conversational principles and maxims

Questions? Problems?

seven

Historical Linguistics: The Study of Language Change

Historical linguistics studies the principles governing language change. This branch of linguistics is concerned with both the description and the explanation of language change. Following are some of the important topics and concepts covered in this chapter. Make sure you are familiar with them.

Sound change
Phonological change
Morphological change
Syntactic change
Lexical change
Comparative reconstruction
Reconstruction and Indo-European

Language Change (Section 1, pp. 246–249)

Some important points concerning language change include:

- Language is always changing. However, for a particular change to take hold, it must be accepted by the language community as a whole.

- Language change is regular and systematic. Some changes affect all words without exception. Other changes begin in a small number of words in the speech of a small number of speakers. These changes may gradually spread through both the vocabulary and the population.

- Languages change because of the way language is acquired. Children are not born with a complete grammar, but must construct a grammar based on the language they are exposed to. Therefore, changes will occur from one generation to the next, and because all children have the same genetic capabilities for language and construct their grammars in similar fashions, the same patterns of change repeat both within and across languages.

- Causes of language change include **articulatory simplification**, **reanalysis**, **analogy**, and **language contact**.

Sequential Sound Change (Section 2.1, pp. 249–256)

While all aspects of a language's structure can change, sound change is often the most noticeable. There are many types of sound change that can occur, but most sound changes involve sequences of segments. The major types of sequential sound changes are outlined below.

- **Assimilation.** Assimilation involves sounds changing to become more like nearby sounds. Assimilation increases the efficiency of the articulations involved in producing the sequence of sounds. Such an increase in efficiency can result in articulatory simplification.

  Some common examples include:

Types of assimilation	**Examples**
a. **Place of articulation assimilation** A sound becomes similar to a nearby sound in terms of place of articulation.	a. Old Spanish [semda] > Modern Spanish [senda]
b. **Manner of articulation assimilation** A consonant changes its manner of articulation to be like a nearby sound.	b. Early Old English [stefn] > Later Old English [stemn]
c. **Total assimilation** A sound assimilates totally to a following sound.	c. Latin [septem] > Italian [sette]
d. **Nasalization** A vowel becomes nasal near a nasal sound.	d. Latin [vinum] > Old French [vĩn]
e. **Palatalization** A nonpalatal sound becomes more palatal. This usually occurs near a sound that is made with the tongue at or near the hard palate—usually [j] or [i].	e. Old English [kirike] > Middle English [ʧirʧe]

  Palatalization is often the first step in the creation of an affricate. The type of change in which a palatalized stop becomes an affricate is called **affrication**. Like palatalization, affrication is often induced by front vowels or [j].

  The above assimilatory processes most often affect adjacent segments; however, assimilation can apply at a distance. **Umlaut**, which is responsible for irregular plurals such as *goose/geese,* is an example of such a change.

- **Weakening.** Full vowels have a tendency to reduce, or weaken, to a schwa-like vowel before they delete. Consonants can be defined along a strength hierarchy, as follows:

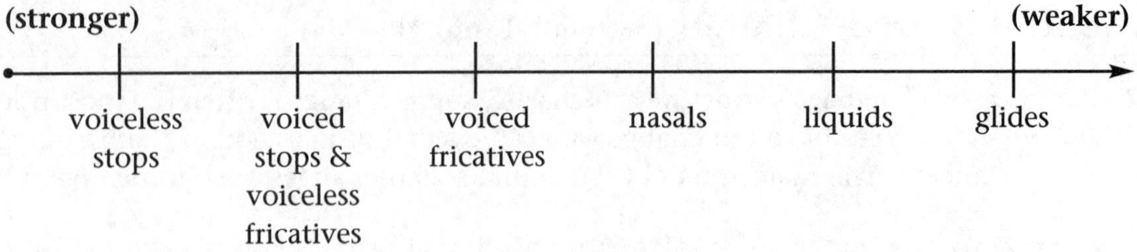

Geminate (long) consonants are stronger than their nongeminate counterparts. The tendency over time is for consonants to weaken along a path determined by this hierarchy.

Some common examples include:

Types of weakening	**Examples**
Vowel weakening	
a. **Vowel reduction** A vowel reduces to schwa. This often occurs in unstressed syllables.	a. Old English [naːma] > Middle English [naːmə]
Consonantal weakening	
a. **Degemination** A long sound becomes short. This is usually the first step in the weakening of consonants.	a. Latin [mittere] > Spanish [meter]
b. **Frication** A stop weakens to a fricative. This often occurs between vowels.	b. Old Spanish [maduro] > Spanish [maðuro]
c. **Voicing** Voiceless stops or fricatives weaken to voiced stops or fricatives.	c. Latin [maturus] > Old Spanish [maduro]
d. **Rhotacism** A fairly common type of weakening in which [z] weakens to /r/.	d. Gothic 'mai [z] a' > English 'mo [ɹ] e'

Consonants can also strengthen. Glides often strengthen to an affricate. This process is called **glide strengthening** and is common in word-initial position.

- **Deletion.** Deletion is often the end result of the weakening processes outlined previously. Both vowels and consonants may delete. Vowels are often subject to deletion when they occur in unstressed syllables.

  Some common examples include:

Types of deletion	**Examples**
Vowel deletion	
a. **Apocope** The deletion of a word-final vowel.	a. Middle English [naːmə] > Modern English [nejm]
b. **Syncope** The deletion of a word-internal vowel	b. Proto-Romance [vivər] > French [vivʁ]
Consonant deletion	
a. Consonants often delete when they occur as part of a consonant cluster, as the final consonant in a word, or as the last step after several weakening processes.	a. Old English [kneː] > Modern English [ni]

- **Others.** There are other types of sound changes as well, many of which will be familiar to you from the phonology chapter. These types of sound changes are not as frequent as those already presented, but like assimilation, they also tend to have the overall effect of making sequences of sounds easier to articulate. Also like assimilation, these changes can affect adjacent segments or segments at a distance.

  Some common examples include:

Types of sound change	**Examples**
a. **Dissimilation** A sound becomes less like a nearby sound. This often occurs so that a sequence of sounds is easier to articulate or perceive.	a. Latin [arbor] > Spanish [arbol]
b. **Epenthesis** A sound is inserted. This sometimes occurs to break up a consonant cluster that is hard to pronounce.	b. Old English [bræməl] > Modern English [bɹæmbl̩]
c. **Metathesis** The position of two sounds has changed relative to each other.	c. Latin 'mira [k] u [l] um' > Spanish 'mi [l] a [g] ro'

PRACTICE 7.1: Identifying types of sound change

Each of the following exemplifies one or more sound changes. The older form is on the left, and the newer, more recent form on the right. Identify the sound change that has taken place for each of the underlined sounds.

1. Proto-Quecha [cumpi] > Tena [cumbi]

____

2. Old English [hlaf] > Modern English [lof]

3. Latin [mare] > Portuguese [mar]

4. Proto-Slavic [kemerai] > Russian [tʃemer]

5. Proto-Tupi-Gurani [puʔam] > Gurani [puʔã]

6. Latin [ornamentum] > Old French [ornəment]

7. Old English [knotta] > Modern American English [nɑt]

8. Proto-Germanic [doːmaz] > Old Icelandic [doːmr]

9. Proto-Romance [venre] > Spanish [vendre]

10. Early Latin [inpossibiliss] > Latin [impossibilis]

11. Proto-Bantu [mukiːpa] > Swahili [mʃipa]

12. Proto-Romance [sekuru] > Spanish [seguro]

13. Latin [pekkatum] > [pekado] > Spanish [pekaðo]

____

14. Proto-Romance [biskɔktu] > Italian [biskotto]

____

Sound change tends to occur in a step-by-step fashion, so a single sound can often be subject to a number of different sound changes. But these multiple sound changes are often not visible in the resulting form. Examine the following change that affected the word *good* in the development from Proto-Germanic to Old Icelandic.

Proto-Germanic [goːdas] > Old Icelandic [goːðr]

Identify all the changes, including any intermediate but not visible changes, that have affected the underlined sounds.

Other Types of Sound Change (Sections 2.2–2.3, pp. 256–257)

The changes considered so far have all involved segments changing under the influence of nearby, though not necessarily adjacent, segments. However, this is not true of all sound change that occurs in language. There are two other common types of sound change: segmental and auditory.

- **Segmental change.** Segmental change involves a change within a segment itself. Segmental change often involves affricates. Affricates are considered a complex segment, since they consist of a stop and a fricative.

  One common example is given below:

Deaffrication	**Example**
An affricate becomes a fricative by eliminating the stop portion of the affricate.	Old French [ts]ent > French [s]ent

- **Auditorily based change.** In addition to the articulatory considerations typically involved in sound change, auditory factors can also have an influence.

  One common example is given below.

Substitution	**Example**
One segment is replaced with a similar-sounding segment.	Middle English lau [x] > English lau [f]

PRACTICE 7.2: Other types of sound change

1. The underlined phones in the following list of words from Lebanese colloquial Arabic are all pronounced as [ʤ] in Modern Standard Arabic. Lebanese Arabic has undergone a second change. Name the process that is responsible.

ʒdiːd	'new'	maʒnuːn	'crazy'
ʒɪbni	'cheese'	rʒaːl	'men'
ʒariːdi	'newspaper'		

2. The Latin word *caput* [k] 'head' became the Old French word *chef* [ʧ] and the modern French word *chef* [ʃ].

   a. List the changes that took place from Latin to modern French, and where possible, name the processes.

   b. The English words *chief* and *chef* were borrowed at different times from French. When in the process was each borrowed?

Phonological Change (Section 2.4, pp. 257–260)

The sound changes described in the previous sections can influence a language's phonological inventory. That is, they can add, eliminate, or rearrange the phonemes within a language.

- **Phonological splits.** A phonological **split** adds phonemes to a language's phonological inventory. In a phonological split, allophones of the same phoneme come to contrast with each other. This is often caused by a loss of the conditioning environment. That is, sounds that were once predictable are no longer predictable and are, therefore, phonemic.

  Consider the following example in the development of English.

  Old English: In Old English, /n/ had two allophones:
  - [ŋ] occurred before velar stops
  - [n] occurred elsewhere

  So a word like *sing* was pronounced as [sɪŋg].

  Middle English: Consonant deletion applied to remove [g] at the end of a word (after a nasal consonant). This created a minimal pair between *sing* now pronounced as [sɪŋ] and *sin* pronounced as [sɪn]. And minimal pairs tell us that sounds contrast. [ŋ] and [n] are now separate phonemes.

  This split can be diagrammed as follows:

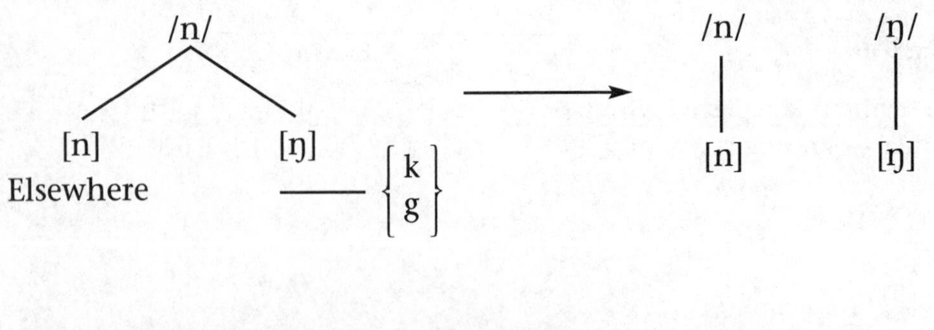

Remember: Spelling often lags behind sound change. We still spell *sing* with the final *g* even though it is now silent. Many silent letters in our English spelling system are a reflection of older pronunciations.

- **Phonological mergers.** While a phonological split adds phonemes to a language, a phonological **merger** reduces the number of contrasts.

  A good example of a phonological merger comes from Cockney English. In Cockney English, the interdental and labiodental fricatives have merged. That is, instances of [θ] and [ð] have become [f] and [v], respectively. In effect, [θ] and [ð] have been lost from the phonemic inventory.

- **Phonological shifts.** A phonological **shift** does not add to or diminish a language's phonemic inventory. Rather, some of the phonemes are reorganized with respect to each other.

  The **Great English Vowel Shift**, beginning in Middle English, is a well-known example of this. The chart below gives the Middle English long vowels before the vowel shift occurred.

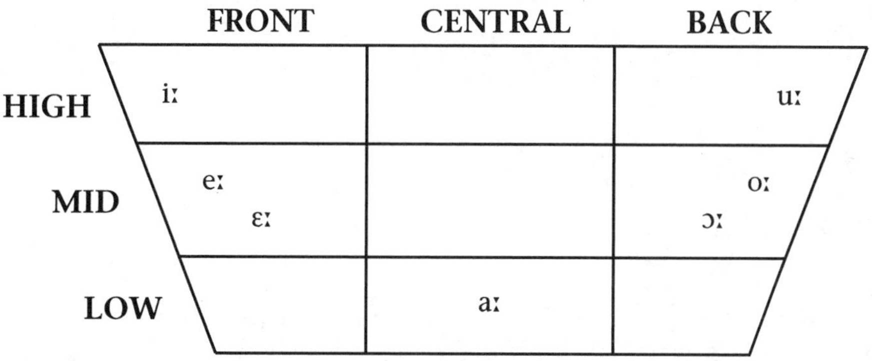

PRACTICE 7.3: The Great English Vowel Shift

Look at the words in Middle English and their pronunciation in Modern English. On the vowel chart that follows the list, draw arrows to show how the pronunciation of the vowel changed. Number each arrow to correspond to the number in the data set. The first one is done for you.

	Middle English	Modern English	
1.	[tiːd]	/tajd/	'tide'
2.	[nuː]	/naw/	'now'
3.	[seːd]	/sid/	'seed'
4.	[sɛː]	/si/	'see'
5.	[goːs]	/gus/	'goose'
6.	[gɔːst]	/gost/	'ghost'
7.	[taːlə]	/tel/	'tale'

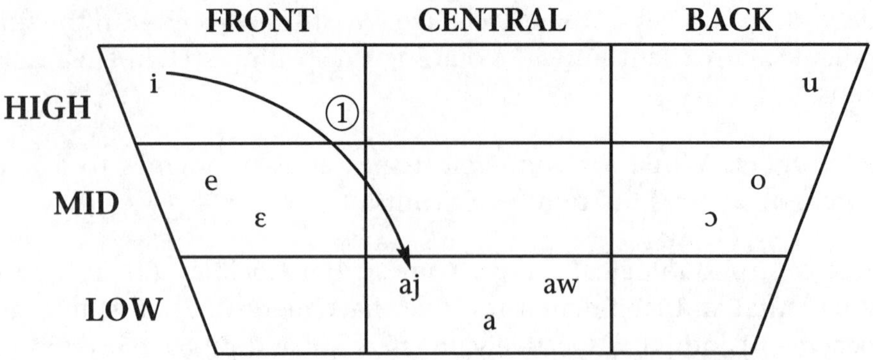

The Great English Vowel Shift probably began with the changes shown in 1 and 2 of the data set on the previous page. It then involved a shift up in vowel articulation of the remaining long vowels to produce the vowels that characterize Modern English.

Fill in the blanks to summarize the vowel shifts:

1. Long [i] became the diphthong ___________.
2. Long [u] became the diphthong ___________.
3. Long [e] became ___________.
4. Long [ɛ] became ___________.
5. Long [o] became ___________.
6. Long [ɔ] became ___________.
7. Long [a] became ___________.

As the vowels shifted, length was lost. After the Great English Vowel Shift, the long vowels now looked like this:

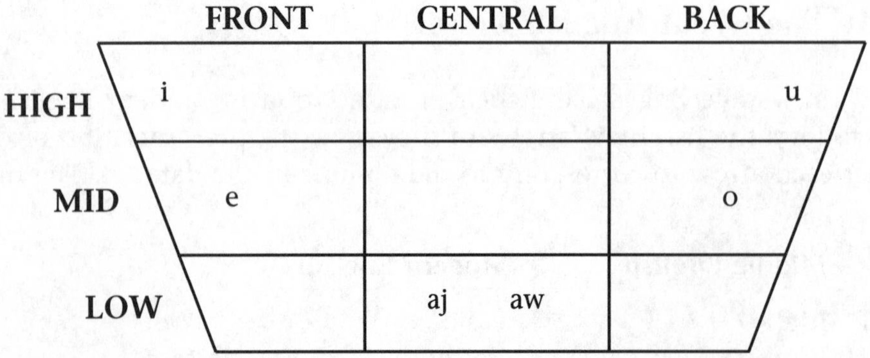

As is evident by comparing the before and after charts, the overall effect of the vowel shift was a reduction in the number of vowels, thereby lessening the crowdedness of the phonological space. Note: Middle English also contained short (lax) vowels, which have not been included on the preceding charts.

Remember: Many of our vowel spellings reflect Middle English pronunciation. For example, *goose* is spelled with *oo* because this orthographic symbol represents [oː]. The word *goose* continues to be spelled this way, even though as a result of the Great English Vowel Shift, Middle English [oː] is now pronounced as [u]. One reason for this mismatch between spelling and pronunciation is that spelling was standardized before the vowels had finished shifting.

Morphological Change (Section 3, pp. 260–265)

Morphological change affects the structure of words within a language. This type of change may increase or reduce a language's inventory of affixes. Recall from morphology that affixes are bound morphemes that attach to a base, and either provide grammatical information (inflection) or are used to create new words (derivation).

- **The addition of affixes.** Some examples of how affixes can be added to a language are given in the box below.

TYPE	DEFINITION	EXAMPLE
Borrowing	Borrowed words frequently consist of a root and at least one affix. Eventually, these affixes may enter the language.	*-ment* and *-able* were borrowed from the French language.
Grammaticalization	Grammaticalization creates new grammatical forms from lexical forms. During grammaticalization, (1) the semantic content of the lexical form is lost, and (2) lexical forms are reduced phonologically.	The Italian future suffix *-ō* developed from the Latin word *habe-ō* 'have/hold/grasp'.
Fusion	Fusion involves the development of an affix (either a prefix or a suffix) from two words that are frequently adjacent to each other. Over time, these words fuse together to form a base and a suffix, or a prefix and a base.	In Latin amāre and *habeam* fused together to become *amābō.*

- **The loss of affixes.** Affixes can also be lost.

Affixes sometimes just simply cease to be used. A good example of this is the Old English derivational suffix *-bora,* which is no longer found in Modern English.

Affixes can also be lost through sound change. Sound changes such as consonant deletion, vowel reduction, and vowel deletion caused the loss of Old English case endings.

- **The effect of adding or losing affixes.** The loss of affixes can result in a synthetic morphological system becoming analytic, while the addition of affixes can result in an analytic morphological system gradually becoming synthetic. An **analytic language** has very few inflectional affixes (e.g., Modern English). In contrast, a **synthetic language** has many inflectional affixes (e.g., Old English).

- **Reanalysis and analogy** can also affect the morphological structure of a language. Reanalysis can result in new morphological structures in a language. Analogy can act to regularize a set of forms. Sometimes, reanalysis is based on a false identification of component morphemes of a word; in such cases, this is known as **folk etymology**.

PRACTICE 7.4: Morphological change

1. Compare the Old English plurals with the Modern English plurals. What happened to the plural morpheme between Old English and Modern English?

Old English	Modern English
handa	hands
gear	years
ēagan	eyes
stānas	stones

2. Look at the data from Welsh. Where did Welsh get the morpheme that is used to reinforce the plurality of a collective noun?

sɛren	'star'
seːr	'stars' (collectively)
seːrs	'stars' (plurally)

3. How did the English forms below arise from the French? What is this process called?

French		English
Bois Brulé	'burnt wood'	Bob Ruly (place name in Michigan)
Purgatoire	'purgatory'	Picketwire (River, in southeastern Colorado)
L'eau Froide	'cold water'	Low Freight (stream in Arkansas)
L'ours	'bear'	Loose (Creek, in Missouri)

4. In the following data from two African languages, the word for 'yesterday' has been used as the basis for which other morpheme? What do we call this type of morphological change?

Baka (spoken by a Pygmy group in Cameroon and Gabon)

pámɛ̀	ʔé	wɔ̀tɔ̀-ngi	ngili
wild boar	3SG	pass-PAST	yesterday

'A wild boar passed [by] (here) yesterday.'

Kru (spoken in Liberia and Côte d'Ivoire) (*kaalaa* 'yesterday')

ma	bóylée	blá	la	mɔ́ɔ
but	foot	kill	PAST	me

'But my foot was killing me.'

5. Examine the data from Latin and Italian. What morphological change has taken place? How has this affected syntax?

Latin

Marcellus Sophiam amat.	'Marcello loves Sophia.'
Marcellus amat Sophiam.	'Marcello loves Sophia.'
Amat Marcellus Sophiam.	'Marcello loves Sophia.'
Sophiam amat Marcellus.	'Marcello loves Sophia.'

Italian

Marcello ama Sophia.	'Marcello loves Sophia.'
Sophia ama Marcello.	'Sophia loves Marcello.'

Syntactic Change (Section 4, pp. 265–268)

Change can also affect the syntactic component of a language's grammar. Change often affects the word-order patterns found in a language. It can also affect the transformations found within a language.

- **Word order.** Languages can change their basic word-order pattern. One common change involves the change from an SOV order to an SVO order. This is a change that happened in the development of English. English descended from a Germanic language having an SOV order.

- **Transformations.** *Yes-no* questions in English are formed using the Inversion transformation. In Old English, both main verbs and auxiliary verbs could be inverted. In Modern English, though, only auxiliary verbs can be inverted. Now, any sentence that does not contain an auxiliary must be made into a *yes-no* question using *do.*

Practice 7.5: Syntactic change in English

Here are some sentences from early seventeenth-century English along with their modern counterparts. How were negatives formed then? How does this differ from today's English?

1. They hearkened not to the voice of their father.
   'They did not listen to their father.'

2. Hide it not from me.
   'Do not hide it from me.'

3. Look not on his countenance or on the height of his stature.
   'Do not look at his appearance or height.'

4. If thou save not thy life, tomorrow thou shalt be slain.
   'If you do not save your life, tomorrow you will be killed.'

5. He cometh not to the king's table.
   'He does not come to the king's table' (i.e., he does not eat with the king).

Connections

Changes can have far-reaching effects. A change that affects the phonology of a language can eventually affect the morphology, which in turn can affect the syntax.

Consider an example (somewhat simplified) of three stages in the development of English:

1. Old English was a highly inflected language. Old English inflectional affixes included:

   - Case: nominative, accusative, dative, genitive
   - Number: singular, dual, plural
   - Person: first, second, third
   - Gender: masculine, feminine, neuter
   - Tense: past, present

   Inflectional affixes were found on pronouns, nouns, articles, adjectives, verbs, etc. As in many inflected languages, Old English had a fairly free word order. Sentences with SVO, VSO, and SOV orders can all be found.

2. During Middle English, sound changes started happening in unstressed syllables. These sound changes included:

   - m → n / ______#
   - n → Ø / ______#
   - a, o, u, i, e → ə / ______#

   These three sound changes affected the inflectional system, since inflectional affixes in Old English were suffixes, and suffixes are typically not stressed. The following examples illustrate the application of the above rules and their effect on the inflectional system.

Old English						Middle English
foxum	>	foxun	>	foxu	>	foxə
helpan	>	helpan	>	helpa	>	helpə

As a result of these sound changes, all the affixes became the same: 'ə'. Since it was now impossible to tell what information was contained in an affix, the Old English affixes were dropped.

3. But speakers still needed to know what the subject of a sentence was, what the object of a sentence was, and what noun an adjective referred to. To get this information, speakers of English began to:

   - rely on prepositions
   - rely on fixed word order (SVO)

   So sound changes can have drastic effects on a language's development over time.

REMINDER

Just as with phonological rules, sound changes often require an order to their application. For example, the three changes presented in the last section require some ordering. [m] has to first change to [n] before it can be deleted. If this change does not occur first, then [n] would not delete and the affixes would not all become [ə].

Lexical Change (Section 5, pp. 268–272)

Lexical change involves modifications to the lexicon. There are two main types of lexical change: addition and loss.

Addition of Lexical Items

New lexical items are typically added to a language's vocabulary in one of two ways.

- **Word formation.** Some of the word-formation processes found in the morphology chapter are frequently used to add new words to a language. These new words often fill a lexical gap resulting from technological innovations. Compounding and derivation are probably the two most frequently used word-formation processes for this purpose, although acronyms, backformation, blending, clipping, and conversion can also be used to add new words to a language.

- **Borrowing.** As languages come into contact with each other, they often borrow words from each other. There are three types of influences that languages can have on each other.

  - **Substratum influence.** This is the influence of a politically or culturally nondominant language on the dominant language in the area. Typically, the dominant language borrows place names as well as names for unfamiliar objects or items from the nondominant language. English borrowed place names such as Thames, London, and Dover from Celtic.

  - **Superstratum influence.** This is the influence of a politically or culturally dominant language on a nondominant language in the area. For example, English borrowed many words from the French language during the Middle English period. After the Norman Conquest, French became the dominant language, and many English speakers borrowed French words to increase their social standing. French loan words are typically found in relation to government (e.g., *government*), religion (e.g., *prayer*), judiciary (e.g., *judge*), science (e.g., *medicine*), culture (e.g., *sculpture*), and warfare (e.g., *army*).

- **Adstratum influence.** This refers to a situation where two languages are in contact, but neither is politically or culturally dominant. Adstratum influence often results in the borrowing of common, everyday words. Such a relationship existed between English and Scandinavian speakers. Scandinavian loan words include *cake, egg, husband, score, window,* and *ugly.*

Loss of Lexical Items

Words can also be lost from the vocabulary of a language. Loan words, nonloan words, compounds, and derived words can also be lost. The most common reason for the loss of a lexical item is some societal change that has rendered an object, and therefore its name, obsolete.

For example, English no longer uses the words *flȳtme* 'bloodletting instrument' and *eafor* 'tenant obligation to the king to convey goods', the compounds *dimhus* 'prison' and *aelfscīene* 'beautiful as a fairy', and the derived words *manscipe* 'humanity' and *heofonisc* 'heavenly'.

PRACTICE 7.6: Lexical change

One of the reasons new and borrowed words are interesting is that they reflect a speech community's history—past conflicts, contacts, and advances. For this exercise, you will need to consult a good dictionary that gives etymologies for words. For each of the following words, find out from what language it is derived and when it entered the English language. Try to figure out why or how English added the word to the language.

Word	Origin	When/Why/How Added
1. plaid	______________	______________________
2. shepherd	______________	______________________
3. cherubim	______________	______________________
4. skin	______________	______________________
5. residence	______________	______________________
6. algebra	______________	______________________
7. portico	______________	______________________
8. theory	______________	______________________

9. moccasin ________________ ________________________

10. jungle ________________ ________________________

11. banana ________________ ________________________

12. automobile ________________ ________________________

13. boondocks ________________ ________________________

Comparative Reconstruction (Sections 6.1–6.2, pp. 273–279)

By comparing languages with each other, it can be determined whether they are genetically related. **Genetically related languages** are languages that have descended from a common ancestor. Using the **comparative method**, this ancestor can be reconstructed. This is typically done by comparing later forms to determine what the earlier form must have looked like. Although it is possible to reconstruct all aspects of a language's grammar, the focus here is on phonological reconstruction.

Some important terms:

- **Cognates** are phonetically and semantically similar words that have descended from a common source. Cognates are compared to reconstruct what this common source must have looked like.

- A **protolanguage** is a language that has been reconstructed using a comparative method. Written evidence of what this language actually looked like typically doesn't exist.

- A protolanguage consists of **protoforms**. These are the individual reconstructed words of the protolanguage. Protoforms are usually indicated with an asterisk (*).

Some important strategies:

Processes underlying language change are systematic. Therefore, as you examine related languages, look for systematic phonetic correspondences that can be generalized for one language in relation to another.

- The **phonetic plausibility strategy** requires that any change posited to account for the differences between the protoform (the ancestor) and the cognates must be phonetically plausible. That is, a sound change that has been found to occur in the course of language development must be able to account for these differences. For our purposes, the sound changes listed under the heading *sequential change* as well as under *segmental* and *auditorily based change* are all plausible.

- The **majority rules strategy** operates in the absence of a phonetically plausible sound change. This strategy states that when no phonetically plausible sound change can be determined, we may reconstruct the segment that occurs in the majority of the cognates.

Practice 7.7: Reconstructing phonemes

The following problems will give you practice in seeing systematic correspondences among phonemes of different languages and will guide you toward reconstruction of protoforms.

1. **Proto-Algonquian: consonant clusters**

Examine the following data and look for regular alternation patterns in the underlined consonant clusters. Note: None of the languages make a phonemic distinction between voiced and voiceless obstruents. In addition, in Menomini, [s] and [ʃ] are allophones of the same phoneme.

First, sort the data so that you can see the four alternation patterns. Then, write the alternations in the list below the data set.

	Fox	Ojibwa	Menomini	Gloss
1.	kiːʃkahamwa	kiːʃkaʔank	keːskaham	'he chops it through'
2.	netehkoma	nintikkom	netɛːhkom	'my louse'
3.	ahteːki	atteːk	aʔtek	'when it is there'
4.	nehtoːwa	nittoːt	nɛʔtaw	'he kills it'
5.	iʃihtoːwa	iʃittoːt	eseːhtaw	'he makes it so'
6.	neʃkiːʃekwi	niʃkiːnʃik	neskeːhsek	'my eye'
7.	ahkohkwa	akkikk	ahkɛːhkok	'kettle'
8.	mehtekwi	mittik	mɛʔtek	'stick'
9.	aʃkotɛːwi	iʃkoteː	eskoːtɛːw	'fire'
10.	noːhkomesa	noːkkomiss	noːhkomɛh	'my grandmother'
11.	poːnihtoːwa	poːnittoːt	poːnehtaw	'he ceases from it'
12.	-----	nantottank	natoːhtam	'he listens for it'

The four consonant cluster alternation patterns are:

Fox	Ojibwa	Menomini	Evidence

Now fill in the chart with the correct pattern beside the protoform:

*PA	Fox	Ojibwa	Menomini
*ʔt			
*ʃk			
*hk			
*ht			

2. **Arabic:** [t], [d], [θ], [ð]

In the following data from Syrian and Iraqi colloquial Arabic, examine the alternations in [t], [d], [θ], and [ð]. First look for regular patterns; then determine what the protoforms were. Fill in the chart to help you. Assume phonetic transcription.
[ɣ] represents a voiced velar fricative.
[ʕ] represents a voiced pharyngeal fricative.
[sˤ] represents a pharyngealized [s].

	Syrian	Iraqi	Gloss
1.	daftar	daftar	'notebook'
2.	tneːn	θneːn	'two'
3.	ɣada	ɣada	'lunch'
4.	ʔaxad	ʔaxað	'he took'
5.	waʔət	wakɪt	'time'
6.	taːlɛt	θaːlɪθ	'third'
7.	dahab	ðahab	'gold'
8.	ʔaktar	ʔakθar	'more'
9.	maktab	maktab	'office'
10.	haːda	haːða	'this'
11.	tɪsʕa	tɪsʕa	'nine'
12.	duːd	duːd	'worm'
13.	sanduːʔ	sˤanduːg	'box'
14.	matal	maθal	'example'

a. Which of the four sounds does each language have in the following positions? Fill in the chart.

Position	Syrian	Iraqi	Evidence
word-initial			
word-final			
between vowels			
after a consonant			

b. How are Syrian and Iraqi different in the use of the four sounds?

c. What were the protoforms?

d. What phonological changes have taken place to lead to the differences between Syrian and Iraqi? **Remember:** Phonological change can involve splits or mergers.

Reconstructing Words in a Protolanguage

We can move from a consideration of specific phonemes to more general reconstruction of words in the protolanguage. We can see it best through an example.

An example:

Reconstruct the protoforms for the data below.

	Language A	Language B	Language C
1.	hauda	hauta	hauta
2.	sav	ʃive	sav

1. Determine the number of sounds that need to be reconstructed. This is straightforward for data set 1 in that all the cognates have the same number of sounds: five. The situation is different in 2. In 2, two of the cognates contain three sounds, and one contains four. If four sounds are reconstructed, then deletion must have occurred in languages A and C. If three sounds are reconstructed, then epenthesis must have occurred in language B. It is more plausible for deletion rather than epenthesis to occur at the end of words. Data set 2, therefore, requires the reconstruction of four sounds.

2. Look for any total correspondences. These are sounds that have not changed; they are the same for all the cognates. Reconstruct these sounds. The protoforms after this step are: *hau?a and *??v?. (The question marks indicate sounds we're not yet sure about.)

3. Examine alternations between the different languages, and determine phonetic plausibility.

   - Data set 1 exhibits an alternation between [t] and [d]. Either [t] or [d] can be reconstructed in the protoform. If [d] is reconstructed, then the change from the protoform to the form in languages B and C ([d] > [t]) does not correspond to a sound change. Therefore, this has a low phonetic plausibility. If [t] is reconstructed, then the change from the protoform to language A ([t] > [d]) can be explained as an instance of weakening (a voiceless stop weakens to a voiced stop). This has a high phonetic plausibility. Reconstruct the change that has the highest phonetic plausibility. The protoform becomes *hauta.

   - Data set 2 exhibits three alternations. First, consider the alternation between [s] and [ʃ]. If [ʃ] is reconstructed, then the change [ʃ] > [s] in languages A and C has low phonetic plausibility since there is no motivation for it. If [s] is reconstructed, then the change [s] > [ʃ] in language B can be explained as palatalization. This has high phonetic plausibility, so [s] is reconstructed. Second, consider the presence or absence of a word-final vowel in the cognates. Recall from above that it is more plausible for a sound to delete than be epenthesized in this position. Therefore, [e] is reconstructed. Third, consider the vowel alternation between [a] and [i]. If [a] is reconstructed, then the change [a] > [i] occurs in language B, and if [i] is reconstructed, then the opposite change [i] > [a] occurs in languages A and C. Neither corresponds to a sound change, so both have a low phonetic plausibility. This strategy, therefore, cannot be used to reconstruct this segment. The protoform, after this step, is *s?ve.

4. Any sounds for which no phonetically plausible sound change could be identified use the majority rules strategy. In data set 2, the alternation between [a] and [i] cannot be accounted for using a sound change; therefore, [a] is reconstructed since it occurs in the majority of the cognates. The protoform becomes *save. Notice that this protoform does not correspond to any of the cognates. This is okay.

5. Put together a summary of the sound changes that have occurred since the different languages split from the protolanguage. Remember that the form you have just reconstructed is older than the cognates from the descendent languages. Both voicing and apocope occurred in the development of language A, while only apocope occurred in the development of language C. Palatalization occurred in the development of language B.

> **REMINDER**
>
> In order to do language reconstruction, you need to be able to identify phonetically plausible sound changes. And in order to do that, you need to know the different types of sequential, segmental, and auditory sound changes. Make sure you are very familiar with them.

PRACTICE 7.8: Reconstructing words

To ease into reconstruction, try a couple of examples from hypothetical languages first. Then move on to real languages for the next exercises.

Each of the following data groups contains some cognate sets. Assume that all the cognates are in phonetic transcription and that all members of the cognate set have the same meaning. Reconstruct the protoforms, and list all the sound changes that have taken place in each language. Remember that for some languages there may be no sound changes, while for others there may be multiple sound changes.

While the data are from hypothetical or highly regularized data, they exemplify processes found in actual languages.

1. **Hypothetical Language Group One**

	Language A	Language B	Protoform
1.	mũtə	mudo	*__________
2.	fumə	vumo	*__________
3.	pippon	bipona	*__________
4.	nõkə	noga	*__________
5.	wusə	juza	*__________
6.	fitə	vido	*__________

Summary of Sound Changes:

Lang A	
Lang B	

Remember: The reconstructed form does not have to be the same as any of the forms found in one of the descendant languages.

2. **Hypothetical Language Group Two**

[x] represents a voiceless velar fricative.
[ʣ] represents a voiced alveolar affricate.

	Language A	Language B	Language C	Language D	Protoform
1.	puxa	buga	puka	puk	* ____________
2.	nizuʣ	nizuz	mizu	nir	* ____________

Summary of Sound Changes:

Lang A	
Lang B	
Lang C	
Lang D	

3. **Austronesian**

The Austronesian languages under investigation here are located in southeast Asia. Malay is spoken on the Malay peninsula and is closely related to Chamic languages. Chamic is a branch of the Austronesian language family brought to southeast Asia about two thousand years ago. Written Cham is the written form of Phan Rang Cham, a Chamic language of Vietnam. Tsat is a Chamic language spoken on the Chinese island of Hainan, off the south coast of China.

Your job is to reconstruct the Proto-Austronesian (*PAN) word for each of the words in the data set. Then below, summarize the sound changes.

	Malay	Written Cham	Tsat	Gloss	*PAN
1.	anak	anəʔ	naʔ	'child'	______
2.	sakit	hakiʔ	kiʔ	'sick, painful'	______
3.	ikat	ikaʔ	kaʔ	'to tie'	______
4.	urat	uraʔ	zaʔ	'vein, tendon'	______

Summary of sound changes:

Malay:	
Written Cham:	
Tsat:	Tsat has also developed into a tone language (tones were not shown here). Why do you think Tsat has developed phonemic tones?

4. **German dialects**

The following data are from two dialects of German. Reconstruct the protoforms for each word, and describe the changes that have occurred in the obstruents (stops and fricatives).

You may not be able to reconstruct all the vowels accurately based on the amount of data here. Assume phonetic transcription.
[x] represents a voiceless velar fricative.
[pf] represents a voiceless labiodental affricate; it is a single segment.
[t͡s] represents a voiceless alveolar affricate; it is a single segment.

	Northern dialect	Southern dialect	Gloss	Protoform
1.	maːkə	maxən	'make'	______
2.	ik	ix	'I'	______
3.	slaːpə	ʃlaːfən	'sleep'	______
4.	pʊnt	pfʊnt	'pound'	______
5.	bejtə	bajsən	'bite'	______
6.	dat	das	'that'	______
7.	tuː	t͡suː	'to'	______

Summary of sound changes:

Northern dialect:	
Southern dialect:	

Reconstruction and Indo-European (Section 6.3, pp. 279–282)

In the late eighteenth century, Sir William Jones discovered that Sanskrit (the ancient language of India), Greek, Latin, and the Celtic and Germanic languages were all related. That is, words from these languages form cognate sets. It was eventually ascertained that at one time the people who now inhabit Europe and northern India all spoke the same language.

Using the comparative method, linguists have been able to reconstruct the protolanguage from which languages such as English, German, Spanish, Welsh, and Russian descended. This ancestral language is called **Proto-Indo-European (PIE)**.

The speakers of Proto-Indo-European began a series of migrations from their homeland (possibly in the steppes north of the Black Sea or in Anatolia). Within each migrating group, changes occurred to the protolanguage until eventually each group spoke a different language.

Grimm's Law

In 1822, Jacob Grimm (of *Grimm's Fairy Tales*) noticed some regular sound correspondences between the Germanic languages and the non-Germanic Indo-European languages. These correspondences are listed below.

Non-Germanic consonant	As in these non-Germanic words	Corresponding Germanic consonant	As in these Germanic cognates
[p]	pater (Latin)	[f]	father (German—Vater)
[t]	tonare (Latin)	[θ]	thunder
[k]	canis (Latin)	[x] → [h]	hound (German—Hund)
[b]	kannabis (Greek)	[p]	hemp
[d]	duo (Latin)	[t]	two
[g]	ager (Latin)	[k]	acre
[bh]	bhrata (Sanskrit)	[b]	brother (German—Bruder)
[dh]	vidhava (Sanskrit)	[d]	widow
[gh]	ghansas (Sanskrit)	[g]	goose (German—Gans)

Grimm explained these correspondences using three sound changes. These sound changes are collectively known as **Grimm's Law**, which is an example of a **sound shift**.

(1) Voiceless stops became voiceless fricatives (i.e., weakening, specifically frication)

PIE		PG (Proto-Germanic)
[p]	>	[f]
[t]	>	[θ]
[k]	>	[x] → [h]

(2) Voiced stops became voiceless stops

PIE		PG
[b]	>	[p]
[d]	>	[t]
[g]	>	[k]

(3) Voiced aspirated stops became voiced unaspirated stops

PIE		PG
[bh]	>	[b]
[dh]	>	[d]
[gh]	>	[g]

The first of Grimm's rules involves the weakening of stops to fricatives. This, of course, is a phonetically plausible sound change. Sound changes that tend to occur across many languages are often referred to as natural. *Naturalness* is an important factor in reconstruction, since language change is regular and systematic. The result of this weakening process left Proto-Germanic without voiceless stops. Since it is rare for a language to completely lack voiceless stops, this gap was filled by devoicing the voiced stops. This change illustrates the role of *typological plausibility* in reconstruction: reconstruction should take into account the universal properties of language. The reintroduction of voiceless stops, in turn, created a lack of voiced stops. This new gap was filled by deaspirating the voiced aspirated stops. This, of course, created yet another gap: a lack of voiced aspirated stops. This gap was not filled.

There are exceptions to Grimm's Law. Some systematic exceptions can be explained with a further rule, notably **Verner's Law**. Still other exceptions can be traced back to borrowings from Latin and French. Such borrowings did not undergo Grimm's Law or even Verner's Law, since these words entered the language long after the sound shift had occurred.

PRACTICE 7.9: Grimm's Law

For each bolded sound in the reconstructed Proto-Indo-European (PIE) word, give the sound change that occurred as a result of Grimm's Law. Then give the Modern English equivalent of the protoform.

	PIE WORD	GERMANIC SOUND (IN IPA)	ENGLISH WORD IN REGULAR SPELLING
1.	***g**el	______________	_____ool
2.	*le**b**	______________	li_____
3.	***g**re**bh**	______________	_____ra_____
4.	***gh**rei**b**	______________	_____ri_____
5.	***p**ulo	______________	_____oul
6.	***k**oimo	______________	_____ome
7.	*swa**d**	______________	swee_____

Review Exercises

The items below provide a review of various topics covered in this chapter, particularly the history of the English language and comparative reconstruction on the basis of sound change.

1. **The Great English Vowel Shift:** For each of the Middle English words below, state the vowel change that would have occurred as a result of the Great English Vowel Shift, and then give the spelling of the corresponding Modern English word.

Middle English	Vowel Change	Modern English Word
a. [noːn]	____________	____________
b. [liːfə]	____________	____________
c. [sweːt]	____________	____________
d. [bɔːst]	____________	____________
e. [guːn]	____________	____________

2. **Changes in English since Shakespeare:** The quotations on the left are all from Shakespeare. Some parts of the quotations are in boldface. To the right are modern "translations" of the boldfaced elements. Compare the early modern English of Shakespeare's time with contemporary English in:

   - the word order of statements (think in terms of subject, verb, and object)
   - the word order in negatives
   - the word order in questions
   - the use of pronouns and verbs that agree with them

   Examine the data and answer the questions after the data.

   1. From *Romeo and Juliet:*

Romeo: By a name	
I know not how to tell thee who I am.	I do not know how to tell you
My name, dear saint, is hateful to myself	
Because it is an enemy **to thee.**	to you
Had I it written, I would tear the word.	If I had written it

   2. From *Hamlet:*

Ghost: But, howsoever **thou pursuest** this act,	you pursue
Taint not thy mind, nor let thy soul contrive	Do not taint your mind or let your soul contrive
Against thy mother aught.	Anything against your mother.

3. From *Macbeth:*

Macb: I have done the deed. **Didst thou not hear** a noise?	Did you not hear/Didn't you hear
Lady: I heard the owl scream and the crickets cry. **Did not you speak?**	Did you not speak?/Didn't you speak?

4. From *Macbeth:*

Macb: **Saw you** the weird sisters?	Did you see
. . . **Came they not** by you?	Did they not come/Didn't they come

a. What is the order of subject (S), verb (V), and object (O) in English today?

What order of S,V, and O did Shakespeare use? Did he always use the same order? Cite evidence.

b. Where do we put the negator *not* in sentences today?

Where did Shakespeare put *not*? Did he always put it in the same place? Cite evidence.

What does Shakespeare's use of negation suggest about the time of the change in negation patterns?

c. What is the word order of *yes-no* questions in English today?

What word order did Shakespeare use? Did he always use the same order? Cite evidence.

d. What pronouns did Shakespeare use that have fallen out of use today?

What verb forms have fallen out of use along with these pronouns?

3. **Sound changes in Romance:** For the following languages, which have all descended from Latin, describe the changes that have taken place in consonants and in vowels on the edges of words. Given the small data set, you will not be able to account for every change, especially in internal vowels; however, you should be able to detail the process of change, including intermediate steps. Note: Latin is the protolanguage here, so you are not expected to reconstruct it but merely to list changes that have occurred.

[ɥ] represents a palatal glide articulated with rounded lips.
[β] represents a voiced bilabial fricative.

	Latin	Italian	Spanish	French	Gloss
1.	spina	[spina]	[espina]	[epin]	'thorn'
2.	scutella	[skodɛlla]	[eskuðija]	[ekɥɛl]	'bowl'
3.	scribere	[skrivere]	[eskriβir]	[ekriːr]	'write'
4.	schola	[skwɔla]	[eskuela]	[ekɔl]	'school'

Summary of changes from Latin to:

Italian:
Spanish:
French:

☑ RECAP

Make sure you know the following material. (See also the Key Terms on pp. 283–284 of the main text.)

- the different types of sound change
- the different types of morphological change
- the different types of syntactic change
- the different types of lexical change
- how to reconstruct protoforms and identify sound changes
- the three sound changes making up Grimm's Law

Questions? Problems?

Sources

The following references provide background information for exercises that are new to the American edition of the *Study Guide*.

Chapter 2

Facial diagrams. Adapted from:
Ladefoged, Peter. 1982. *A Course in Phonetics*. 2nd ed. San Diego: Harcourt Brace Jovanovich.

Chapter 3

Practice 3.4, #3, Japanese. Data derived from a number of sources:
Fromkin, Victoria, and Robert Rodman. 1993. *An Introduction to Language*. 5th ed. New York: Harcourt Brace, 267.
Okada, Hideo. 1999. "Japanese." In *Handbook of the International Phonetic Association*. Cambridge: Cambridge University Press, 117–119.
Takahashi, Naoko. Personal communication.

Practice 3.5, #2, Biblical Hebrew. Data from:
Weingreen, J. 1959. *A Practical Grammar for Biblical Hebrew*. 2nd ed. Oxford: Clarendon.

Practice 3.5, #3, German. Data from:
Cowan, W., and J. Rakušan. 1998. *Source Book for Linguistics*. Amsterdam: John Benjamins, 7, 31.
Kohler, Klaus. 1999. "German." In *Handbook of the International Phonetic Association*. Cambridge: Cambridge University Press, 86–89.
Kurtz, John W., and Heinz Politzer. 1966. *German: A Comprehensive Course for College Students*. New York: W.W. Norton, 8.

Practice 3.5, #4, Zinacantec Tzotzil. Data from:
<www.zapata.org/Tzotzil/Audio/index.html>
<www.zapata.org/Tzotzil/Chapters/Chapt1.html>

Practice 3.6, #3, Inuktitut. Data from:
<www.shindale.com/inuktitut>

Practice 3.6, #5, Yakut. Adapted from:
O'Grady, William, Michael Dobrovolsky, and Mark Aronoff. 1989. *Contemporary Linguistics*. 1st ed. New York: St. Martin's Press, 85.

Practice 3.13, #1, Polish. Data from:
Cohn, Abigail. 2001. "Phonology." In *The Handbook of Linguistics*. Edited by Mark Aronoff and Janie Rees-Miller. Oxford: Blackwell, 206–209.

Practice 3.14, #2, Standard Spanish and Andalusian Spanish. Data from:
Danford, Richard. Personal communication.

Review Exercise, #1, Passamaquoddy. Data from:
Leavitt, Robert M., and David A. Francis. 1986. *Philip S. LeSourd's English and Passamaquoddy-Maliseet Dictionary*. Perry, ME: Passamaquoddy/Maliseet Bilingual Program.
Waponahki Museum and Resource Center. 1986–1987. *I Know How to Speak Indian*. Perry, ME: Passamaquoddy/Maliseet Bilingual Program.

Review Exercise, #2, Kpelle. Data from:
Welmers, Wm. E. 1973. *African Language Structures*. Berkeley: University of California Press, 30.

Review Exercise, #3, Hausa. Data from:
Schuh, Russell G., and Lawan D. Yalwa. 1999. "Hausa." In *Handbook of the International Phonetic Association*. Cambridge: Cambridge University Press, 90–95.
<www.humnet.ucla.edu/humnet/aflang/Hausa/Hausa_online_grammar/Grammar_frame.html>

Review Exercise, #4, Bemba. Data from:
Spitulnik, Debra, and Mubanga Kashoki. 1998. "Bemba: A Brief Linguistic Profile." Available at <www.emory.edu/COLLEGE/ANTHROPOLOGY/FACULTY/ANTDS/Bemba/profile.html>

Review Exercise, #5, Syrian Arabic. Data from:
Cowell, Mark W. 1964. *A Reference Grammar of Syrian Arabic*. Washington, DC: Georgetown University Press, 6–7.
Stowasser, Karl, and Moukhtar Ani. 1964. *A Dictionary of Syrian Arabic*. Washington, DC: Georgetown University Press.

Chapter 4

Practice 4.14, #1, Toba Batak. Data from:
Crowhurst, Megan. 1998. "*Um* Infixation and Prefixation in Toba Batak." *Language* 74, no. 3: 595.

Practice 4.14, #2, Turkish. Data from a variety of sources:
Bender, Byron. Accessed through <http://www2.hawaii.edu/~bender/toc.html>.
Lewis, G. L. 1953. *Teach Yourself Turkish*. London: The English Universities Press.

Practice 4.14, #3, Classical Nahuatl. Data from:
Jordan, D. K. 1997. "Inadequate Nahuatl Reference Grammar" and "Nahuatl Lessons." Accessed through <http://weber.ucsd.edu/~dkjordan/nahuatl>.
Karttunen, Frances. 1983. *An Analytical Dictionary of Nahuatl*. Austin: University of Texas Press, xxvi–xxvii.

Practice 4.15, #2, Turkish. Data from:
O'Grady, William, Michael Dobrovolsky, and Mark Aronoff. 1997. *Contemporary Linguistics*. 3rd ed. New York: St. Martin's Press, 242–243.

Practice 4.15, #3, Dutch. Data from:
King, Peter, and Margaretha King. 1958. *Concise Dutch and English Dictionary*. London: Teach Yourself Books, Hodder and Stoughton.
<www.sr.net/srnet/InfoSurinam/dutch.html>

Review Exercise, #1, Ancient Egyptian. Data from:

Allen, James P. 2000. *Middle Egyptian: An Introduction to the Language and Culture of Hieroglyphs.* Cambridge: Cambridge University Press, 36–37.

Review Exercise, #2, Luganda. Data from:

<www.buganda.com/ggulama.htm#noun>

Chapter 6

Practice 6.3, #2, Menomini. Data from:

Bloomfield, Leonard. 1962. *The Menomini Language.* Edited by Charles F. Hockett. New Haven: Yale University Press.

Practice 6.3, #3, Kiswahili. Data from:

Erickson, Helen, and Marianne Gustafsson. "Kiswahili Grammar Notes: Nouns." Accessed at <www.cis.yale.edu:80/swahili/grammar/Noun_Classes.htm>

<victorian.fortunecity.com/louver/88/Swahili/lessons6.htm>

Practice 6.3, #4, German. Data from:

Buckley, R. W. 1965. *Living German.* London: Hodder and Stoughton, 75–77.

Review Exercise, #1, Burmese. Data from:

Ladefoged, Peter, and Ian Maddieson. 1996. *The Sounds of the World's Languages.* Cambridge, MA: Blackwell, 69.

Chapter 7

Practice 7.4, #1, English. Data from:

Arlotto, Anthony. 1972. *Introduction to Historical Linguistics.* Lanham, MD: University Press of America, 132.

Practice 7.4, #2, Welsh. Data from:

Weinreich, Uriel. 1968. *Languages in Contact.* The Hague: Mouton, 32.

Practice 7.4, #3, Folk etymology. Data from:

Mencken, H. L. 1963 [1951]. *The American Language: An Inquiry into the Development of English in the United States.* 4th ed. Edited by Raven I. McDavid. New York: Alfred A. Knopf, 648–649.

Practice 7.4, #4, African languages. Data from:

Childs, G. Tucker. 2003. *An Introduction to African Languages.* Amsterdam: John Benjamins, 160.

Practice 7.4, #5, Latin and Italian. Data from:

Arlotto, Anthony. 1972. *Introduction to Historical Linguistics.* Lanham, MD: University Press of America, 151-152.

Practice 7.5, Seventeenth-century English:

All sentences from the book of I Samuel in the King James Version of the Bible.

Practice 7.7, #1, Proto-Algonquian. Data from:

Bloomfield, Leonard. 1946. "Algonquian." In *Linguistic Structures of Native America.* Edited by Harry Hoijer. New York: Viking Fund Publications in Anthropology, no. 6, 85–129.

Practice 7.7, #2, Syrian and Iraqi Arabic. Data from:

Clarity, Beverly E., Karl Stowasser, and Ronald Wolfe. 1964. *A Dictionary of Iraqi Arabic.* Washington, DC: Georgetown University Press.

Stowasser, Karl, and Moukhtar Ani. 1964. *A Dictionary of Syrian Arabic.* Washington, DC: Georgetown University Press.

Practice 7.8, #3, Austronesian. Data from:

Thurgood, Graham. 1996. "Language Contact and the Directionality of Internal Drift: The Development of Tones and Registers in Chamic." *Language* 72, no. 1: 21.

Practice 7.8, #4, German dialects. Data from:

Bloomfield, Leonard. 1984 [1933]. *Language.* Chicago: University of Chicago Press, 342.

Review Exercise, #3, Romance. Data from:

Bloomfield, Leonard. 1984 [1933]. *Language.* Chicago: University of Chicago Press, 335.

Collins Concise Italian Dictionary. 1985. Glasgow: William Collins.

Danford, Richard. Personal communication.

Answer Key

Chapter 1

Practice 1.1

1.–2. Possible sentences include:
The early bird catches every worm.
Every early bird catches the worm.
Every bird catches the early worm.
3. Examples of unacceptable sentences:
Worm early the bird catches every.
Bird every early worm the catches.
4. One possible answer is that words must be in a specific order in a sentence; e.g., the subject comes before the verb, and the object follows the verb; adjectives come before the nouns they modify.

Practice 1.2

1. Possible English words: b, d, e, h
2. Possible English words: b, d
3. Possible English sentences: b, c, d, e

Practice 1.3

1. All are examples of prescriptive grammar.
2. a. The first is prescriptive, the second descriptive.
   b. The first is prescriptive, the second descriptive.
   c. The first is descriptive, the second prescriptive.
   d. The first is prescriptive, the second descriptive.

Review Exercise

a. 4 (answer supplied in text)
b. 1 c. 3 d. 2 e. 4 f. 4 g. 3 h. 2 i. 3 j. 4 k. 1

Chapter 2

Practice 2.1

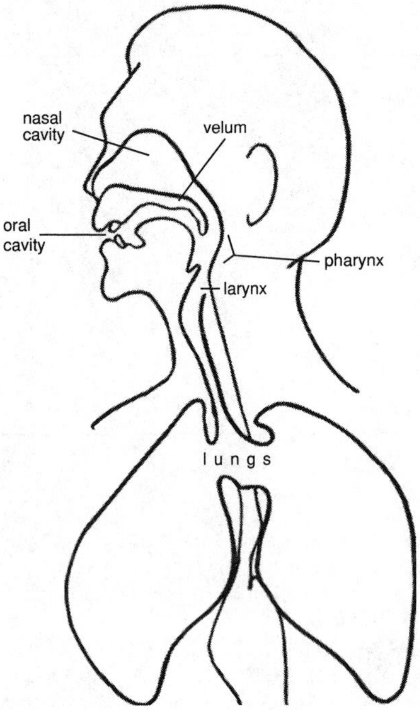

Practice 2.2

1. consonant (answer supplied in text)
2. vowel
3. consonant
4. glide
5. consonant
6. glide
7. vowel
8. consonant

Practice 2.3

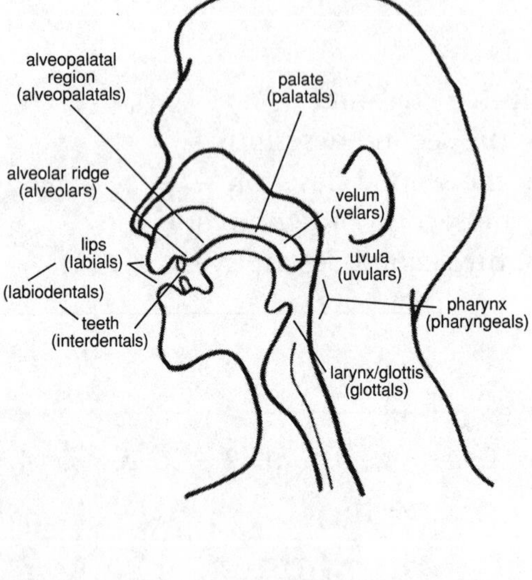

Practice 2.4

MANNER OF ARTICULATION	GLOTTAL STATE	Bilabial	Labiodental	Interdental	Alveolar	Alveopalatal	Palatal	Velar	Glottal
Stop	voiceless	p			t			k	ʔ
	voiced	b			d			g	
Fricative	voiceless		f	θ	s	ʃ			h
	voiced		v	ð	z	ʒ			
Affricate	voiceless					ʧ			
	voiced					ʤ			
Nasal	voiced	m			n			ŋ	
Liquid a. lateral	voiced				l				
Liquid b. retroflex	voiced				ɹ				
Glide	voiced	w					j	w	

Practice 2.5

Words with aspirated voiceless stops: 2, 4, 6

Practice 2.6

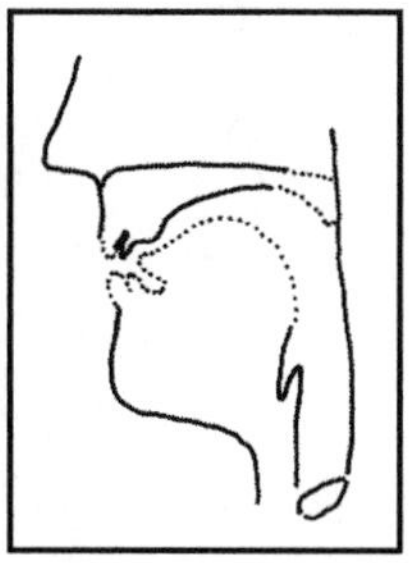

1. [s]

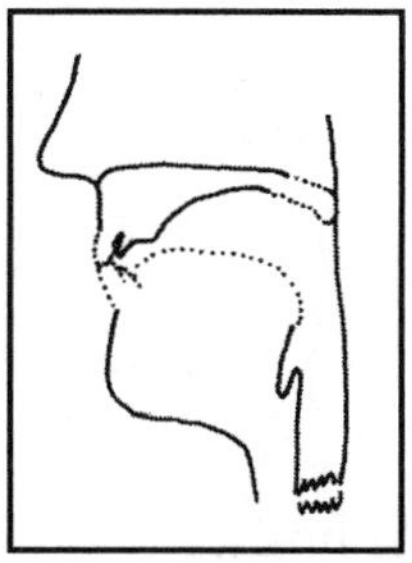

2. [b]

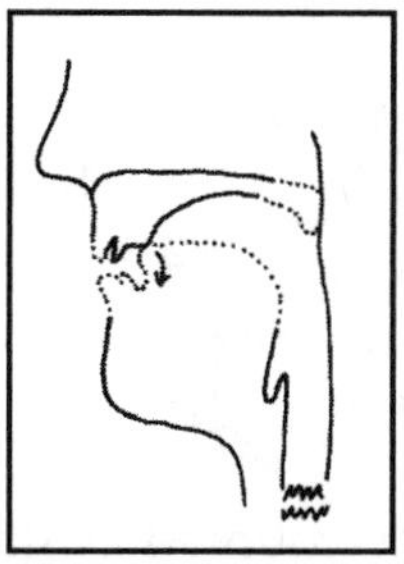

3. [ʤ]

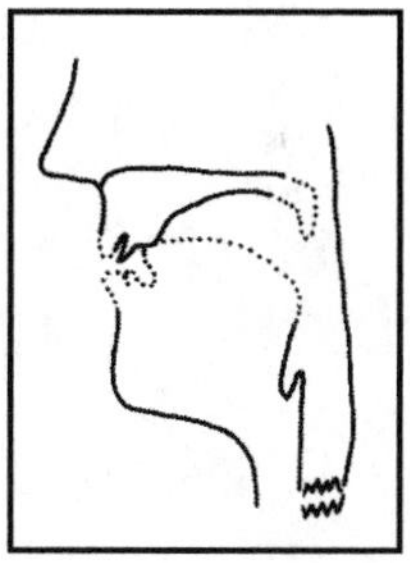

4. [n]

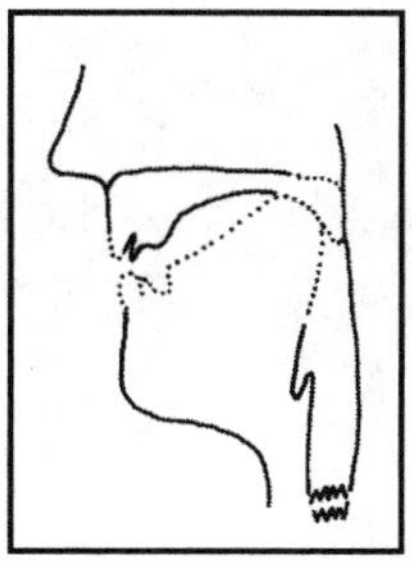

5. [g]

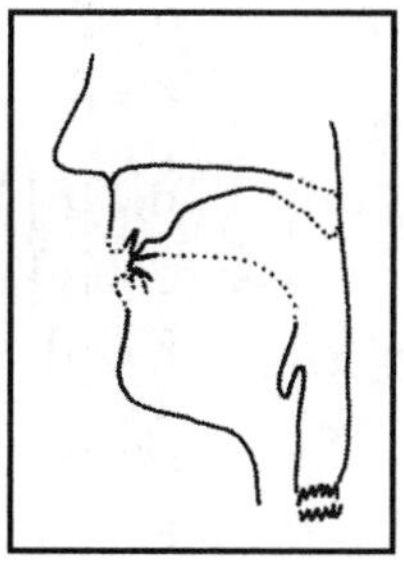

6. [ð]

Practice 2.7

1. [k]
2. [m]
3. [z]
4. [θ]
5. [f]
6. [d]

Practice 2.8

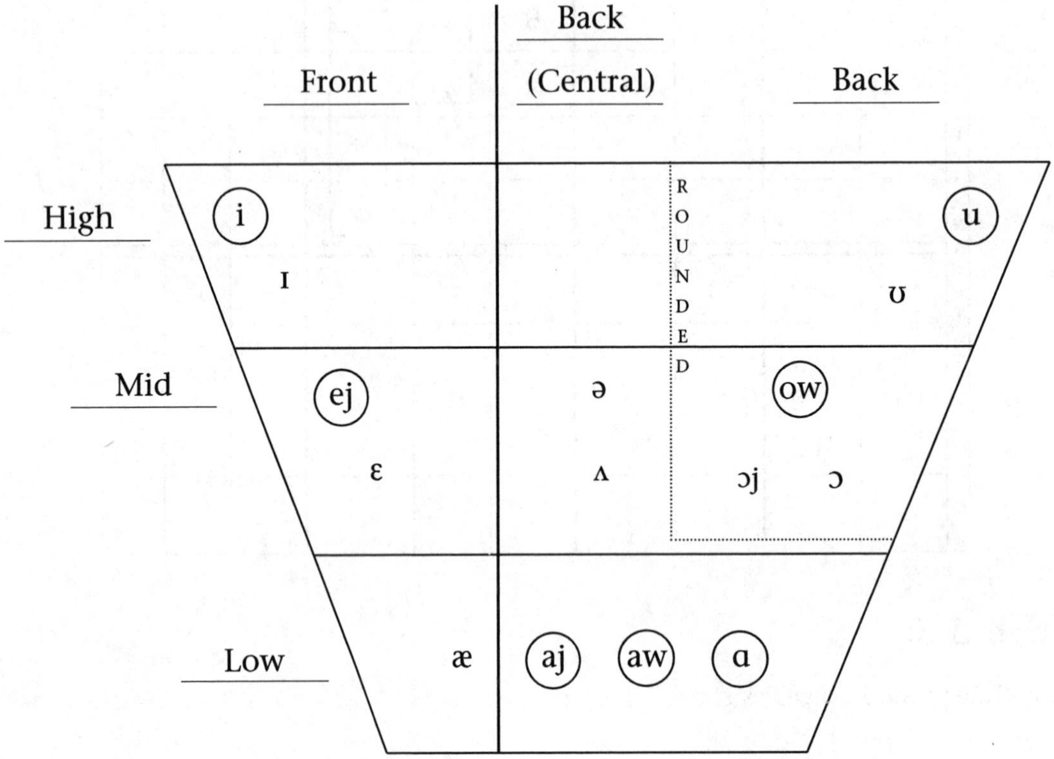

Practice 2.9

1. [æ̃]
2. [ɛ]
3. [ɔ]
4. [ĩ]

Practice 2.10

1. Diphthongs are counted as single sounds.
   a. 3
   b. 3
   c. 5
   d. 6
   e. 3
   f. 4
2. a. [t]
   b. [ʌ], [ə]
   c. [k]
   d. [n]
   e. [ʧ]
   f. [i]
3. a. [f]
   b. [ŋ]
   c. [ow], [aw]
   d. [m]
   e. [z] or [s]
   f. [s]

Practice 2.11

1. [kɹæft]
2. [saj]
3. [hɛlθ]
4. [bejʒ]
5. [fɹɔg], [fɹɑg]
6. [pʰædl̩]
7. [ejnʤl̩]
8. [ɹɪʧ]
9. [tʰejp]
10. [vejg]
11. [ɹustɹ̩]
12. [ɪnstɛd]
13. [bɑɹm̩]
14. [ʧɹ̩ʧ]
15. [θɔt], [θɑt]
16. [hæd]
17. [ɛgzɪt], [ɛksɪt]
18. [ʃʊgɹ̩]
19. [junɪt]
20. [kwɛsʧn̩]

Practice 2.12

1. [kʰi]
2. [du], [dju]
3. [lowf]
4. [mejd]
5. [ʧiz]
6. [ejt]
7. [wiz], [ʍiz]
8. [θɹu]
9. [bown]
10. [ist]
11. [bejbi]
12. [θɹow]

Practice 2.13 (Note: Answers are subject to dialectal variation.)

1. [ʧɪɹ], [ʧiɹ]
2. [kʰɑɹ]
3. [sɹ̩]
4. [ɔɹ], [oɹ]
5. [hɑɹt]
6. [ʃɑɹp]
7. [ðɛɹ]
8. [stɑɹ]
9. [hɹ̩]
10. [hɔɹs], [hoɹs]
11. [hɑɹd]
12. [ʃɹ̩t]
13. [ʧɛɹ], [ʧejɹ]
14. [skɔɹ], [skoɹ]
15. [flɔɹ], [floɹ]
16. [kʰɔɹs], [kʰoɹs]
17. [hɑɹm]
18. [θwɔɹt]

Practice 2.14 (Note: Numbers 4, 6, 13, 14, 17 will be different for raising dialects.)

1. [vɔjs]
2. [awɹ̩]
3. [ajz]
4. [sajt]
5. [pɹawl]
6. [najft]
7. [tɹajl̩]
8. [ɔjli]
9. [pɹajz]
10. [saj]
11. [kʰawntɹ̩]
12. [dawn]
13. [bajsɪkl̩]
14. [pɹajs]
15. [ɛmbrɔjdɹ̩]
16. [sajd]
17. [ajs]
18. [ʤɔjnt]

Practice 2.15

1. [slʌʤ]
2. [kwɑləɾi]
3. [lʌk]
4. [nowɾəs]
5. [θʌndɹ̩]
6. [bəhejv]
7. [ɛmfəsɪs]
8. [ənawns]
9. [hʌŋ]
10. [ʌvn̩]
11. [stʌf]
12. [ʌndɹ̩stænd]

Practice 2.16

1. leisure
2. axe
3. worthy
4. once
5. shade
6. shy
7. sweet
8. tube
9. choice
10. mutton
11. pipe
12. soften
13. phony
14. statue
15. square

Practice 2.17

1. voiced (oral) stops (answer supplied in text)
2. voiced consonants
3. strident consonants
4. voiced sonorant consonants
5. back vowels
6. lax front vowels

Practice 2.18

1. metathesis
2. assimilation (voicing, manner)
3. epenthesis
4. assimilation (place), nasalization (of the vowel)
5. dissimilation

Review Exercises

1. a. The lungs provide the air necessary for making speech sounds.
   b. The larynx is responsible for different glottal states such as voicing.
   c. The velum is one place of articulation in the oral cavity. Also, opening and closing the velum allows or prevents air from passing through the nasal cavity, creating nasal or oral sounds.
2. a. (bi)labial
   b. palatal
   c. uvular
   d. laryngeal
3. a. [ʔ]
   b. [i]
   c. [m]
   d. [f]
4. a. low front unrounded lax vowel
   b. voiced labiodental fricative
   c. (voiced) palatal glide
   d. mid back (or central) unrounded lax vowel
5. a. [u]
   b. [aj]
   c. [i]
   d. [ɑ]
   e. [ɪ]
   f. [ʊ]
6. Note: There may be dialectal variation in vowels and syllabic consonants.
   a. [skɔ́ɹnd]
   b. [dɪskʰʌ́vɹ̩]
   c. [ɛksplówʒn̩]
   d. [ʤínjəs]
   e. [mækəɹówni]
   f. [dúpləkət] or [dúpləkʰèjt]
   g. [díktejt] or [dɪktʰéjt]
   h. [ɑ́kjəpajd]
   i. [ɪnfɔ́ɹməɾɪv]
   j. [ajdɑ́lətɹi]

7. Note: There may be dialectal variations. Vowels in unstressed syllables may also vary.
   1. [dejz]
   2. [zɪɹɑks], [ziɹɑks]
   3. [gɛs]
   4. [jɛlow]
   5. [mɛɾl̩]
   6. [junəsajkl̩]
   7. [ɛkstɪŋgwɪʃ]
   8. [pʰɑpjəlɹ̩]
   9. [ajsəlejt]
   10. [fɹajtn̩], [fɹajʔn̩]
   11. [æʤɪtʰejt]
   12. [ɹowst]
   13. [θʌm]
   14. [bɑɹgn̩]
   15. [məʃin]
   16. [səɹawndəd]
   17. [kʰɑstjum]
   18. [ɹajɾɹ̩]
   19. [tʰajmtʰejbl̩]
   20. [jufəmɪzm̩]
   21. [nowm]
   22. [sɪksθs]
   23. [mæskjəlɪn]
   24. [pɹɛʃəs]
   25. [fɔɹmjələ]
   26. [kʰɑmədi]
   27. [gɹæʤuejt], [gɹæʤuɪt]
   28. [ɪɹɪgejt]
   29. [ʌnfɹ̩gɪvəbl̩]
   30. [kʰɔld], [kʰɑld]

8. a. m: fricatives; ð: labials
   b. n: oral stops; g: alveolar consonants; t: voiced consonants
   c. ɪ: back vowels or tense vowels

9. a. epenthesis
   b. deletion, nasalization
   c. epenthesis, voicing
   d. deletion, place assimilation, nasalization
   e. metathesis, nasalization

Chapter 3

Practice 3.1

1. no
2. yes
3. no
4. yes

Practice 3.2 (Sample answers are given; answers will vary.)

1. (answer supplied in text)
2. tuck: duck — wrote: rode
3. cut: gut — buck: bug
4. fine: vine — safe: save
5. sip: zip — bus: buzz
6. more: nor — sum: sun
7. red: led — peer: peel
8. tank: thank — bat: bath
9. cheer: jeer — batch: badge
10. pine: fine — cup: cuff

Practice 3.3

1. [p] occurs after [s] and between vowels when the first vowel is stressed.
   [pʰ] occurs word-initially and between vowels when the second vowel is stressed.
   [p̚] occurs word-finally and before a consonant.

2. [l] occurs word-initially, between a consonant and a vowel, and between vowels when the second vowel is stressed.
   [ɫ] occurs word-finally after a vowel, before a consonant, and between vowels when the first vowel is stressed.
   [l̩] occurs word-finally after a consonant (in an unstressed syllable).

Practice 3.4

1. Oneida: [s] occurs elsewhere.
   [z] occurs between vowels (V____V).
   Since they do not occur in the same environment, they are in complementary distribution.
2. Oneida: [s] occurs elsewhere.
   [ʃ] occurs before [j].
   Since they do not occur in the same environment, they are in complementary distribution.
3. Japanese: [ts] occurs before [u].
   [tʃ] occurs before [i].
   [t] occurs elsewhere.
   Since they do not occur in the same environment, they are in complementary distribution.

Practice 3.5

1. Arabic: [h] and [ʔ] are separate phonemes.
   Minimal pairs: 1–5; 2–6; 3–7; 4–8
2. Biblical Hebrew: [ð] occurs after a vowel; [d] occurs elsewhere.
   They are in complementary distribution and are allophones of the same phoneme.
3. German: [χ] occurs after a back vowel; [ç] occurs elsewhere.
   They are in complementary distribution and are allophones of the same phoneme.
4. Zinacantec Tzotzil:
   [p'] and [p] are separate phonemes.
   Minimal pair: 5–12
   Near-minimal pairs: 1–7; 4–10
   [k'] and [k] are separate phonemes.
   Minimal pair: 3–6
   Near-minimal pair: 9–11

Practice 3.6

1. English:
   Note: We assume diphthongs are single sounds.
   Corresponding short and long vowels are allophones of the same phoneme. They are in complementary distribution. Long vowels occur before word-final voiced obstruents; short vowels occur elsewhere.

Sample representation:

/i/

[iː] [i]

2. Korean:

   [ɾ] and [l] are allophones of the same phoneme.

   [ɾ] occurs intervocalically; [l] occurs elsewhere.

   Representation:

   /l/

   [ɾ] [l]

3. Inuktitut:

   [k] and [q] are separate phonemes that occur in similar environments (word-initially, word-finally, between front and back vowels).

   /k/ /q/

   | |

   [k] [q]

4. English:

   All are allophones of one phoneme.

   They are in complementary distribution: [gʷ] occurs before [u]; [gʲ] occurs before [i]; [g] occurs elsewhere.

   Representation:

   /g/

   [g] [gʷ] [gʲ]

5. Yakut:

   All are separate phonemes.

   Minimal pairs:

[i] : [ɨ]	3–7
[i] : [y]	1–10
[i] : [u]	4–12
[ɨ] : [y]	5–9
[ɨ] : [u]	6–13
[y] : [u]	9–14

   Representations:

   /i/ /ɨ/ /y/ /u/

   | | | |

   [i] [ɨ] [y] [u]

Practice 3.7

Sample answers are provided:

Practice 3.6:

1. English
   2. /ɹɑbd/ (vowel length is not shown)
   4. /mod/ (vowel length is not shown)

2. Korean
   3. /ilumi/ (intervocalic flapping is not shown)
   4. /kili/ (intervocalic flapping is not shown)
4. English
   6. /ɹægu/ (lip rounding of /g/ is not shown)
   12. /gis/ (fronting of /g/ is not shown)

Practice 3.8

1. a. (answer supplied in text)
   b. [+/–continuant]
   c. [+/–strident]
   d. [+/–nasal], [+/–sonorant]
   e. [+/–continuant], [+/–delayed release]

2. Note: Sample answers are given. Other answers are possible.
   a. (answer supplied in text)
   b. [ʃ] [+continuant], [–voice]
   c. [d] [–continuant]
   d. [w] [+sonorant]
   e. [z] [+anterior], [–sonorant], [+continuant]

3. a. glides
   b. voiced fricatives

4. a. [t] [+voice], *or* [v] [–continuant]
   b. [ʒ] [+sonorant], *or* [m] [–nasal]
   c. [m] [–nasal]
   d. [ʧ] [–delayed release]

5. a. [p, f, m, w] are all LABIAL
   [K, ŋ, J] are all DORSAL and [+high]

   b. [p, t, k, ʔ] are all [–sonorant, –continuant, –voice]
   [t, s, ʃ, ɹ] are all CORONAL
   [s, ʃ] are both [+strident]

   c. [m̩, n̩, l̩, i, u, ɑ] are all [+syllabic, +sonorant]
   [i, u] are both [+high]

   d. [b, d, g] are all [–sonorant, –continuant, +voice]
   [m, n, ŋ ,l] are all [+sonorant]

6. a. The sounds in the group share the following features:

   [
   +consonantal
   –sonorant
   –syllabic
   –nasal
   +continuant
   –lateral
   –delayed release
   ]

The following features distinguish each sound:

[f]	[v]	[θ]	[ð]
[–voice]	[+voice]	[–voice]	[+voice]
O LABIAL	O LABIAL	O CORONAL	O CORONAL

b. The sounds share the following features:

$$\begin{bmatrix} \text{+consonantal} \\ \text{–sonorant} \\ \text{–syllabic} \\ \text{–nasal} \\ \text{–continuant} \\ \text{–lateral} \\ \text{+voice} \end{bmatrix}$$

The following features distinguish each sound:

[g]	[ʤ]
[–delayed release]	[+delayed release]
O DORSAL	O CORONAL

c. The sounds share the following features:

$$\begin{bmatrix} \text{–consonantal} \\ \text{+sonorant} \\ \text{+syllabic} \\ \text{+continuant} \\ \text{+voice} \\ \text{O LABIAL} \\ \text{+round} \\ \text{O DORSAL} \\ \text{–low} \\ \text{+back} \\ \text{+tense} \\ \text{–reduced} \end{bmatrix}$$

The following features distinguish each sound:

[u]	[o]
[+high]	[–high]

d. The sounds share the following features:

$$\begin{bmatrix} \text{–consonantal} \\ \text{+sonorant} \\ \text{+syllabic} \\ \text{+continuant} \\ \text{+voice} \\ \text{O DORSAL} \\ \text{–back} \\ \text{–reduced} \end{bmatrix}$$

The following features distinguish each sound:

[i]	[ɪ]	[e]	[ɛ]	[æ]
+high	+high	–high	–high	–high
–low	–low	–low	–low	+low
+tense	–tense	+tense	–tense	–tense

Practice 3.9

Note: For the purpose of space, the word level is shown for the first answer only. However, the word level should be assumed for all subsequent words in the data set.

1.

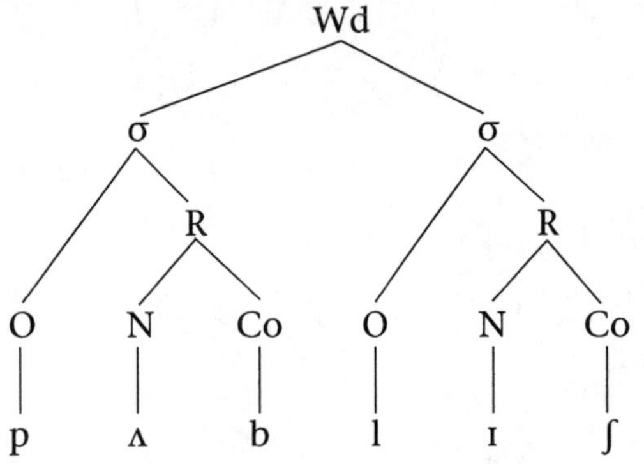

2.

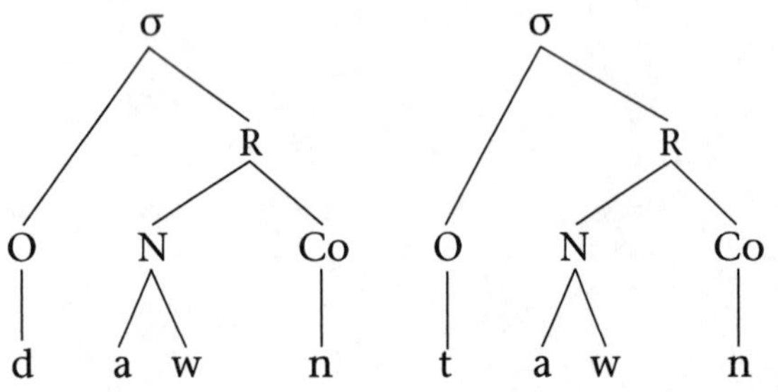

3.

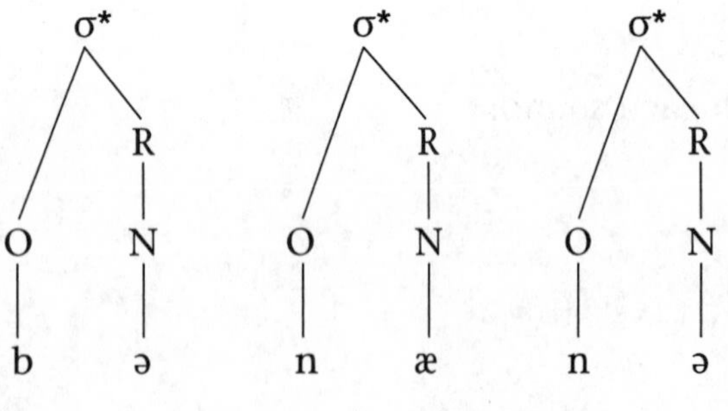

*open syllables

4.

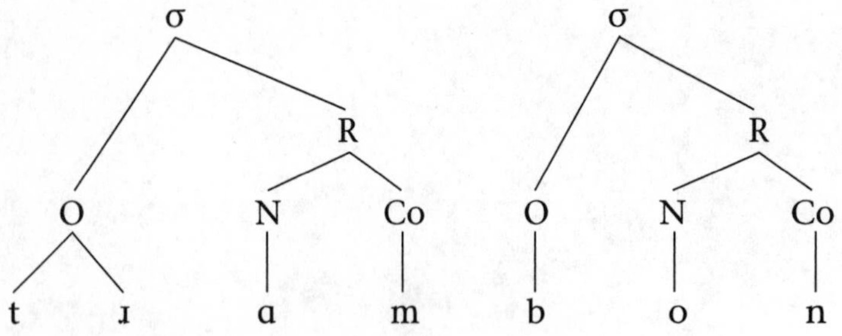

5.

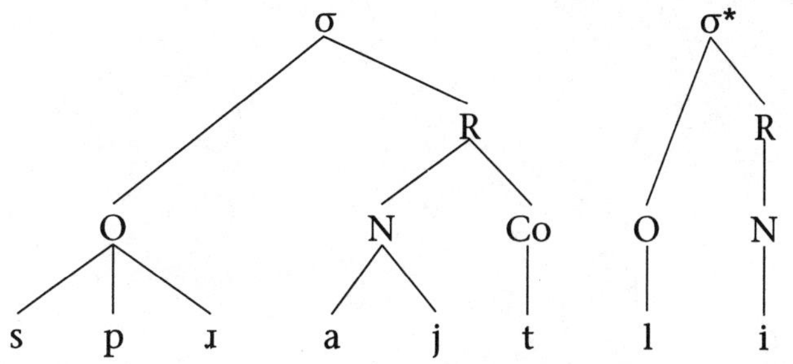

*open syllable

6.

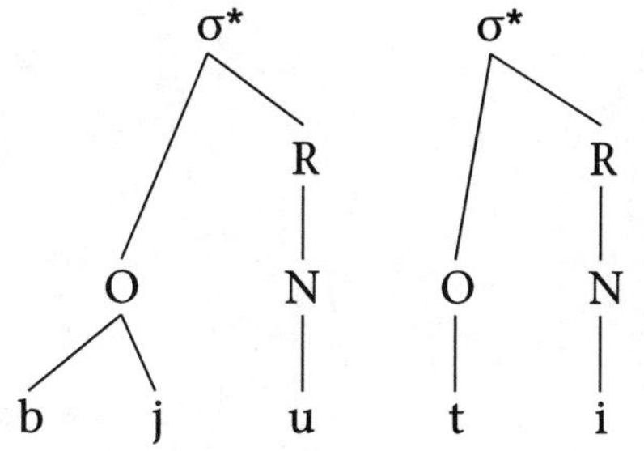

*open syllables

7.

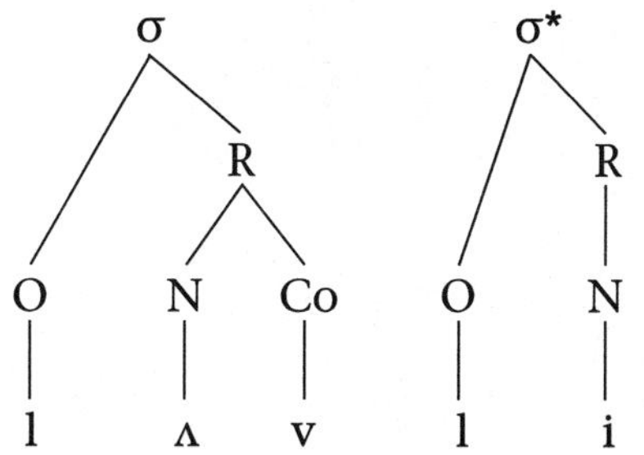

*open syllable

8.

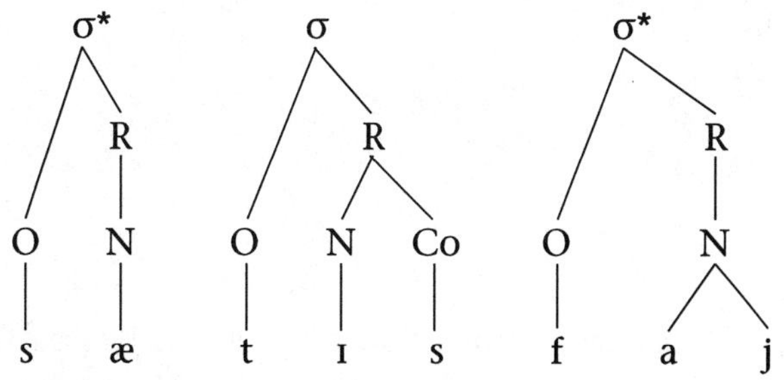

*open syllables

9.

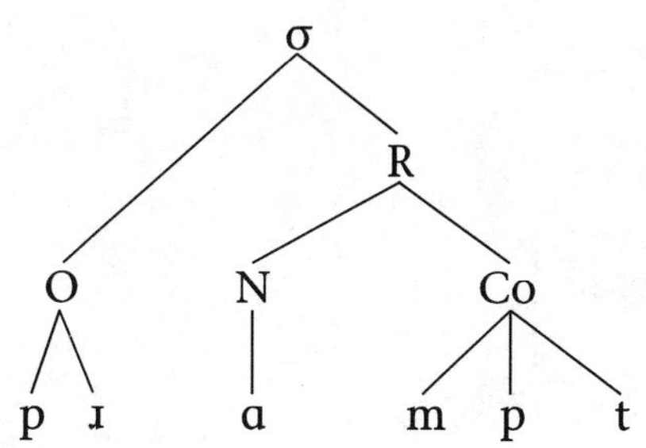

Practice 3.10

1.

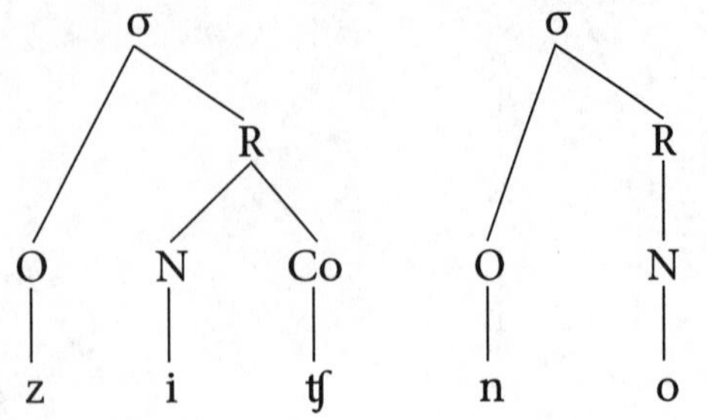

2.

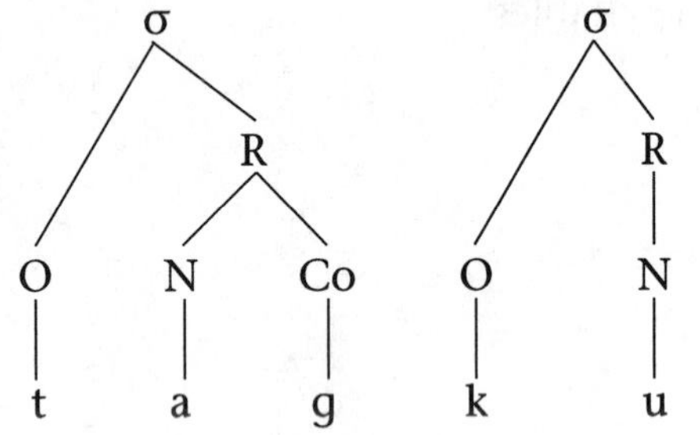

3.

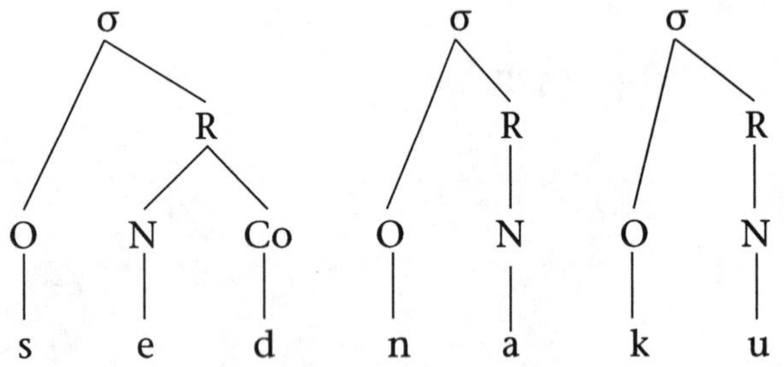

Practice 3.11

Stress in this language is on closed syllables.

Practice 3.12

1, 3. Rules and feature matrices:

Note: Full feature matrices are not given; only those features that distinguish the particular sounds are included in the feature matrices. For the sake of brevity, we use V to mean any vowel [–consonantal, +syllabic] and C to mean any consonant [+consonantal, –syllabic].

a. $\begin{bmatrix} -\text{sonorant} \\ -\text{continuant} \\ +\text{voice} \end{bmatrix} \longrightarrow [-\text{voice}] \quad / \quad \#\_\_\_\_$

b. $\begin{bmatrix} +\text{delayed release} \\ \text{OCORONAL} \\ -\text{anterior} \end{bmatrix} \longrightarrow \begin{bmatrix} -\text{delayed release} \\ +\text{continuant} \end{bmatrix} \quad / \quad \text{V}\_\_\_\_\text{V}$

c. $$\text{V} \longrightarrow [+\text{nasal}] \;/\; \_\_\_\_ \underset{[+\text{nasal}]}{\text{C}}$$

d. $$[\text{ə}] \longrightarrow \text{Ø} \;/\; \_\_\_\_\#$$

e. $$\text{Ø} \longrightarrow [\text{ə}] \;/\; [\text{p}]\_\_\_\_[\text{l}]$$

2, 3. Statements and feature matrices:

Note: The rule using feature matrices follows each statement.

a. A voiceless alveolar stop becomes glottalized following a glottal stop.

$$\begin{bmatrix} -\text{sonorant} \\ -\text{continuant} \\ -\text{voice} \\ -\text{SG} \\ \text{OCORONAL} \end{bmatrix} \longrightarrow [+\text{CG}] \;/\; \begin{bmatrix} -\text{sonorant} \\ -\text{continuant} \\ +\text{CG} \end{bmatrix} \_\_\_\_$$

b. Voiceless fricatives become voiced intervocalically.

$$\begin{bmatrix} -\text{sonorant} \\ +\text{continuant} \\ -\text{voice} \end{bmatrix} \longrightarrow [+\text{voice}] \;/\; \begin{bmatrix} -\text{consonant} \\ +\text{syllabic} \end{bmatrix} \_\_\_\_ \begin{bmatrix} -\text{consonant} \\ +\text{syllabic} \end{bmatrix}$$

c. Nonlow tense front vowels become lax word-finally.

$$\begin{bmatrix} -\text{consonant} \\ +\text{syllabic} \\ \text{ODORSAL} \\ -\text{low} \\ -\text{back} \\ +\text{tense} \end{bmatrix} \longrightarrow [-\text{tense}] \;/\; \_\_\_\_\#$$

d. A voiceless oral stop becomes aspirated word-initially before a stressed vowel.

$$\begin{bmatrix} -\text{sonorant} \\ -\text{continuant} \\ -\text{voice} \\ -\text{CG} \\ -\text{SG} \end{bmatrix} \longrightarrow [+\text{SG}] \;/\; \#\_\_\_\_ \begin{bmatrix} -\text{consonant} \\ +\text{syllabic} \\ +\text{stress} \end{bmatrix}$$

Practice 3.13

1. Polish:
Voiced stops are devoiced word-finally.

$$\begin{bmatrix} -\text{sonorant} \\ -\text{continuant} \\ +\text{voice} \end{bmatrix} \longrightarrow [-\text{voice}] \;/\; \_\_\_\_\#$$

2. South Midland and Southern American English:
[ɛ] becomes [ɪ] before a nasal consonant.

$$\begin{bmatrix} -\text{consonant} \\ +\text{syllabic} \\ -\text{high} \\ -\text{low} \\ -\text{back} \\ -\text{tense} \end{bmatrix} \longrightarrow [+\text{high}] \quad / \quad \underline{\quad\quad} \begin{bmatrix} +\text{consonant} \\ +\text{nasal} \end{bmatrix}$$

Practice 3.14

1. Tamil:
Voiceless stops become voiced intervocalically.

$$\begin{bmatrix} -\text{sonorant} \\ -\text{continuant} \\ -\text{voice} \end{bmatrix} \longrightarrow [+\text{voice}] \quad / \quad \text{V} \underline{\quad\quad} \text{V}$$

Derivation:

UR	#kappal#	#mukil#	#kuṯi#
Voicing	——	#mugil#	#kuḏi#
PR	#kappal#	#mugil#	#kuḏi#

2. Standard and Andalusian Spanish: Note that the answers given here are based on the data set. The situation is actually somewhat more complicated.

a. In Standard Spanish, [d] becomes [ð] after [r] and after a vowel.

We could write: [d] → [ð] / [+continuant] _____
But what is happening (manner assimilation) is clearer if we use features:

$$\begin{bmatrix} -\text{sonorant} \\ -\text{continuant} \\ +\text{voice} \\ \text{O CORONAL} \\ -\text{strident} \end{bmatrix} \longrightarrow [+\text{continuant}] \ / \ [+\text{continuant}] \underline{\quad\quad}$$

b. In Andalusian Spanish, [d] becomes [ð] after [r] and after a vowel.
[d] → [ð] / [+continuant] _____

$$\begin{bmatrix} -\text{sonorant} \\ -\text{continuant} \\ +\text{voice} \\ \text{O CORONAL} \\ -\text{strident} \end{bmatrix} \longrightarrow [+\text{continuant}] \ / \ [+\text{continuant}] \underline{\quad\quad}$$

c. In Andalusian Spanish, [r] is deleted syllable finally: [r] → Ø ____$_\sigma$
(Note it is *not* just when it comes after a vowel—see # 12 [floriːo].)

d. [ð] is deleted after a vowel.
[ð] → Ø / V ____

$$\begin{bmatrix} -\text{sonorant} \\ +\text{continuant} \\ +\text{voice} \\ \text{O CORONAL} \\ -\text{strident} \end{bmatrix} \longrightarrow \emptyset \ / \ V \ \_\_\_\_$$

Note that in both cases of deletion, there is compensatory lengthening of the vowel. This may require a separate rule, but we will assume here for the sake of simplicity that it happens automatically.

e. Note: [ð] deletion must come before [r] deletion.

UR	#berdad#	#merkado#
[d] frication	berðað	merkaðo
[ð] deletion	berðaː	merkaːo
[r] deletion	beːðaː	meːkaːo
PR	#beːðaː#	#meːkaːo#

Review Exercise

1. Passamaquoddy:
   [p] and [b] are in complementary distribution.
   [b] occurs between vowels; [p] occurs elsewhere. (Actually, the situation is a bit more complex, but this statement fits the data given here.)

   [p] ⟶ [b] / V____V

2. Kpelle:
   Nasalized and oral vowels are separate phonemes.
   Minimal pair: 4–8

3. Hausa:
   [r] and [ɽ] are separate phonemes.
   Near-minimal pairs: 2–8; 3–7

4. Bemba:
   [s] and [ʃ] are in complementary distribution.
   [ʃ] occurs before [i]; [s] occurs elsewhere. This is a case of palatalization.

   [s] ⟶ [–anterior] / ____ [i]

5. Syrian Arabic:
   The plain and pharyngealized consonants are separate phonemes.
   Minimal pair: 4–9
   Near-minimal pairs: 2–14; 6–16

Chapter 4

Practice 4.1

1. desert = 1
2. memory = 1
3. format = 1
4. flowchart = 2
5. bug = 1
6. debug = 2
7. supply = 1
8. supplies = 2
9. supplier = 2
10. faster = 2
11. power = 1
12. processor = 2

Practice 4.2

	# of Morphemes	Free	Bound
1.	(answer supplied in text)		
2.	1	wicked	
3.	2	valid	in-
4.	1	invalid	
5.	2	Jack	-s
6.	4	opt	-tion, -al, -ity
7.	2	furnish	re-
8.	4	able	in-, -ity, -s
9.	4	nation	de-, -al, -ize
10.	1	deride	
11.	4	act	-ive, -ate, -tion

Practice 4.3

	# of Morphemes	Root	Root Category	Word Category
1.	(answer supplied in text)			
2.	2	amaze	verb	noun
3.	3	use	verb	adjective
4.	2	honest	adjective	adjective
5.	1	Baltimore	noun	noun
6.	3	love	noun	adjective
7.	3	history	noun	adjective
8.	3	control	verb	adjective
9.	3	person	noun	adjective
10.	2	tree	noun	noun
11.	2	fast	adjective	adjective
12.	3	read	verb	verb
13.	2	beauty	noun	adjective
14.	1	child	noun	noun

Practice 4.4

1.
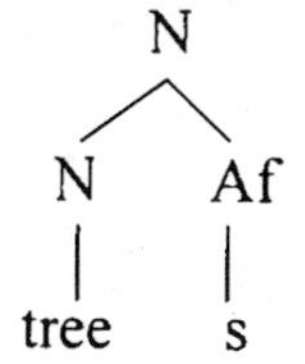

2.
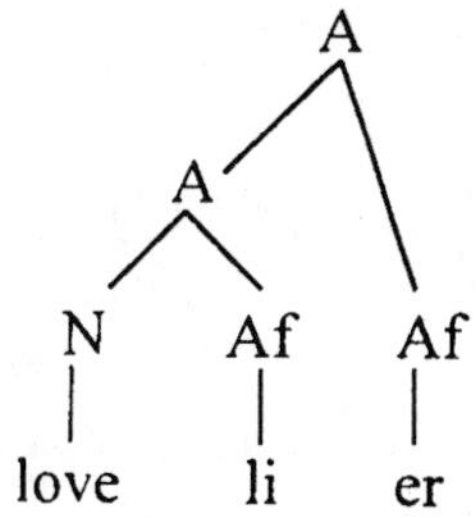

3.
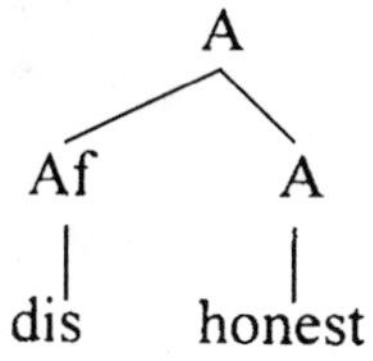

4.
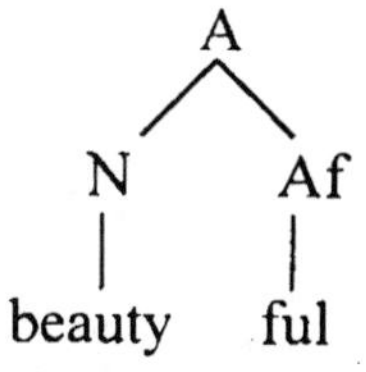

5.
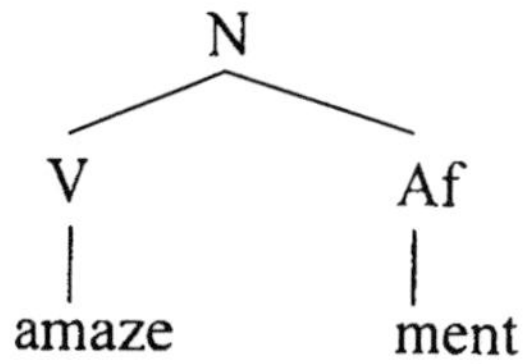

6.
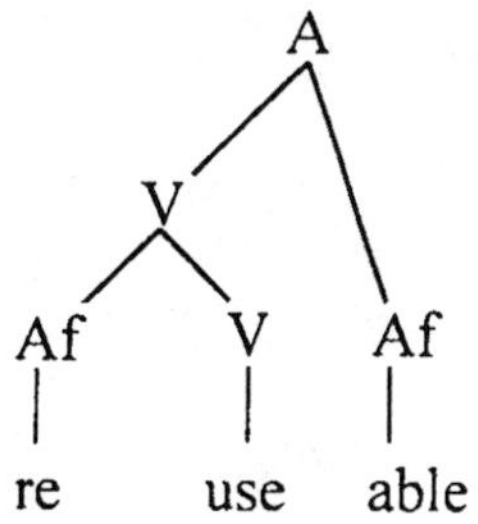

7.
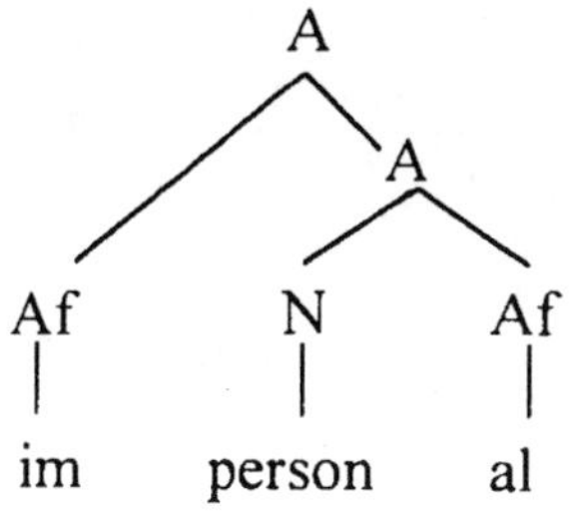

8.

Practice 4.5

1. a.
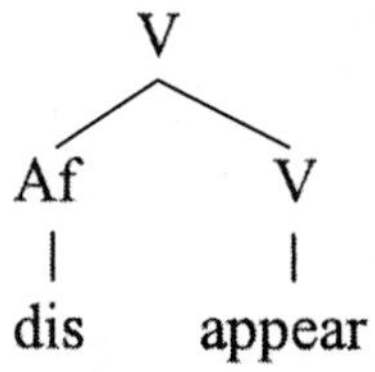

b.
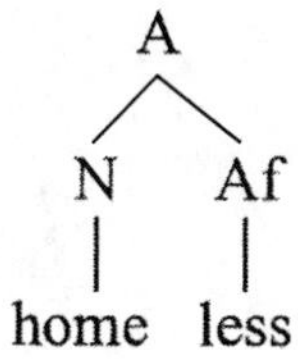

c.
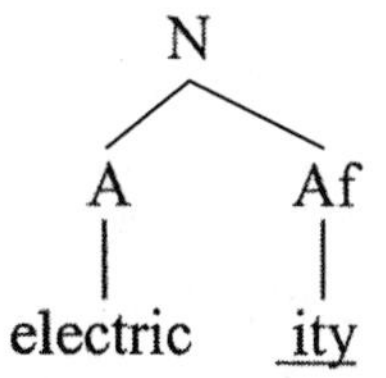

Class I

d.
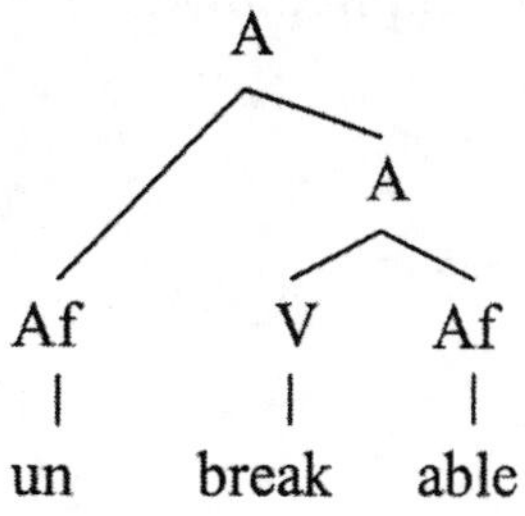

e.

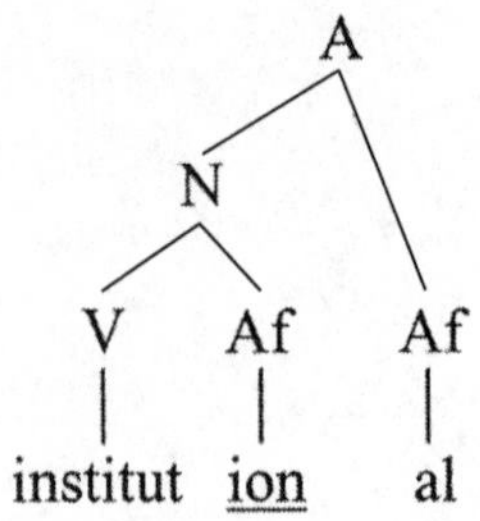

Class I

f.

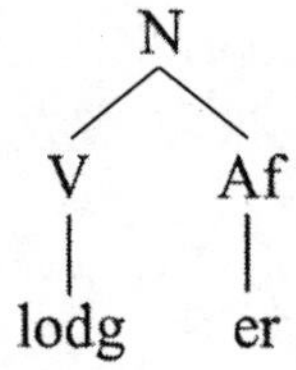

2.

1.	-able	V → A	8.	-ity	A → N
2.	-ial	N → A	9.	re-	V → V
3.	-ness	A → N	10.	-ian	N → A
4.	dis-	V → V	11.	-ize	N → V
5.	-ize	N → V	12.	-ate	A → V
	-ation	V → N	13.	-en	A → V
6.	-ive	V → A	14.	un-	A → A
7.	-ous	N → A		-ant	V → A
			15.	un-	V → V

Practice 4.6

(Note: Sample examples are given in the tree diagrams; answers will vary.)

1. a.

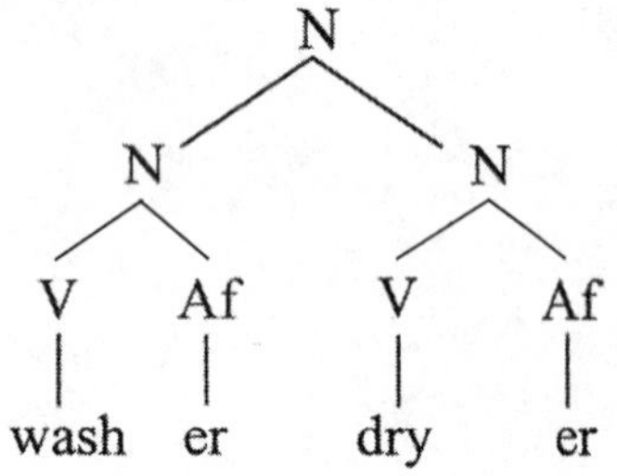

c.

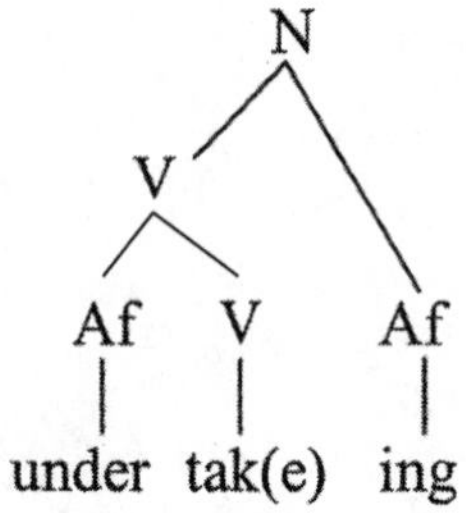

b.

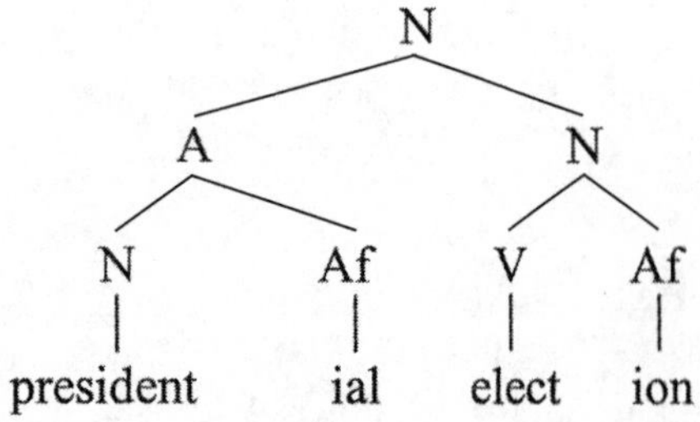

d.

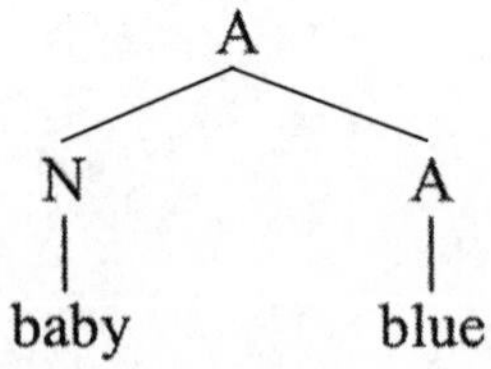

2.

COMPOUND		LEXICAL CATEGORIES
1.	bathroom (answer supplied in text)	
2.	scarecrow	V + N
3.	skin-deep	N + A
4.	bittersweet	A + A
5.	upstairs	P + N

1.

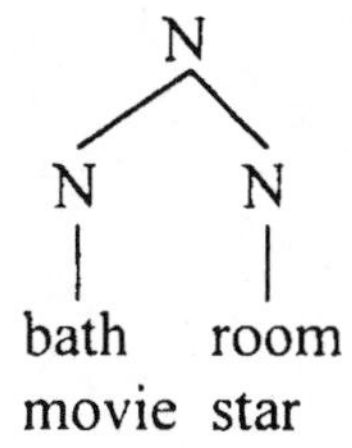

2.

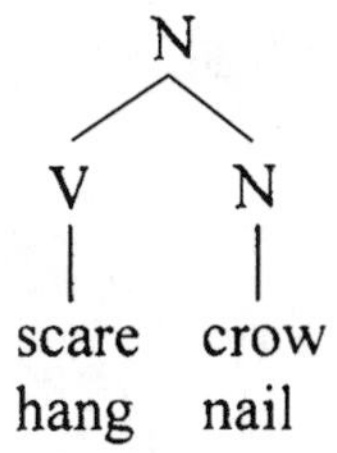

3.

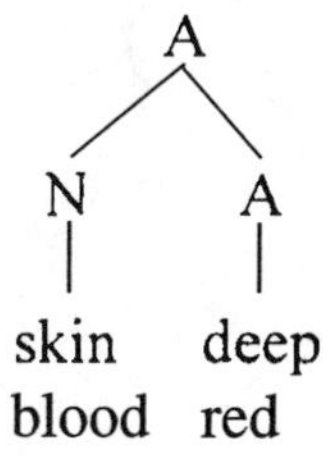

4.

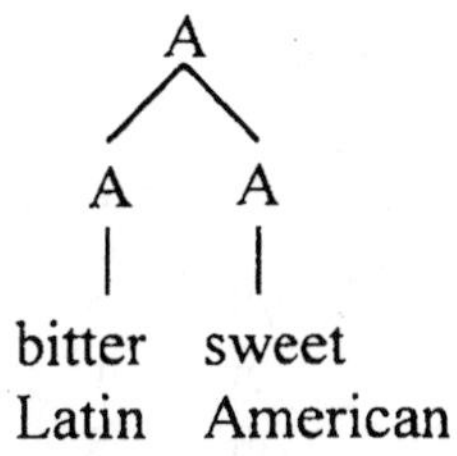

5.

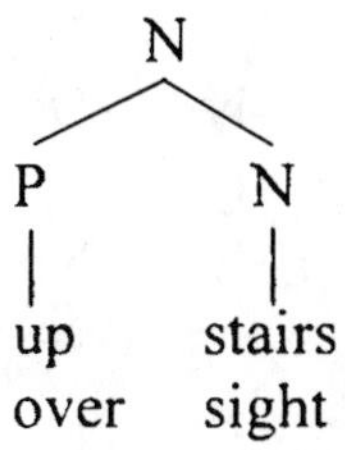

Practice 4.7

	Lexical Category	Inflectional Information
1.	(answer supplied in text)	
2.	V	third-person singular nonpast
3.	A	superlative
4.	N	plural
5.	V	progressive
6.	V	past participle
7.	A	comparative

Practice 4.8

	WORD	SIMPLE/COMPLEX	INFL/DERIV
1.	(answer supplied in text)		
2.	fly	simple	——
3.	prettier	complex	inflectional
4.	stringy	complex	derivational
5.	delight	simple	——
6.	reuse	complex	derivational
7.	fastest	complex	inflectional
8.	mistreat	complex	derivational

Practice 4.9

(Note: The affix is supplied.)

1. (answer supplied in text)

2. -y S
   N
   -y D
   -y S

3. N
   -en S
   -en D
   -en S

4. -er S
   -er D
   N
   -or S

5. -er S
   -er D
   -er S
   N

6. -ly D
   -ly S
   -ly S
   N

7. N
   in- D
   in- S
   in- S

8. -ed D
   -ed S
   -ed S
   N

Practice 4.10

1. inflection

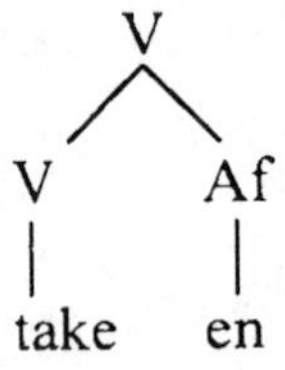

2. compound inflection

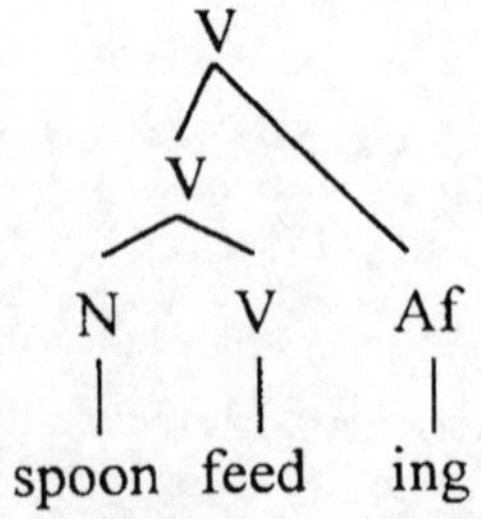

3. inflection

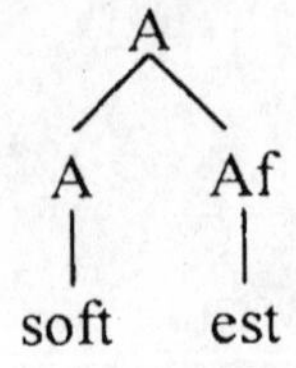

4. derivation, inflection

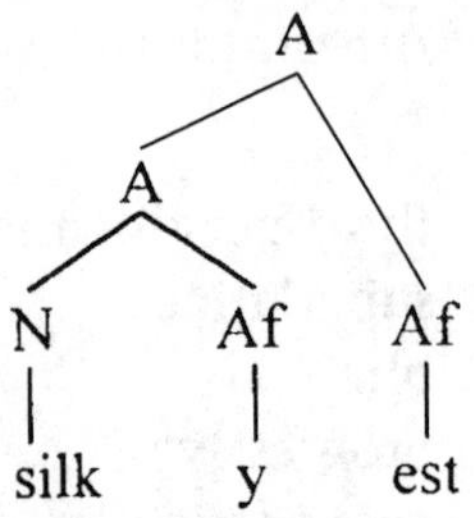

5. derivation, inflection

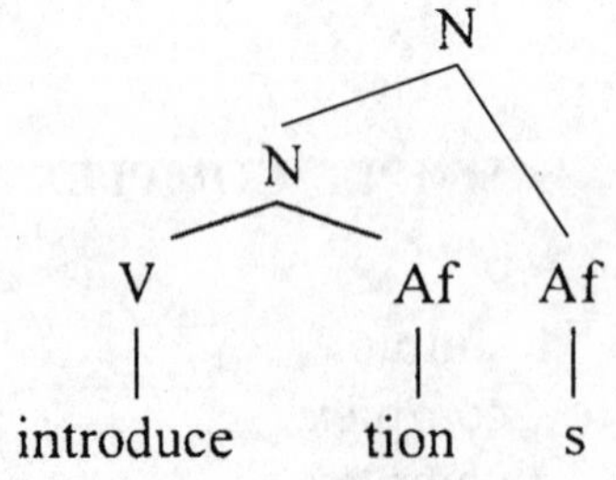

6. inflection

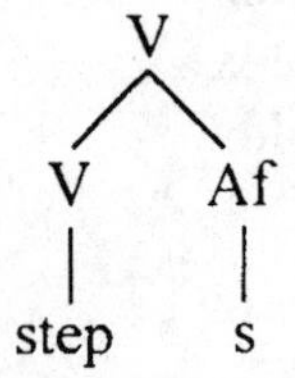

7. inflection

8. derivation, inflection

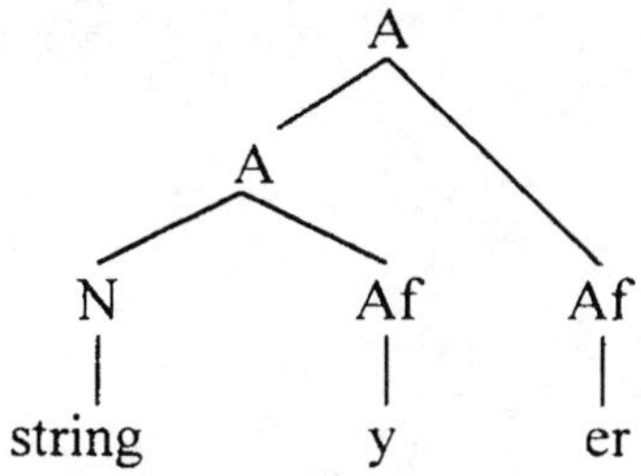

9. derivation, inflection

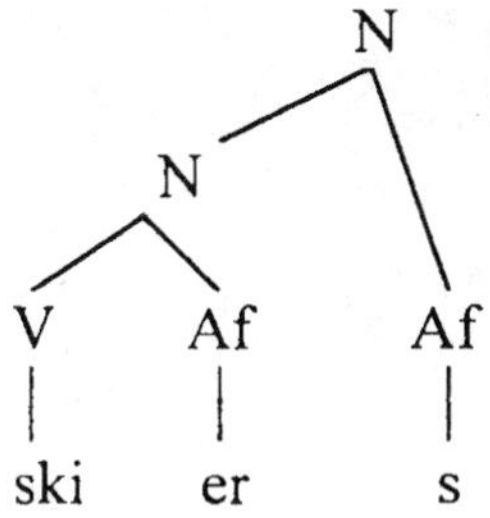

10. -----

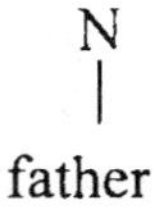

11. compound

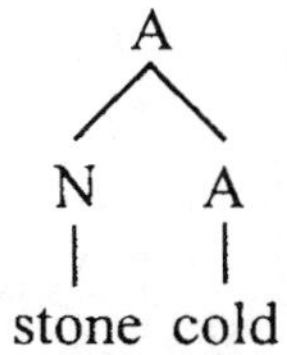

12. inflection

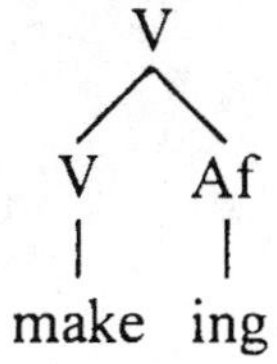

13. derivation

14. derivation

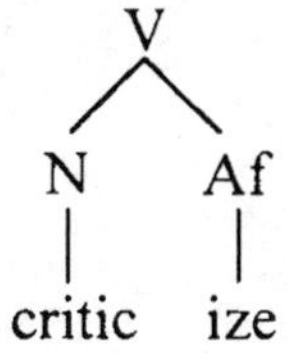

15. derivation

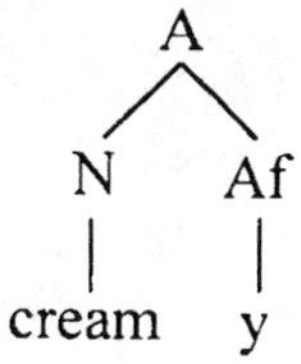

16. derivation, inflection

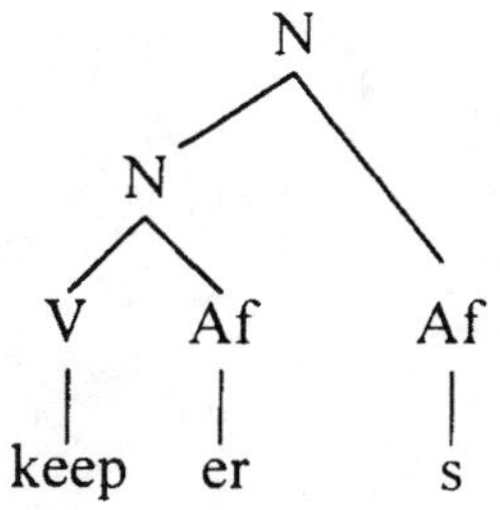

17. derivation

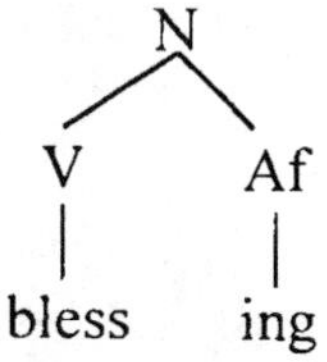

18. inflection

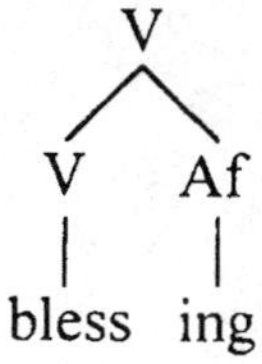

19. derivation, compound

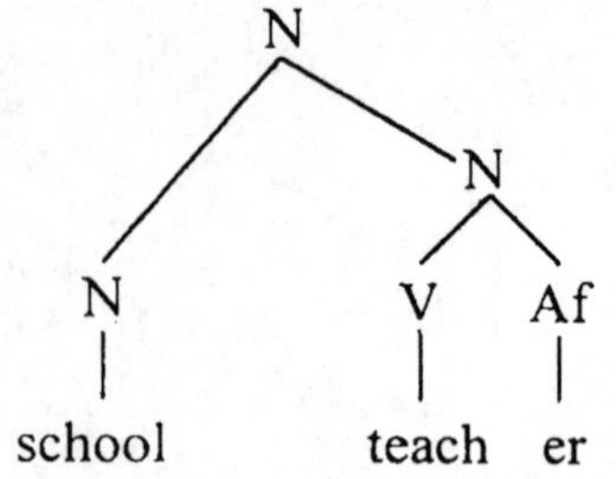

20. derivation

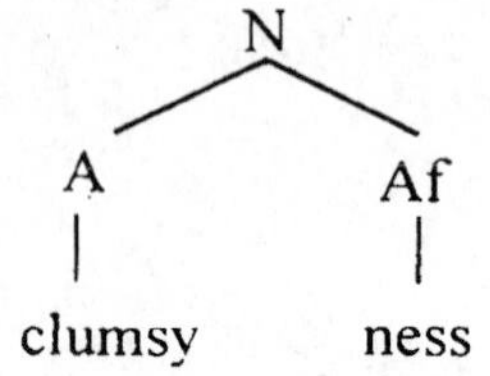

21. compound, inflection

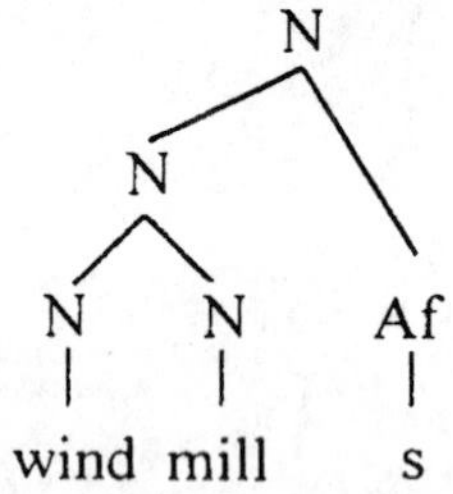

22. inflection

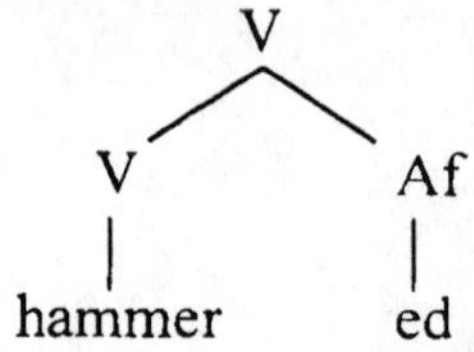

23. derivation, inflection

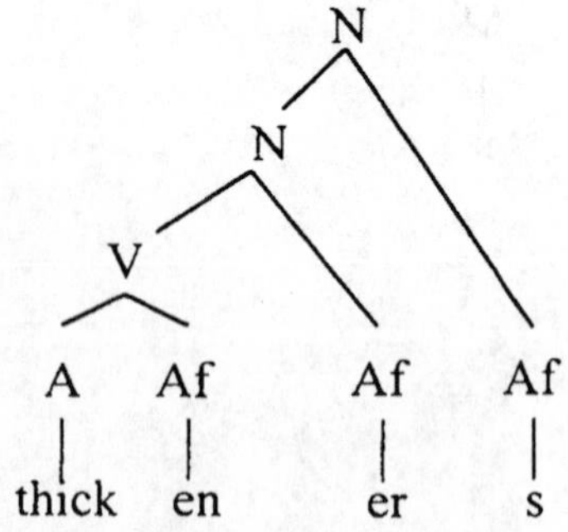

24. derivation, inflection

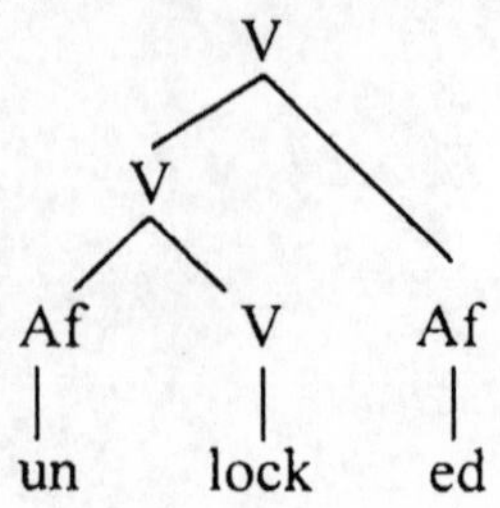

25. derivation

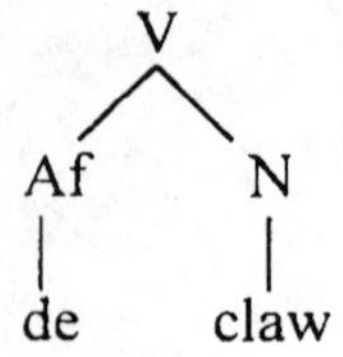

26. derivation

27. compound

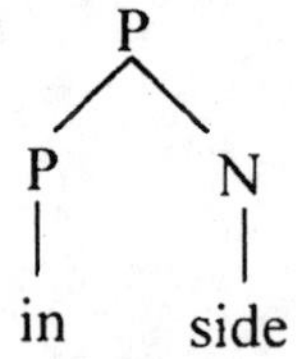

28. derivation

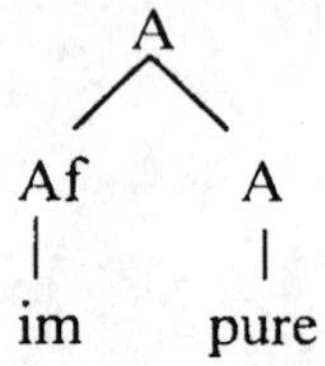

29. compound, derivation

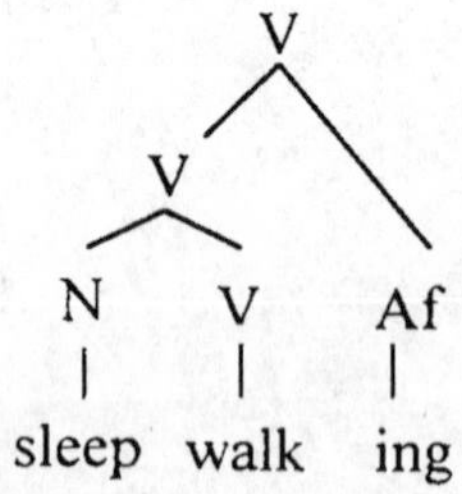

30. derivation, inflection

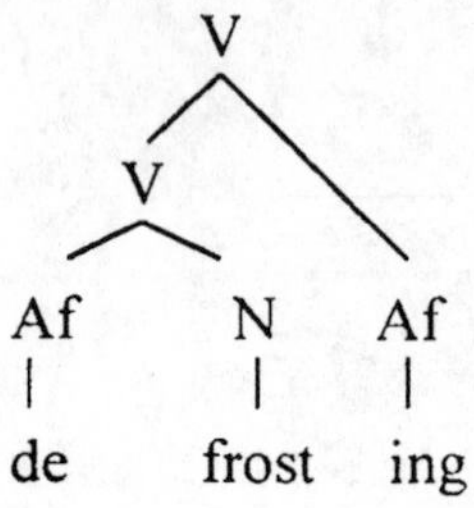

Practice 4.11

1. (answer supplied)
2. suppletion
3. affixation
4. (full) reduplication
5. suppletion
6. affixation
7. affixation
8. (partial) reduplication
9. internal change

Practice 4.12

1. 1. (answer supplied in text)
   2. conversion
   3. inflection (internal change)
   4. compounding
   5. onomatopoeia
   6. inflection (affixation)
   7. derivation
   8. clipping
   9. derivation
   10. cliticization
   11. compounding
   12. onomatopoeia
   13. acronym

2. Words from the passage:

Dave	clipping
brunch	blending
chirping	onomatopoeia
outside	compounding
buzz	onomatopoeia
infomercial	blending
(TV is not technically an	acronym)
headache	compounding
hammering	conversion
eyeball	compounding
Kleenex	coinage
scuba	acronym
flu	clipping
fingered	conversion
med	clipping
enthused	backformation
off-putting	compounding
CAT	acronym
blood test	compounding

laser	acronym
laze	backformation
Coke	clipping of a coinage
sandwiches	coinage (from the Earl of Sandwich)
channel-surfing	compounding

Practice 4.13

1. Mende
   a. -i
   b. [salei]
   c. 'night'
2. Ganda
   a. omu-
   b. aba-
   c. [omulanga]
3. Kanuri
   a. prefix
   b. [nəm]
   c. [nəmkəji]
   d. [gəla]
   e. derivation
   f.

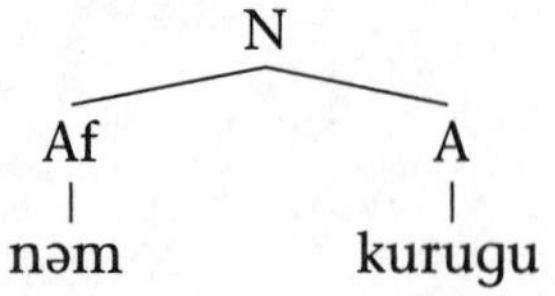

Practice 4.14

1. Toba Batak
   a. -um- indicates comparative
   b. infix (after the first consonant)
   c. [dumatu] 'wiser'
   d. [sumɔmal] 'more usual'
   e. [ʤɛppɛk] 'short'
   f. [lógo] 'dry'
2. Turkish
   a. Morphemes

1. 'city'	[ʃehiɾ]	8. 'from'	-[den]
2. 'hand'	[el]	9. 'to'	-[e]
3. 'bridge'	[kœpɾy]	10. 'on, in'	-[de]
4. 'bell'	[zil]	11. 'my'	-[im]
5. 'house'	[ev]	12. 'your'	-[iniz]
6. 'voice'	[ses]	13. PLURAL	-[leɾ]
7. 'bus'	[otobys]		

   b. Order of morphemes: ROOT + PLURAL + POSSESSIVE + POSTPOSITION

c. English translation
   1. 'in a city'
   2. 'your hands'

d. Turkish translation
   'to the buses' [otobyslere]

3. Classical Nahuatl
   a. Morphemes

1. 'sing'	[kʷiːka]
2. 'eat'	[kʷa]
3. 'bathe'	[aːltia]
4. you (SG) (subject)	[ti]-
5. s/he (subject)	Ø (not marked)
6. it (object)	[ki]-
7. we (subject)	[ti]- (STEM)-[ʔ]
8. you (PL) (subject)	[an]- (STEM)-[ʔ]
9. they (subject)	-[ʔ]

   b. suffix marking plural subject in present: -[ʔ]
   c. customary present marked with lengthening of final vowel plus suffix: -[ːni]

Practice 4.15

1. English
   a. Three allomorphs: [ɪn], [ɪm], [ɪŋ]
      1. [ɪm] occurs before labials.
      2. [ɪŋ] occurs before velars.
      3. [ɪn] occurs elsewhere.
   b. [ɪn] is the elsewhere allomorph and is thus the underlying representation.
   c. UR of *inedible, impossible,* and *incapable* would all start with [ɪn].
   d. Place assimilation is at work.
   e. Rules: [ɪn] ⟶ [ɪm] / ___ C_{LABIAL}

      [ɪn] ⟶ [ɪŋ] / ___ C_{DORSAL}

2. Turkish
   a. [laɾ], [leɾ]
   b. [+/–back]
   c. [+/–back] If the last V in the root is [+back], the allomorph is [laɾ]. If the last V in the root is [–back], the allomorph is [leɾ].

3. Dutch
   a. -en
   b. ge-(STEM)-t/d
      -t is used when stem ends with a voiceless C.
      -d is used when stem ends with a voiced C or V.

c. Both are pronounced as [t] because of word-final consonant devoicing.
d. ge-
e. *gestolen* is a strong verb. It has no -t/d suffix as would be expected with a weak verb.

Review Exercises

1. Ancient Egyptian
   a. Morphemes:

1. 'sibling'	sn	4. MASCULINE	Ø (not marked)
2. 'deity'	nt^jr	5. DUAL	-j
3. FEMININE	-t	6. PLURAL	-w

   b. Order of morphemes:

1. M SG:	ROOT	4. F PL:	ROOT/PLURAL/FEMININE
2. F SG:	ROOT/FEMININE	5. M DU:	ROOT/PLURAL/DUAL
3. M PL:	ROOT/PLURAL	6. F DU:	ROOT/FEMININE/DUAL

2. Luganda

SG	PL	STEMS	GLOSS
mu-	ba-	-ntu (1, 20)	'person'
		-wala (12, 18)	'girl'
ka-	bu-	-ti (2, 16)	'stick'
		-tiko (9, 14)	'mushroom'
ki-	bi-	-tabo (3, 4)	'book'
		-ntu (10, 17)	'thing'
ku-	ma-	-gulu (5, 13)	'leg'
		-tu (8, 15)	'ear'
mu-	mi-	-ti (7, 6)	'tree'
		-sege (11, 19)	'wolf'

3. Fore
   a. Morphemes:

1. I	-[uw]	6. they (DUAL)	-[aːs]
2. he	-[iy]	7. eat	-[na]
3. we	-[un]	8. yesterday	-[t]
4. they	-[aːw]	9. today	-[gas]
5. we (DUAL)	-[us]	10. will	-[k]

   b. QUESTION -[aw]
   STATEMENT -[i]
   c. Order of morphemes:
   V; adverb (tense); personal pronoun; question/statement marker
   d. Translations:

1. 'He ate yesterday?'	[natiyaw]
2. 'They (DUAL) will eat?'	[nakaːsaw]
3. 'They ate today.'	[nagasaːwi]

Chapter 5

Practice 5.1

1.

V	Conj	Pron	P
beat	and	she	to

Det	N	V	N	N	N	V
the	door	located	hobo	jungle	bum	heard

2.

N	V	P
leg	said	in

3.

Conj	Det	A	N	V	Pron	Aux	V	P
and	the	great	explorer	says	it	could	be	in

4.

Pron	V	N	N	N	V	Aux	A	N
I	turned	key	lab	door	thought	would	dull	day

V	C	Pron	Aux	V	V
noticed	that	my	had	flopped	waving

Pron	V
I	realized

5.

V	A	N	V	Aux
was	green	clarity	diluted	was

V	A	N	Pron	V	N
making	cutting	remarks	she	drank	scotch

6.

V	N	Adv
hate	pineapples	dolefully

7.

Det	N	A	N	Pron	Aux	V	N
a	fortune	male	deer	you	will	have	bucks

Practice 5.2

	HEAD (Lexical category)	**SPECIFIER**	**COMPLEMENT**
1.	(answer supplied in text)		
2.	men (N)	——	——
3.	in (P)	——	the barn
4.	mean (A)	really	——
5.	worked (V)	——	——
6.	worked (V)	——	at the station
7.	boring (A)	extremely	——
8.	destruction (N)	that	of the city
9.	walks (V)	never	to the park
10.	small (A)	very	——
11.	in (P)	——	the room
12.	cute (A)	awfully	——
13.	smiles (V)	seldom	——

	HEAD	SPECIFIER	COMPLEMENT
14.	swept (V)	—	the floor
15.	poem (N)	the	about love
16.	pancakes (N)	—	—

Practice 5.3

Note: Sample answers are given. Some answers may vary.

1. Substitution test:

    1. [They] arrived [there] [then].
    2. *The cabbage [them] salty.
       Not a phrase.
    3. They moved [it].
    4. Little Andrew swallowed [them].
    5. Mike is [doing so].

2. Movement test:

    1. *[Army was surrounded] the by the enemy.
       Not a phrase.
    2. [Viennese waltzes and Argentinean tangos] Leona likes.
    3. [In the revolving restaurant], Jean ate his lunch.
    4. *[Be merry for] eat, drink, and today will become yesterday.
       Not a phrase.
    5. *[Were swimming among] the polar bears the ice floes.
       Not a phrase.

3. Coordination test:

	Conjunction	Substitution	Type of phrase
1.	[the new desk] and [the old chair]	they	NP
2.	[assembled the new desk] and [painted the old chair]	did so	VP
3.	[new] and [expensive]	(no proform)	AP
4.	[in a hole] or [under a rock]	there	PP
5.	[rather huge] but [somewhat ugly]	(no proform)	AP
6.	[worked on a movie] and [played in a band]	did so	VP
7.	[beside the fence] or [near the tree]	there	PP
8.	[really lovely] but [hideously expensive]	(no proform)	AP
9.	[talked to the girls] and [played with the boys]	did so	VP
10.	[a dentist] or [a lawyer]	she	NP

Practice 5.4

1.

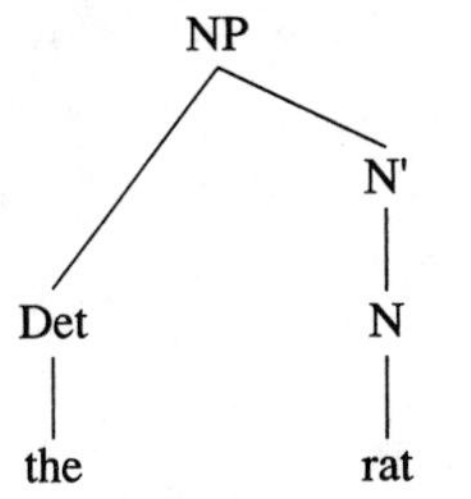

2.

3.

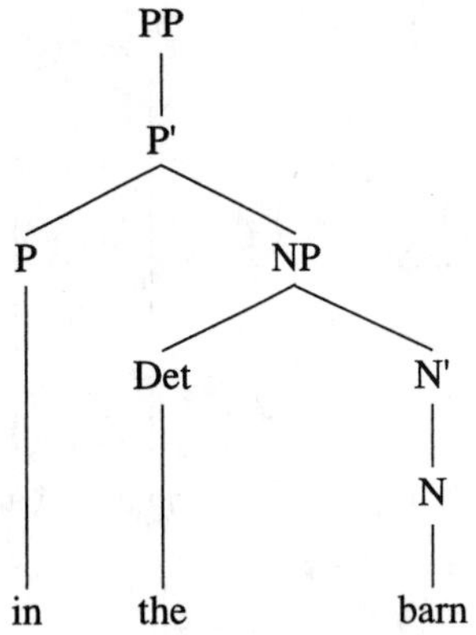

4.

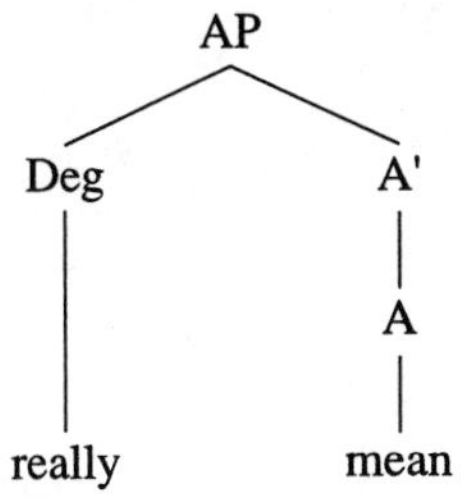

5.

6.

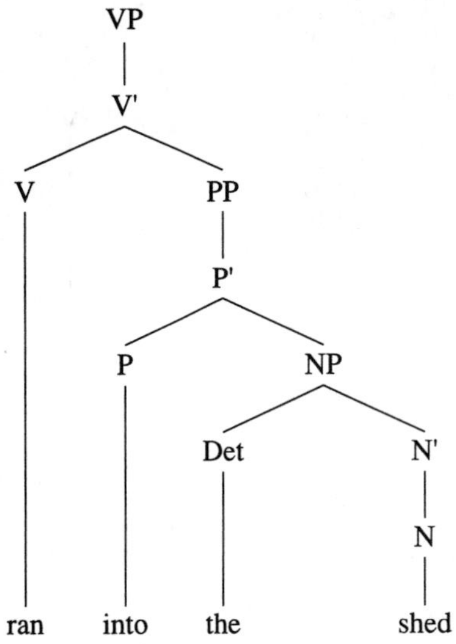

7.

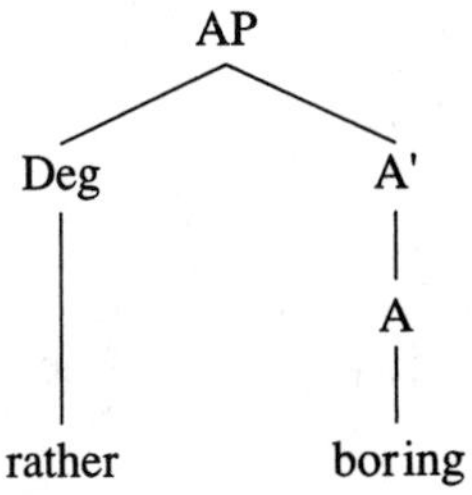

8.

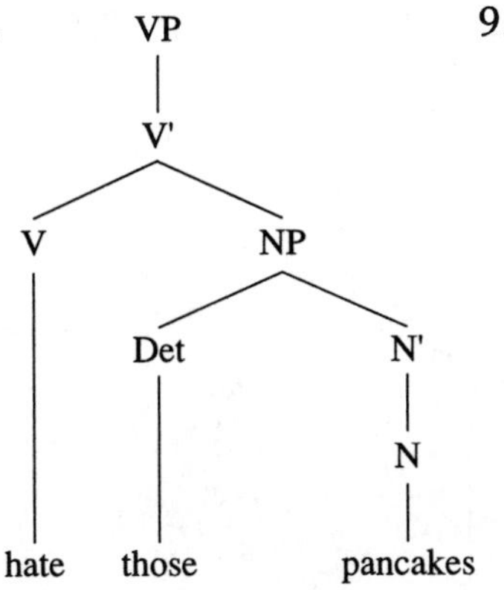

9.

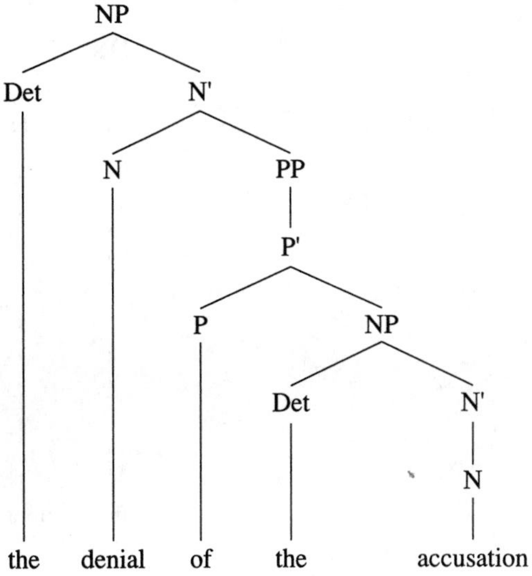

10.

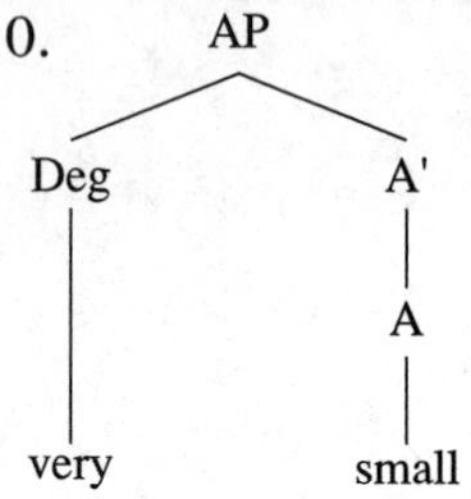

11.

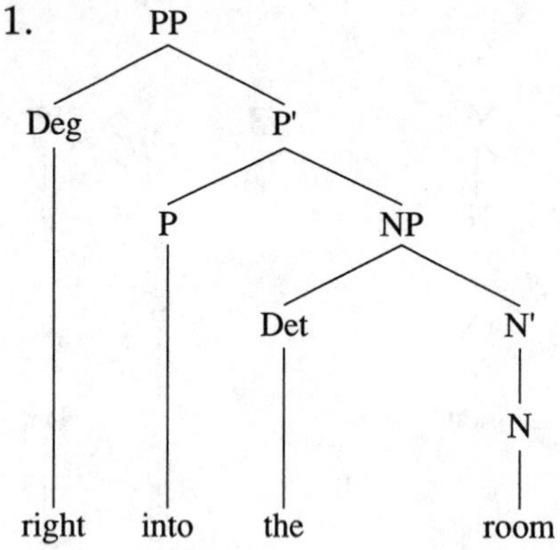

12.

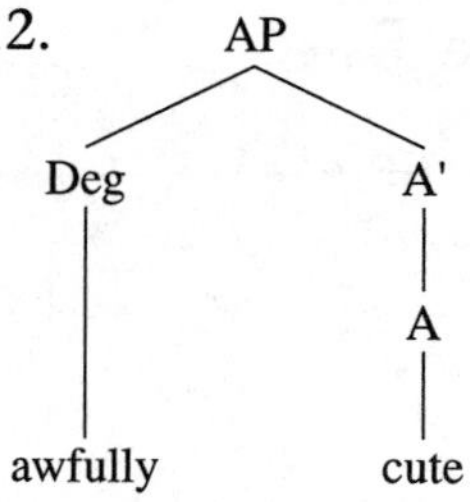

13.

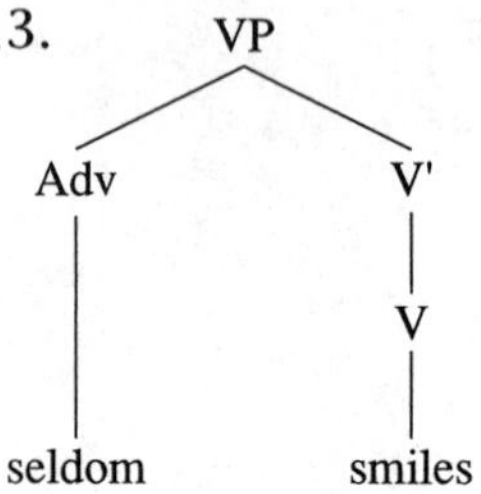

14.

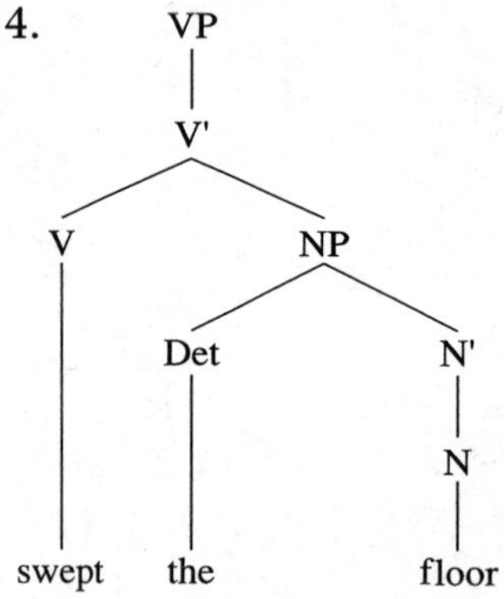

15.

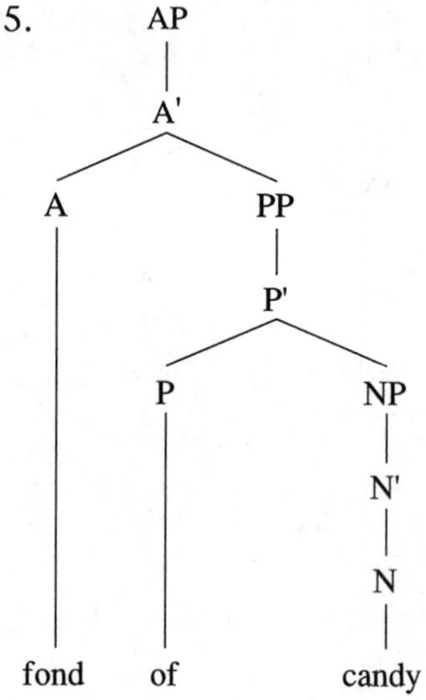

16.

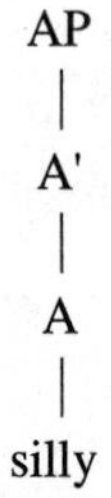

17.

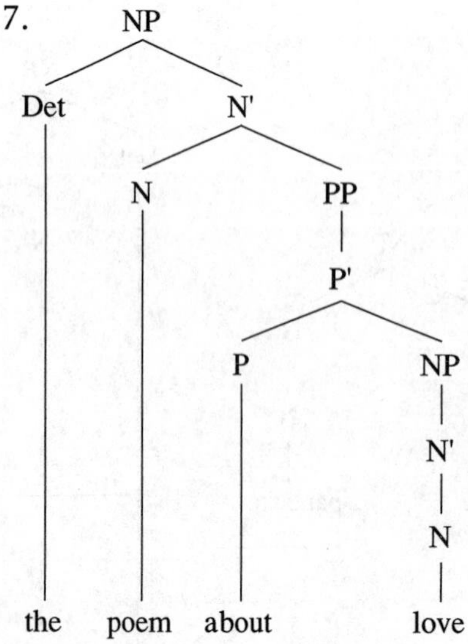

18.

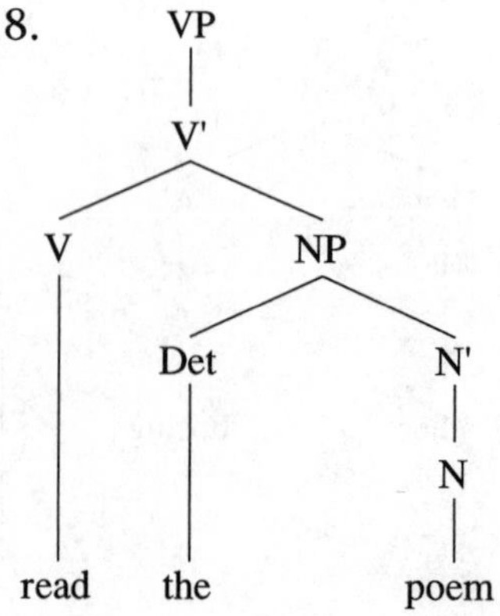

19.

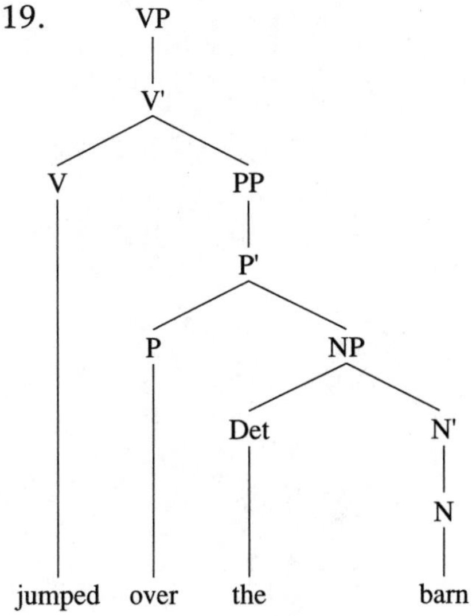

20.

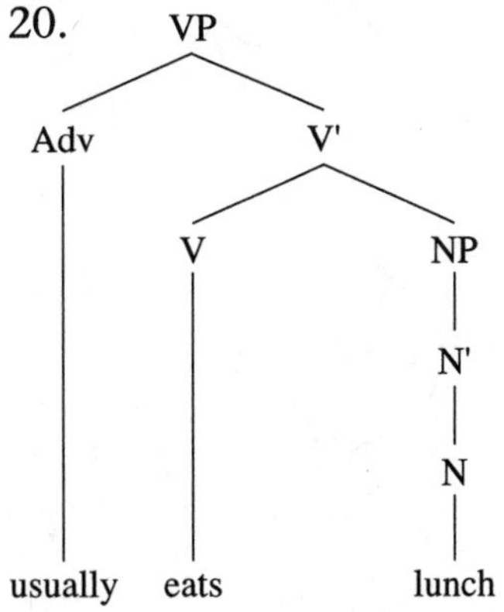

Practice 5.5

1.

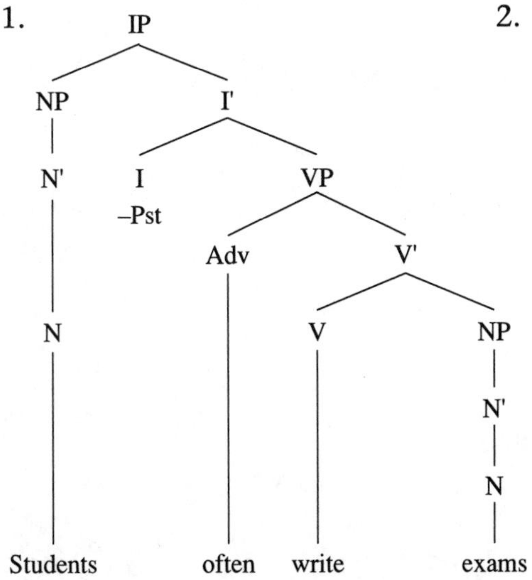

2.

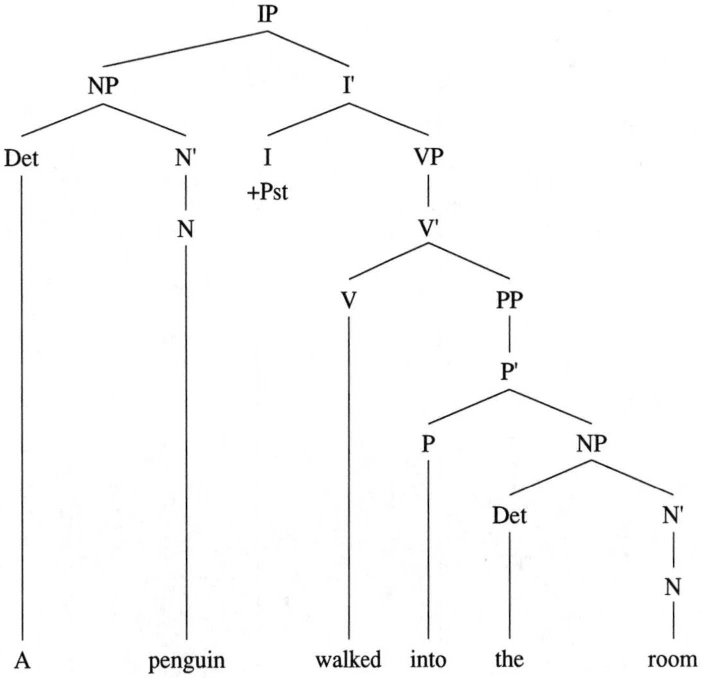

3.

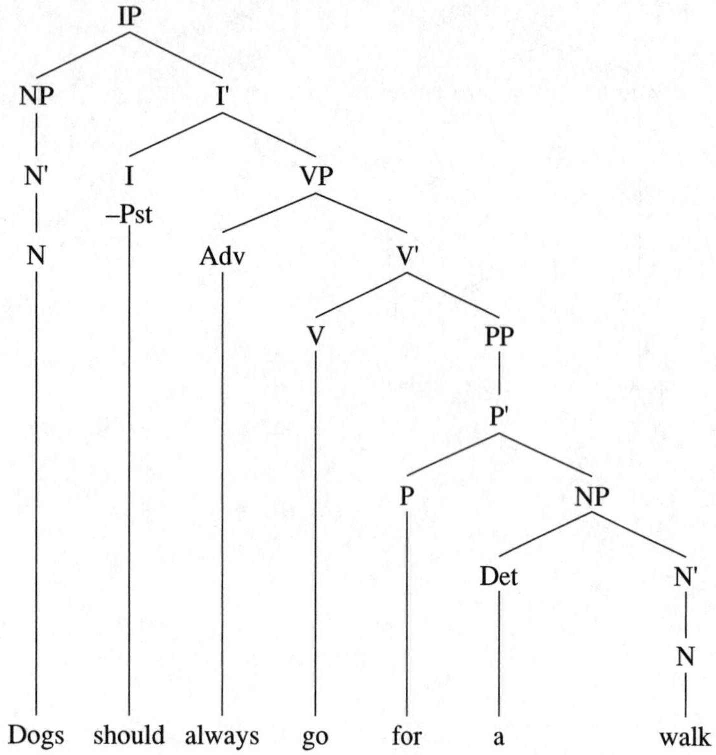
IP
NP
I'
N'
I
VP
–Pst
N
Adv
V'
V
PP
P'
P
NP
Det
N'
N
Dogs should always go for a walk

4.

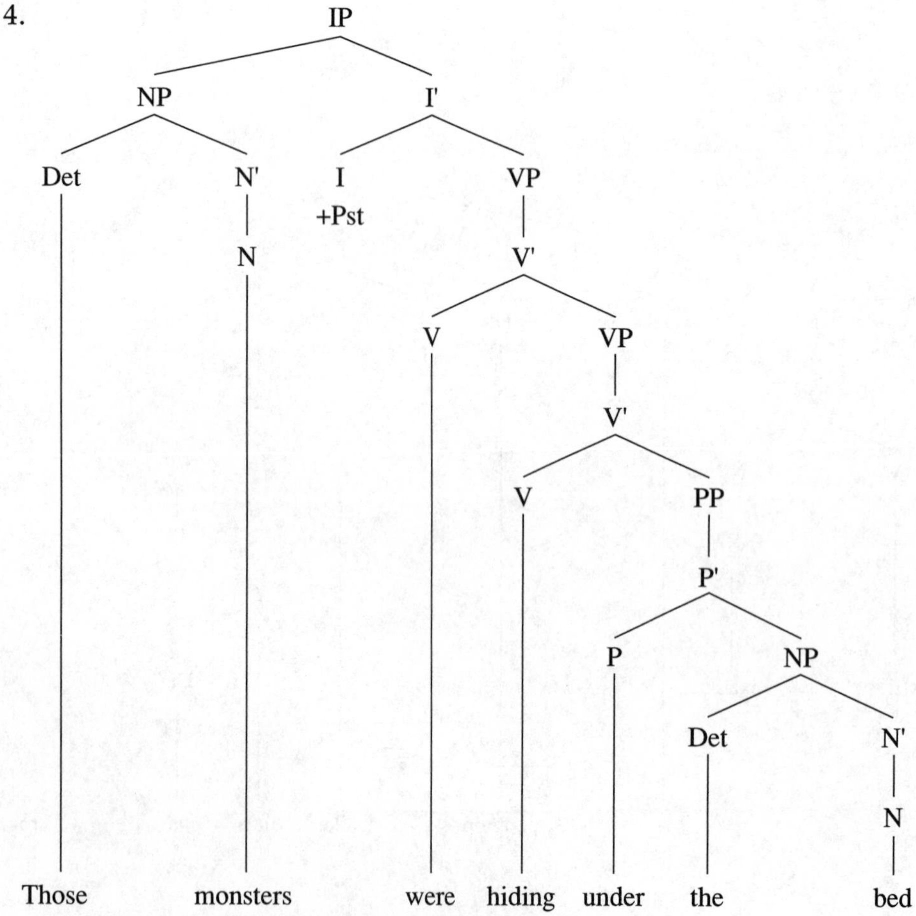
IP
NP
I'
Det
N'
I
VP
+Pst
N
V'
V
VP
V'
V
PP
P'
P
NP
Det
N'
N
Those monsters were hiding under the bed

5.

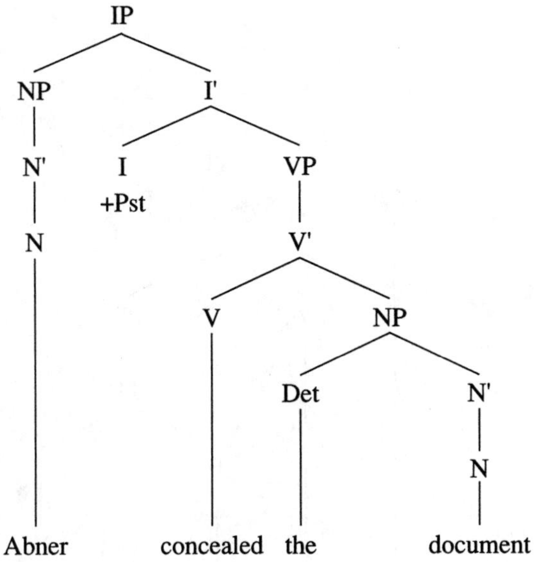
IP
NP
I'
N'
I
+Pst
VP
N
V'
V
NP
Det
N'
N
Abner
concealed
the
document

6.

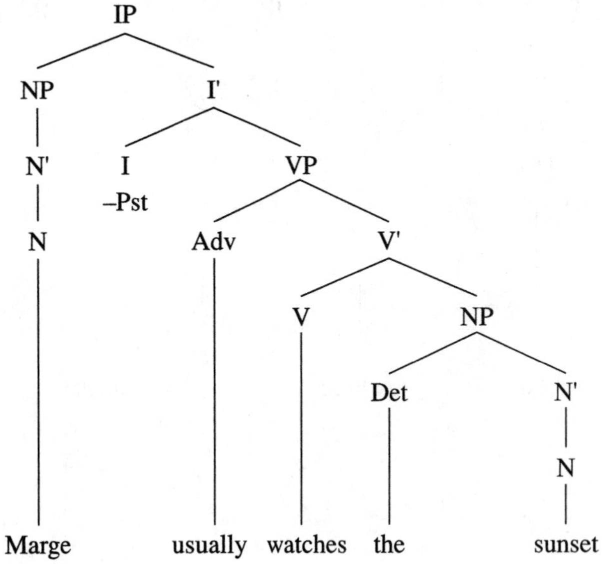
IP
NP
I'
N'
I
–Pst
VP
N
Adv
V'
V
NP
Det
N'
N
Marge
usually
watches
the
sunset

7.

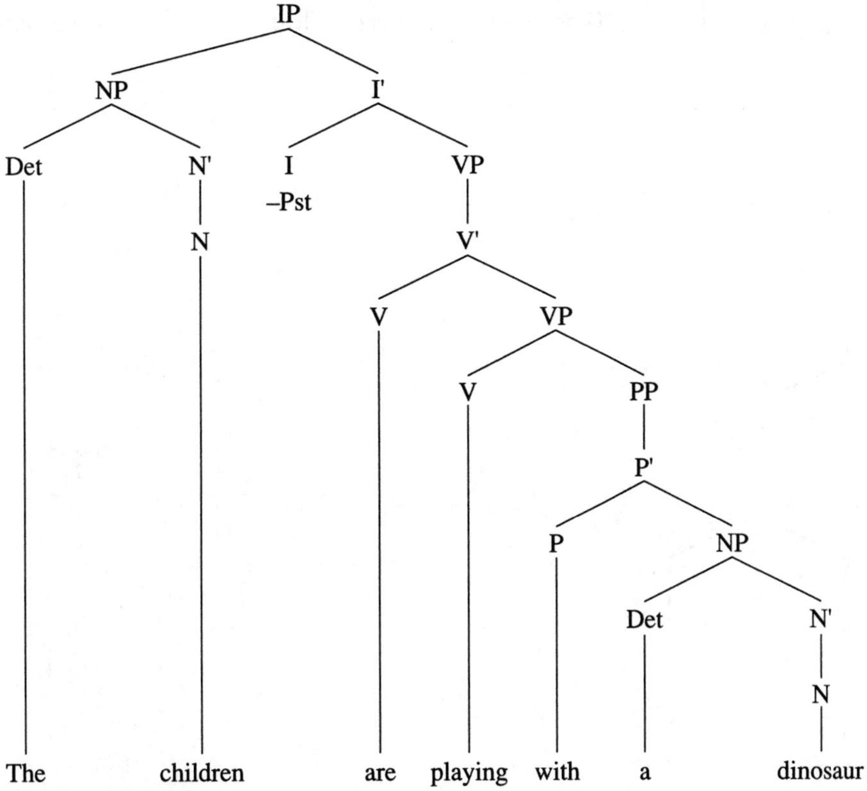
IP
NP
I'
Det
N'
I
–Pst
VP
N
V'
V
VP
V
PP
P'
P
NP
Det
N'
N
The
children
are
playing
with
a
dinosaur

8.

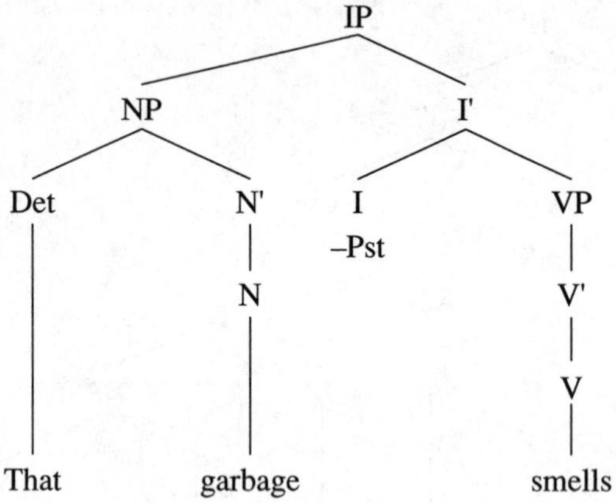

9.

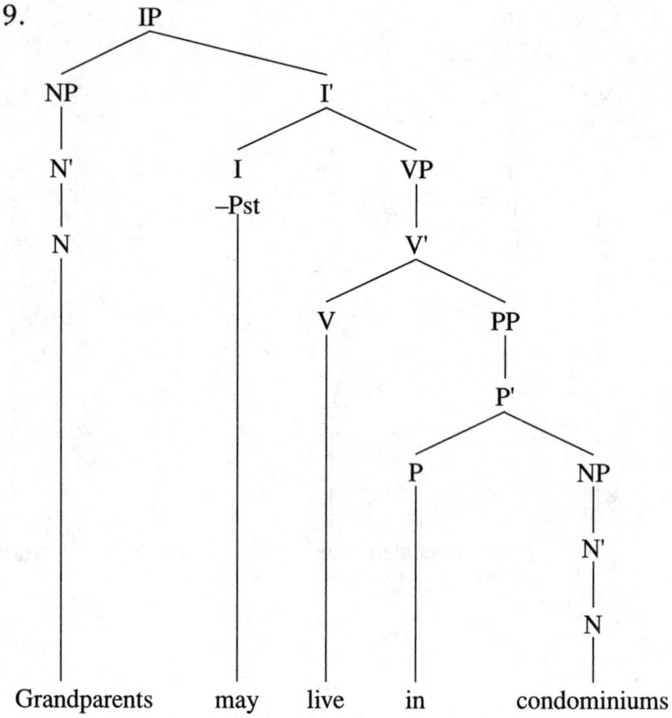

10.

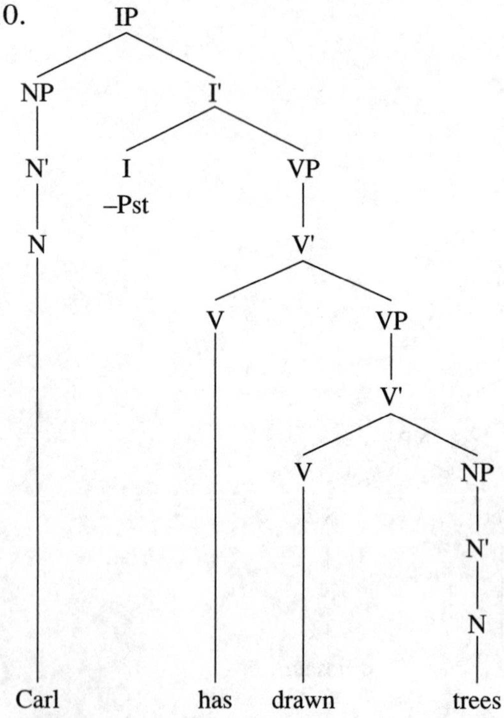

Practice 5.6

1. Complement options for verbs:
   (Note: Sample sentences are given, but answers will vary.)

	Complement options	Sample sentences
1.	No complement:	When we saw the price of the dinner, we panicked. *We panicked the price.
2.	NP	We watched the show.
3.	NP or CP	I can't imagine it. The child imagined that she was an astronaut.
4.	NP or NP, PP or NP, NP	Mark Twain wrote a book. He wrote a letter to his sister. He wrote his sister a letter.
5.	CP or PP	We wondered what was happening. They wondered about the story.
6.	Ø or NP	The children played. The Cardinals play baseball.

2. Complement options for nouns, adjectives, prepositions:

1. PP or CP	4. Ø
2. NP	5. NP
3. PP	6. PP or Ø

Practice 5.7

1.

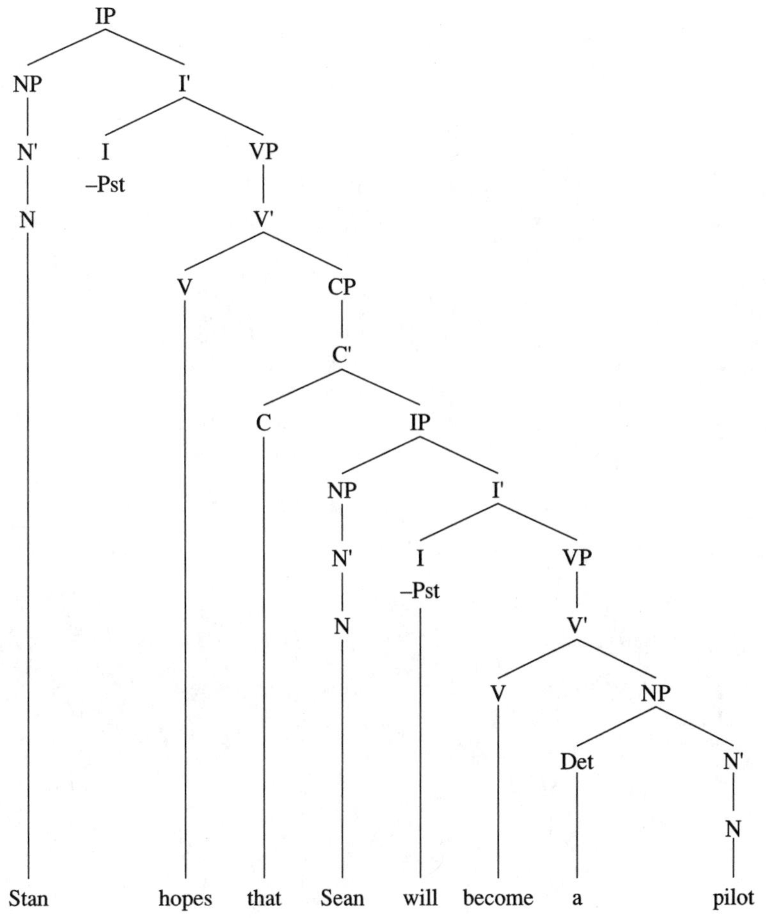

2.

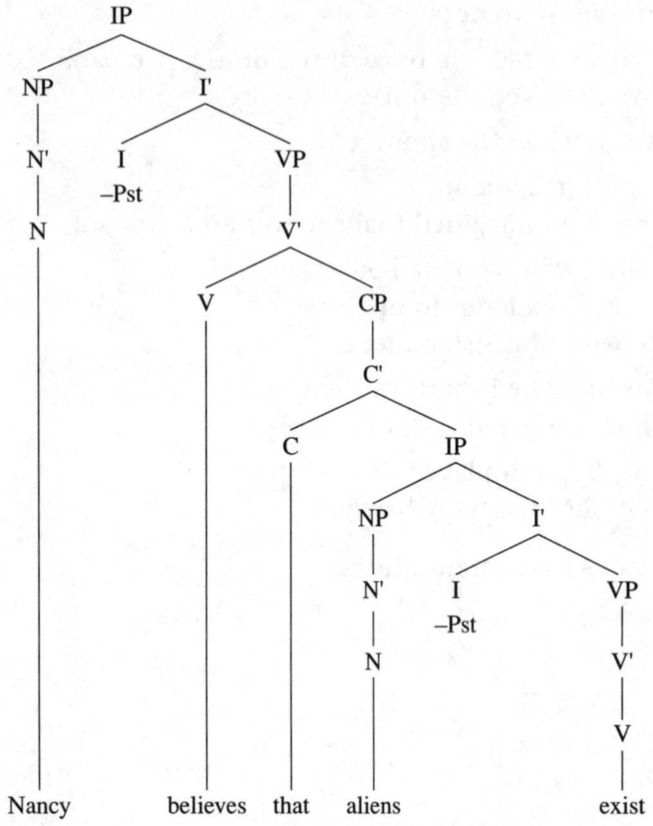
IP
NP
I'
N'
I
–Pst
VP
N
V'
V
CP
C'
C
IP
NP
I'
N'
I
–Pst
VP
N
V'
V
Nancy
believes
that
aliens
exist

3.

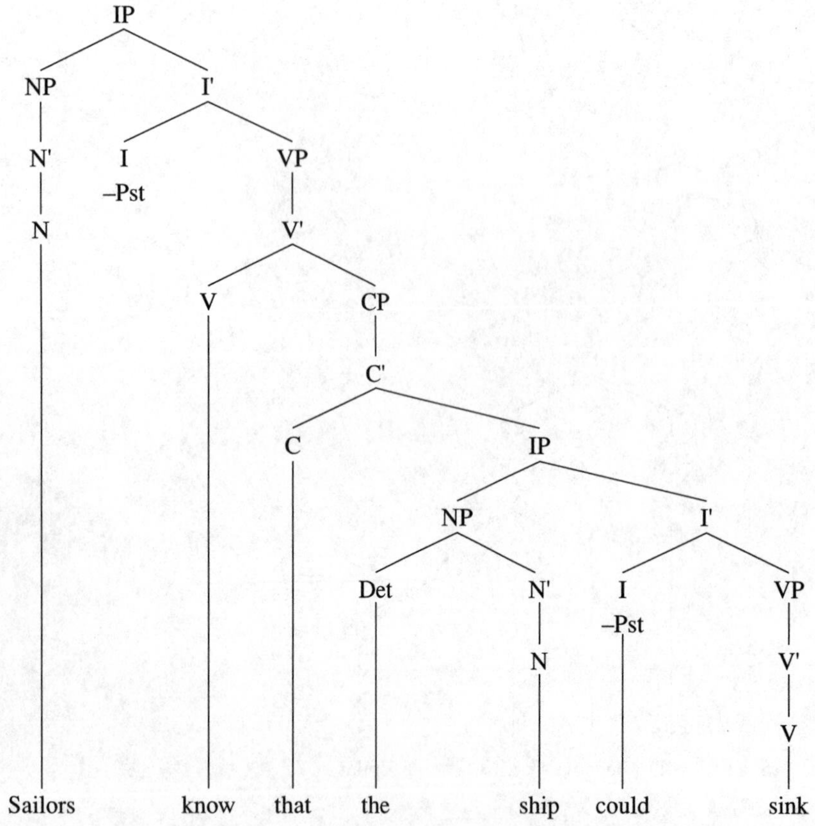
IP
NP
I'
N'
I
–Pst
VP
N
V'
V
CP
C'
C
IP
NP
I'
Det
N'
I
–Pst
VP
N
V'
V
Sailors
know
that
the
ship
could
sink

4.

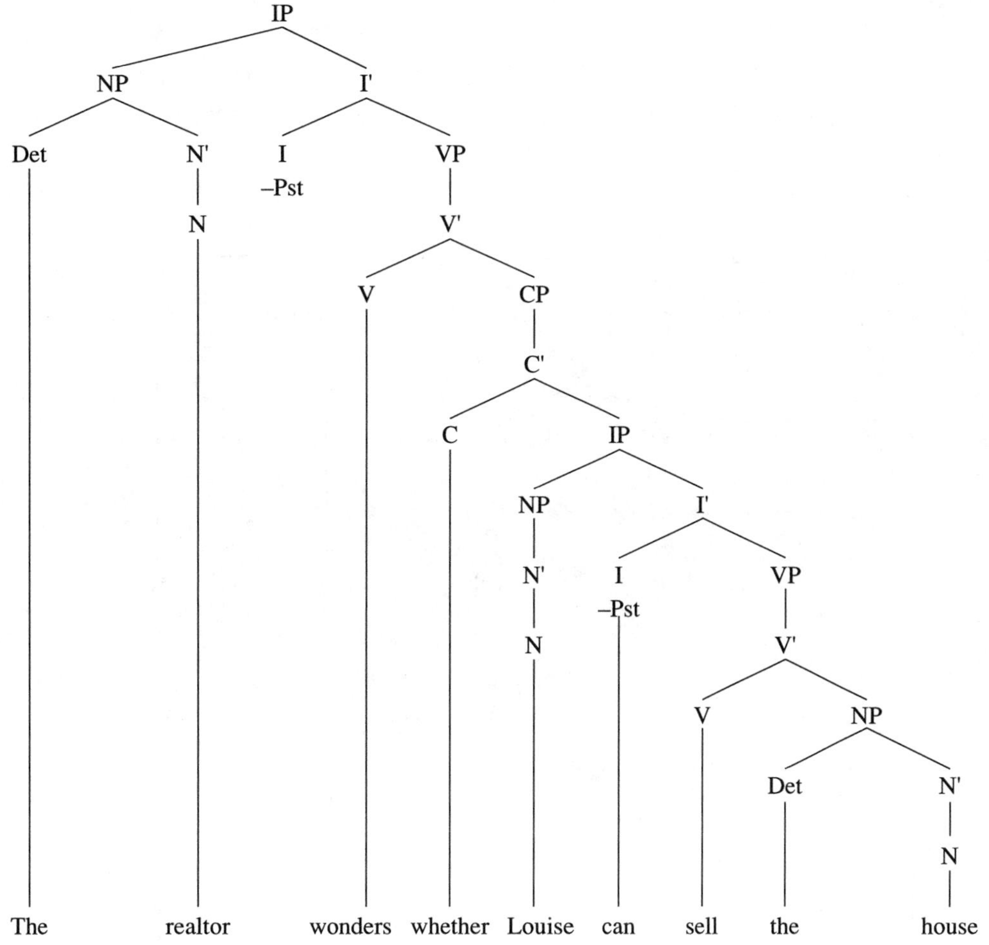
IP
NP
I'
Det
N'
I
VP
–Pst
N
V'
V
CP
C'
C
IP
NP
I'
N'
I
VP
–Pst
N
V'
V
NP
Det
N'
N
The
realtor
wonders
whether
Louise
can
sell
the
house

5.

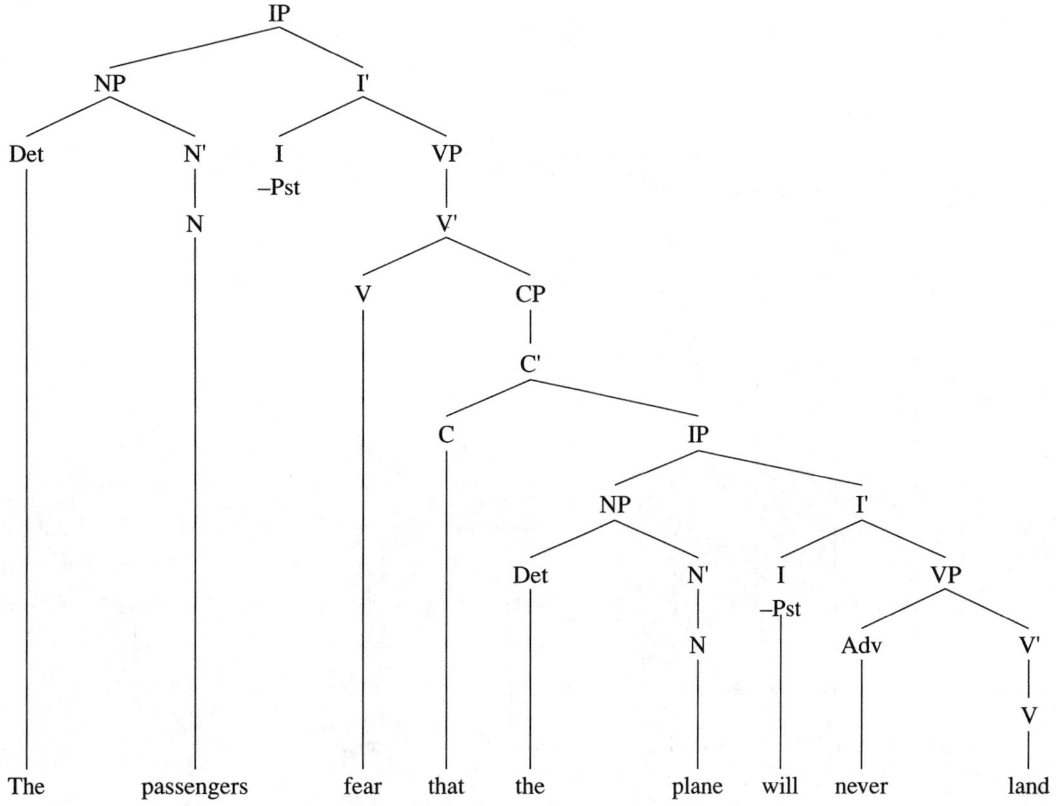
IP
NP
I'
Det
N'
I
VP
–Pst
N
V'
V
CP
C'
C
IP
NP
I'
Det
N'
I
VP
–Pst
N
Adv
V'
V
The
passengers
fear
that
the
plane
will
never
land

Practice 5.8

1.

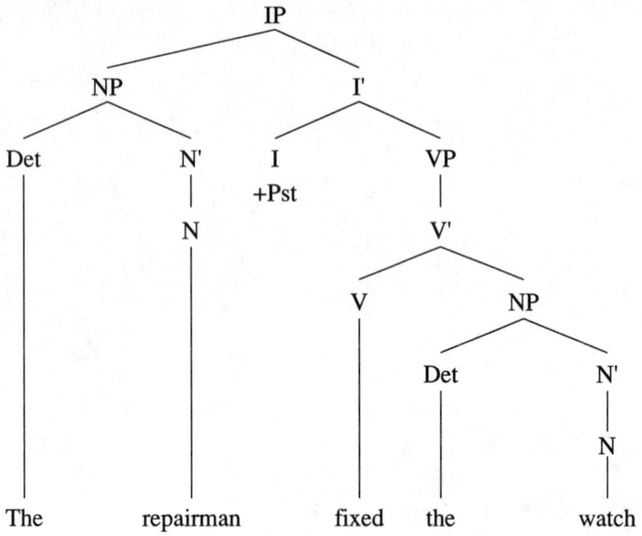

2.

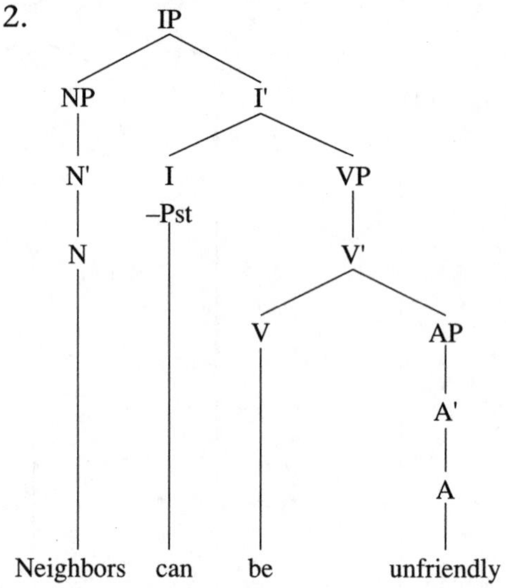

3.

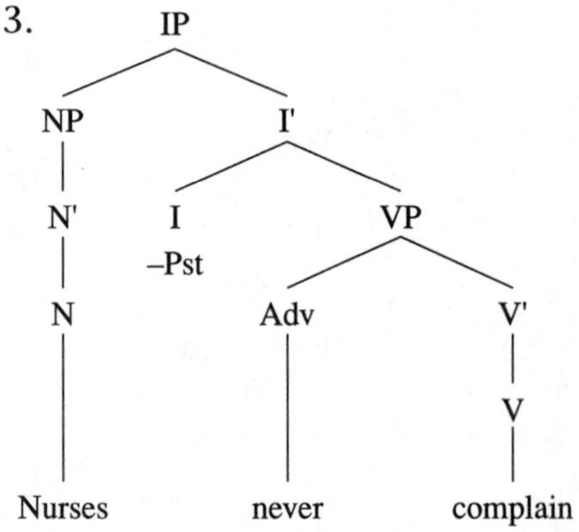

4.

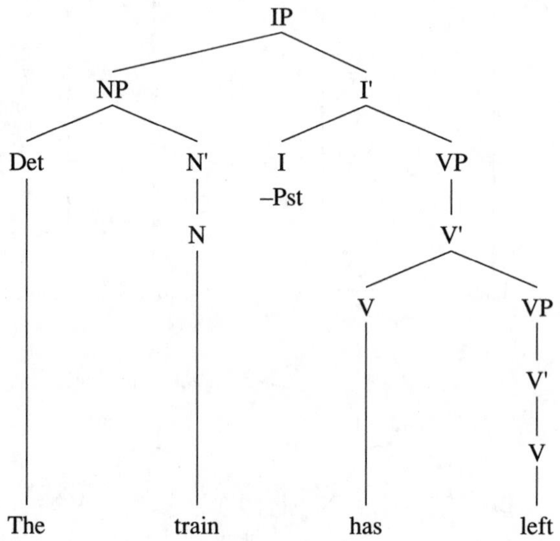

5.

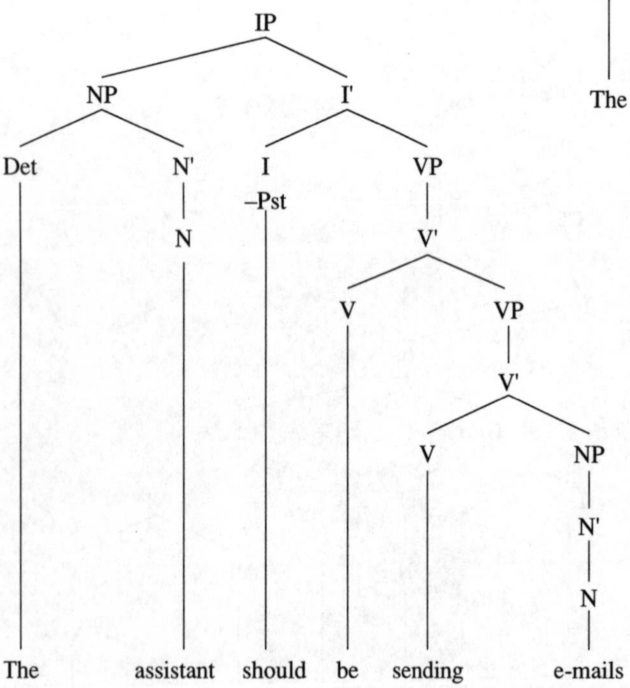

6.

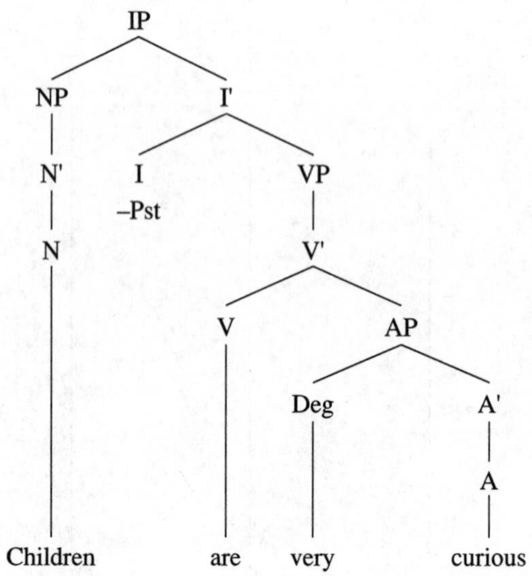

7.

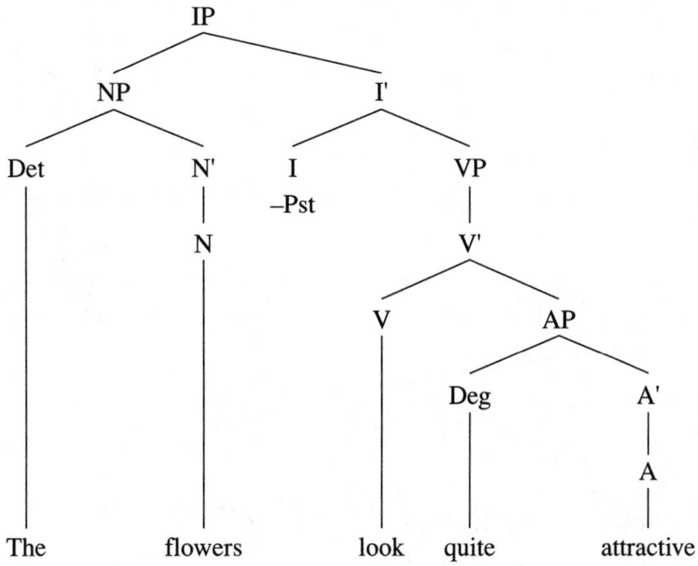
IP
NP
I'
Det
N'
I
–Pst
VP
N
V'
V
AP
Deg
A'
A
The
flowers
look
quite
attractive

8.

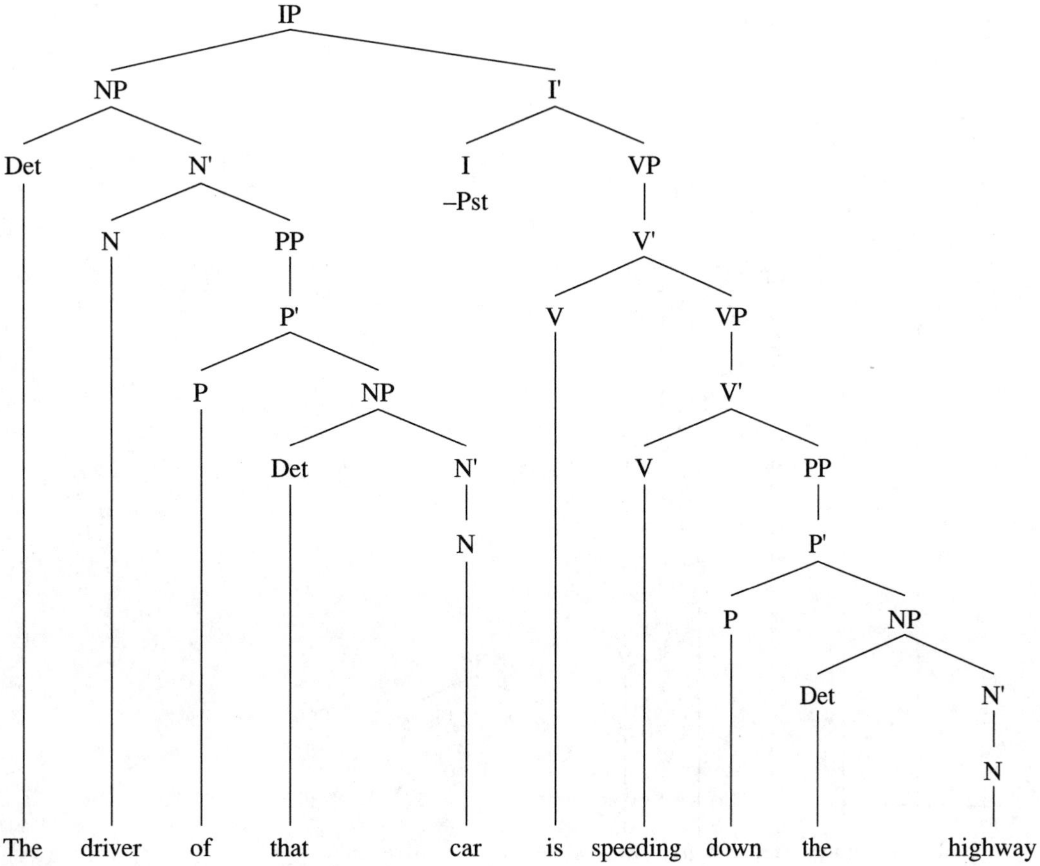
IP
NP
I'
Det
N'
I
–Pst
VP
N
PP
V'
P'
V
VP
P
NP
V'
Det
N'
V
PP
N
P'
P
NP
Det
N'
N
The
driver
of
that
car
is
speeding
down
the
highway

9.

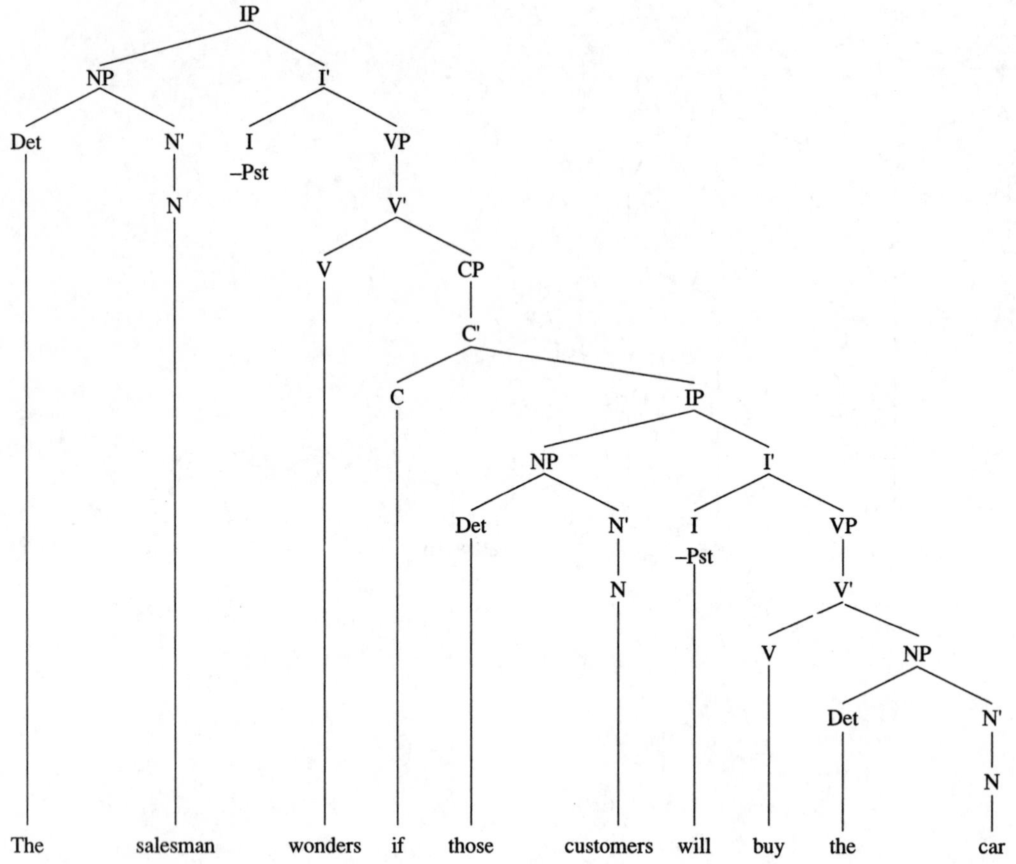
IP
NP
I'
Det
N'
I
–Pst
VP
N
V'
V
CP
C'
C
IP
NP
I'
Det
N'
I
–Pst
VP
N
V'
V
NP
Det
N'
N
The
salesman
wonders
if
those
customers
will
buy
the
car

10.

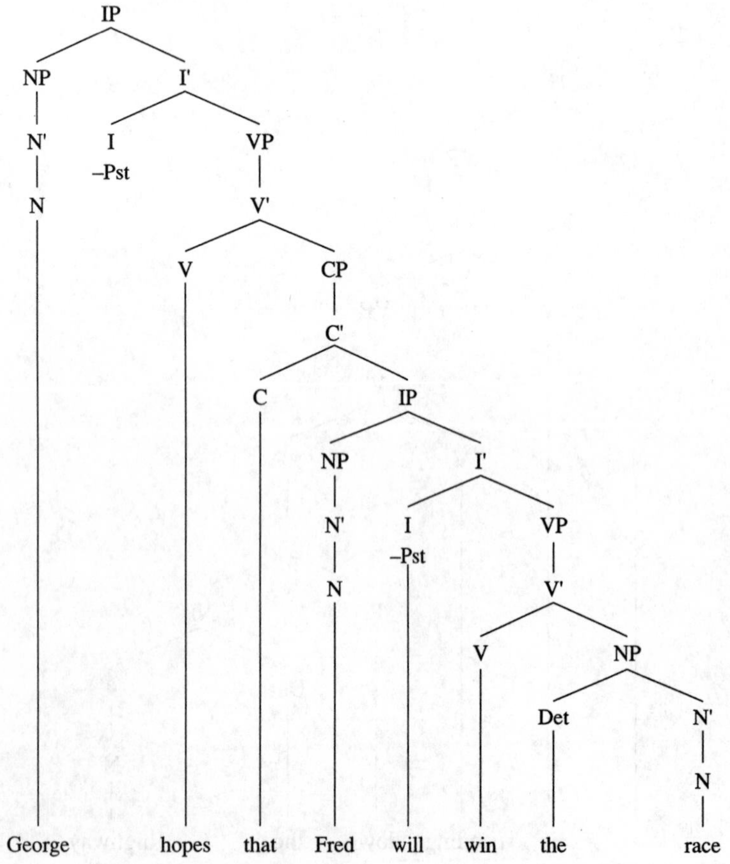
IP
NP
I'
N'
I
–Pst
VP
N
V'
V
CP
C'
C
IP
NP
I'
N'
I
–Pst
VP
N
V'
V
NP
Det
N'
N
George
hopes
that
Fred
will
win
the
race

11.

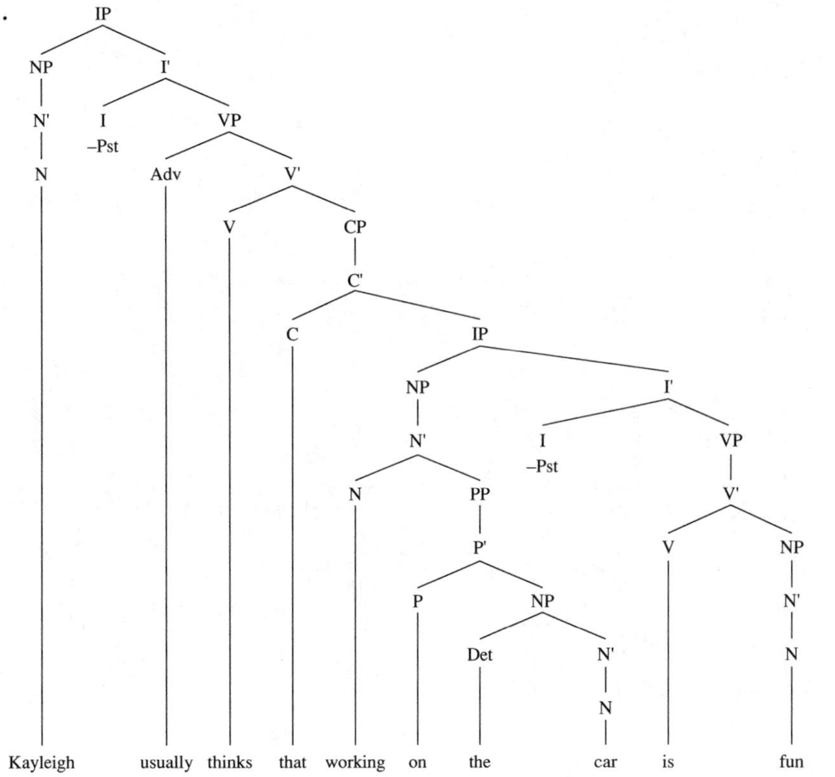
IP
NP I'
N' I VP
–Pst
N Adv V'
V CP
C'
C IP
NP I'
N' I VP
–Pst
N PP V'
P' V NP
P NP N'
Det N' N
N
Kayleigh usually thinks that working on the car is fun

12.

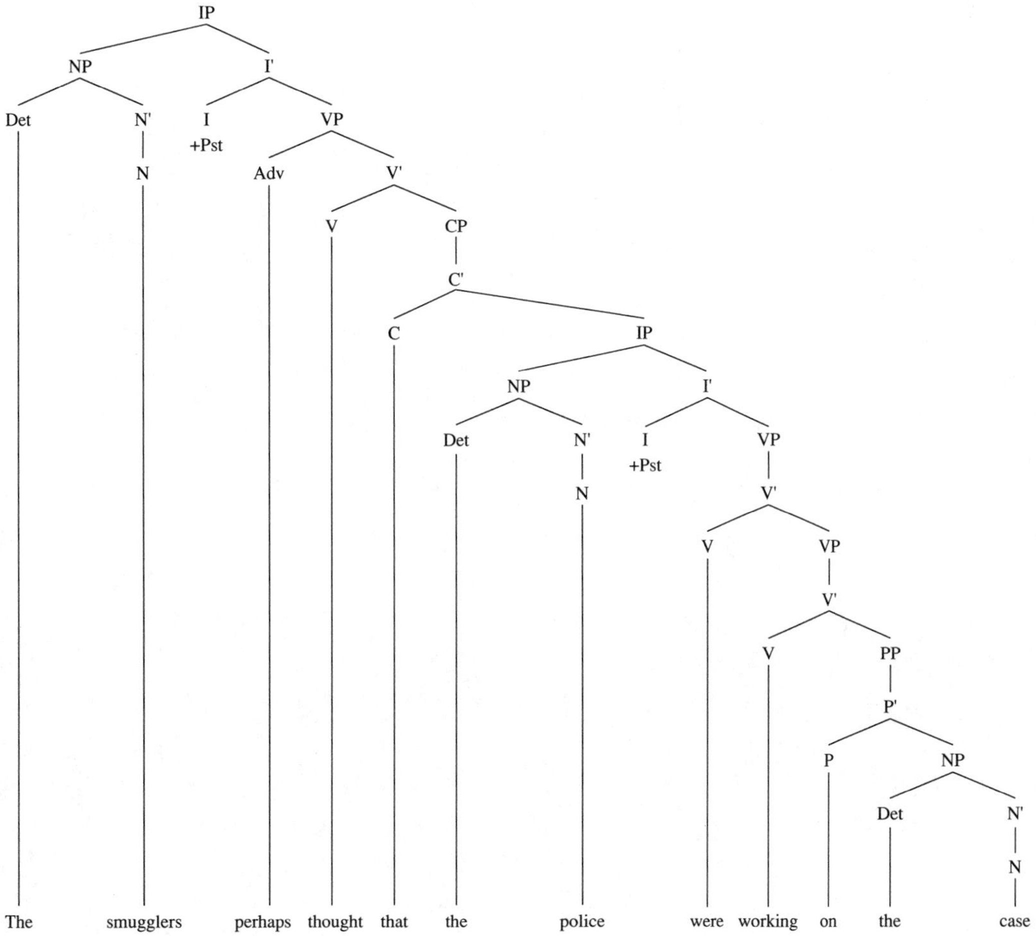
IP
NP I'
Det N' I VP
+Pst
N Adv V'
V CP
C'
C IP
NP I'
Det N' I VP
+Pst
N V'
V VP
V'
V PP
P'
P NP
Det N'
N
The smugglers perhaps thought that the police were working on the case

13.

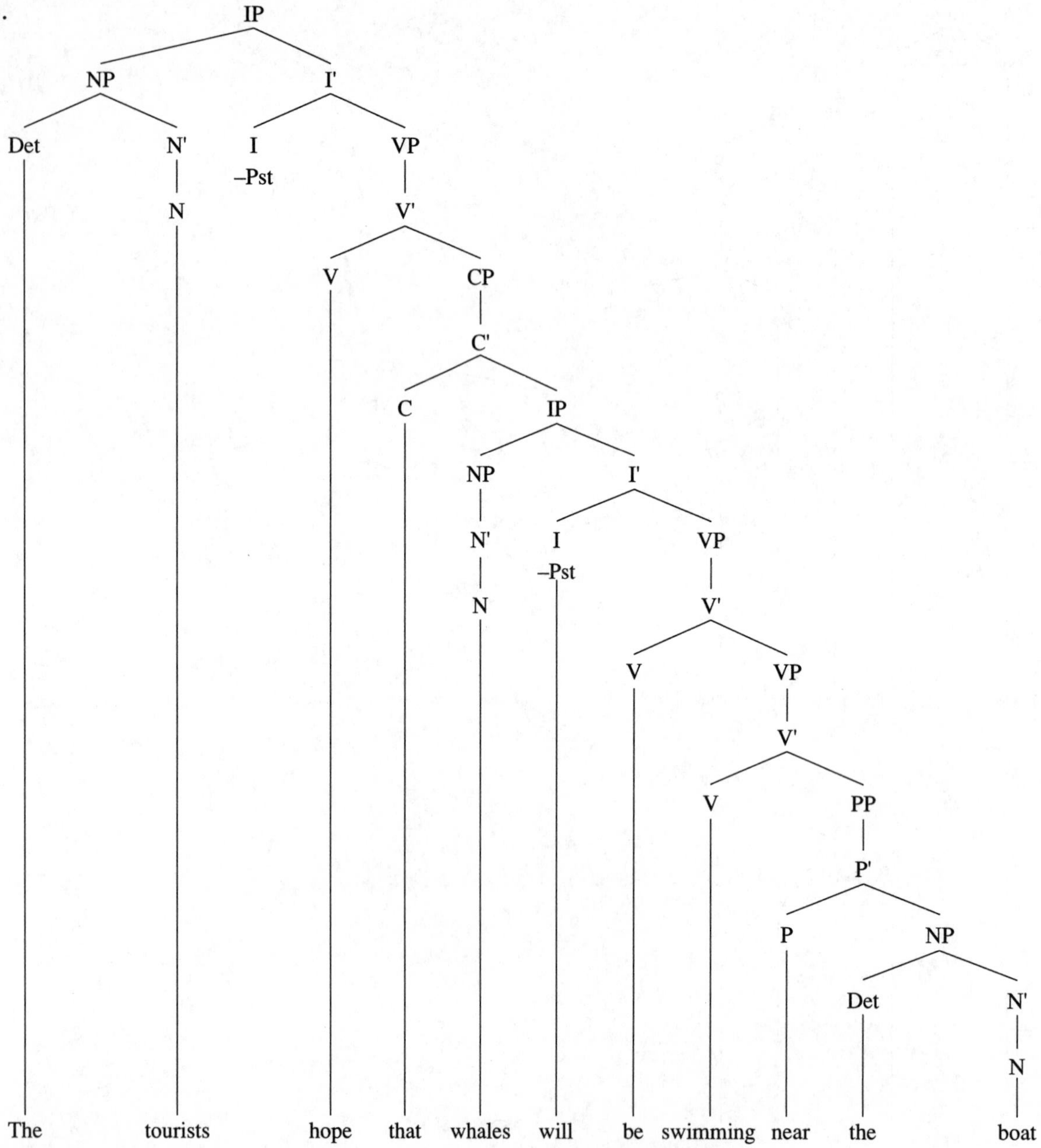
IP
NP
I'
Det
N'
I
–Pst
VP
N
V'
V
CP
C'
C
IP
NP
I'
N'
I
–Pst
VP
N
V'
V
VP
V'
V
PP
P'
P
NP
Det
N'
N
The tourists hope that whales will be swimming near the boat

Practice 5.9

Note: In S-structure, some phrases unaffected by transformations are shown without the intermediate structure.

1. D-structure:

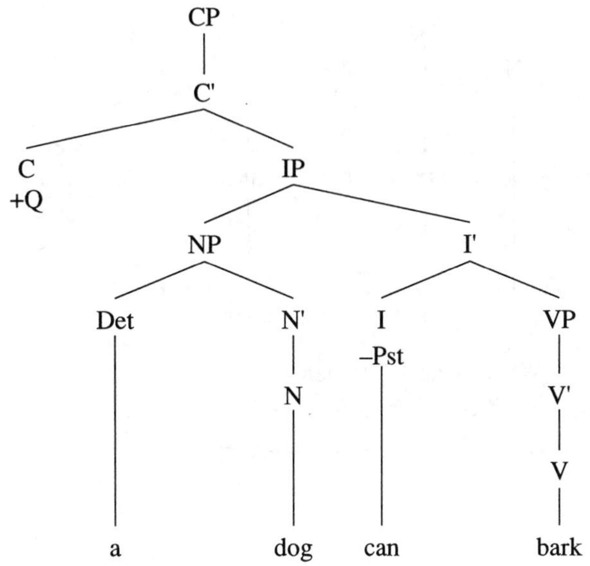

S-structure:

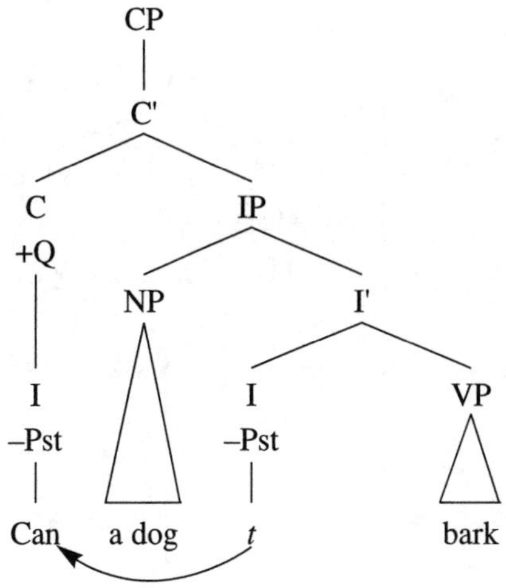

2. D-structure:

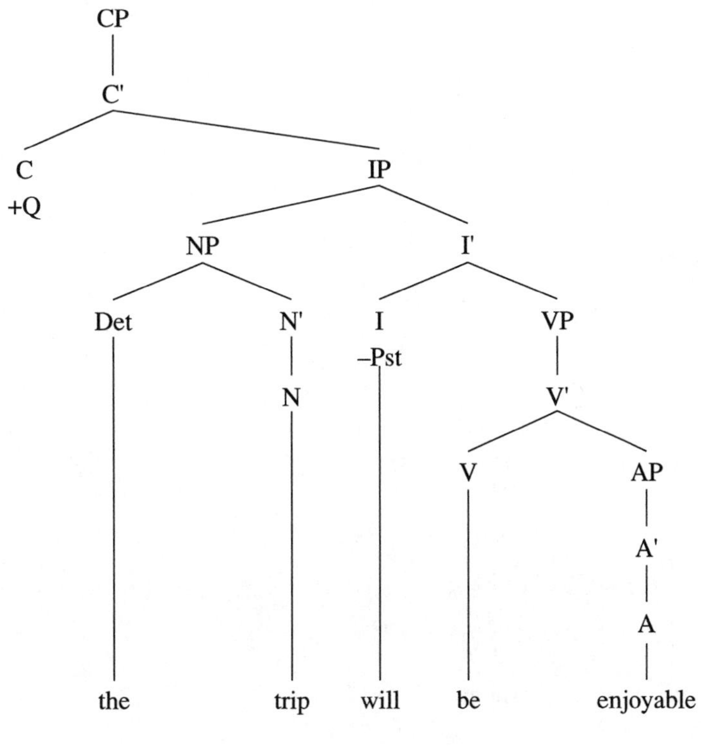

S-structure:

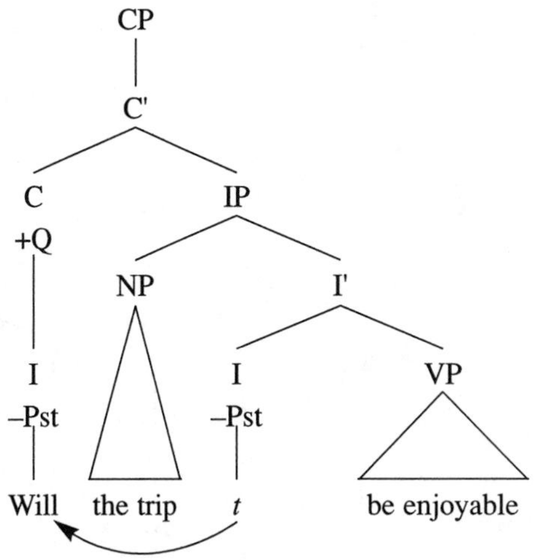

3. D-structure:

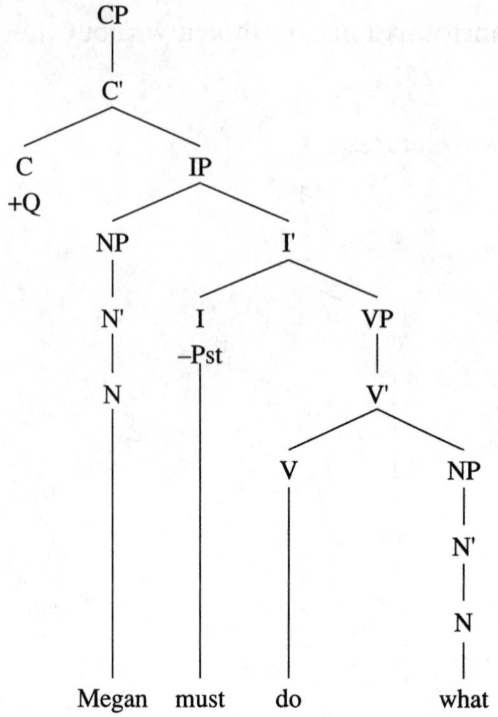

S-structure:

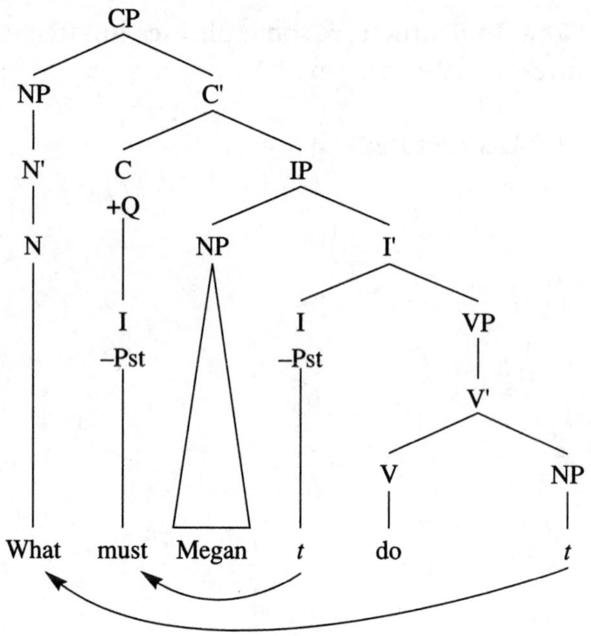

4. D-structure:

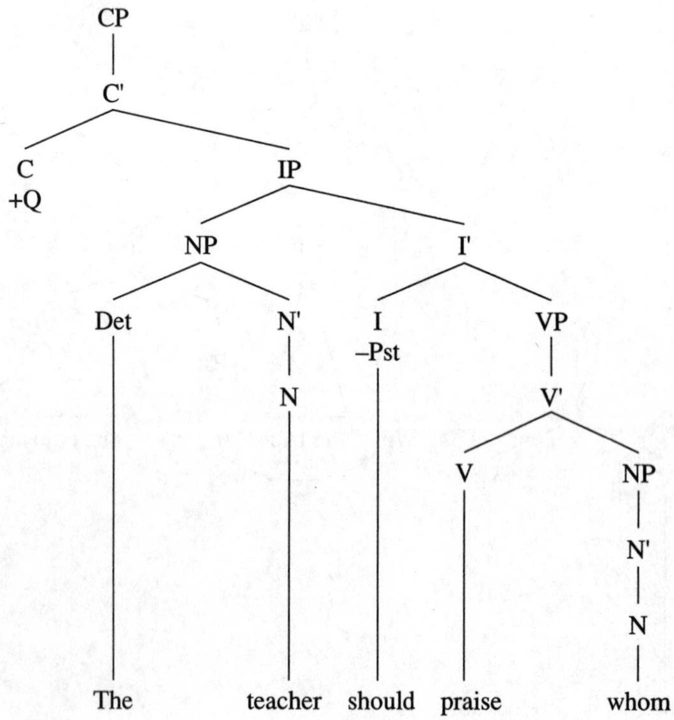

S-structure:

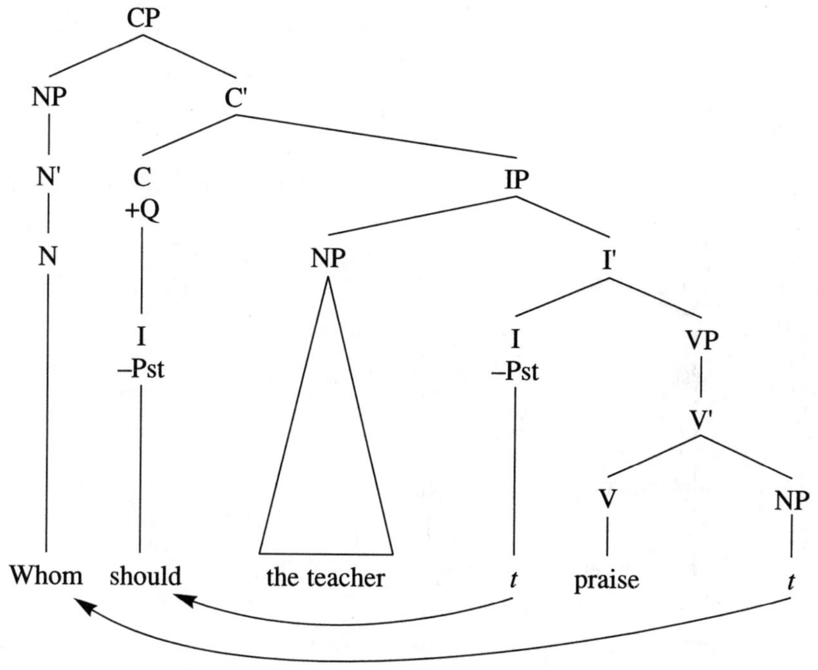

5. D-structure:

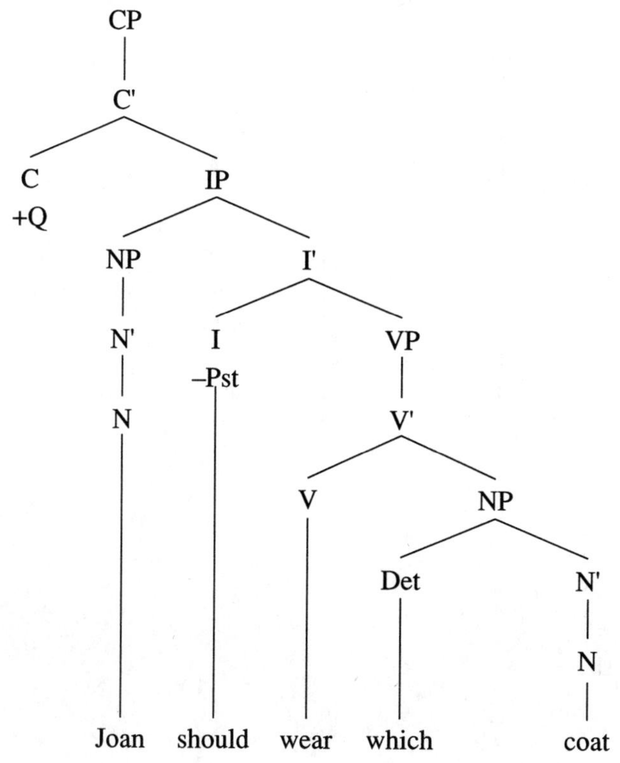

S-structure:

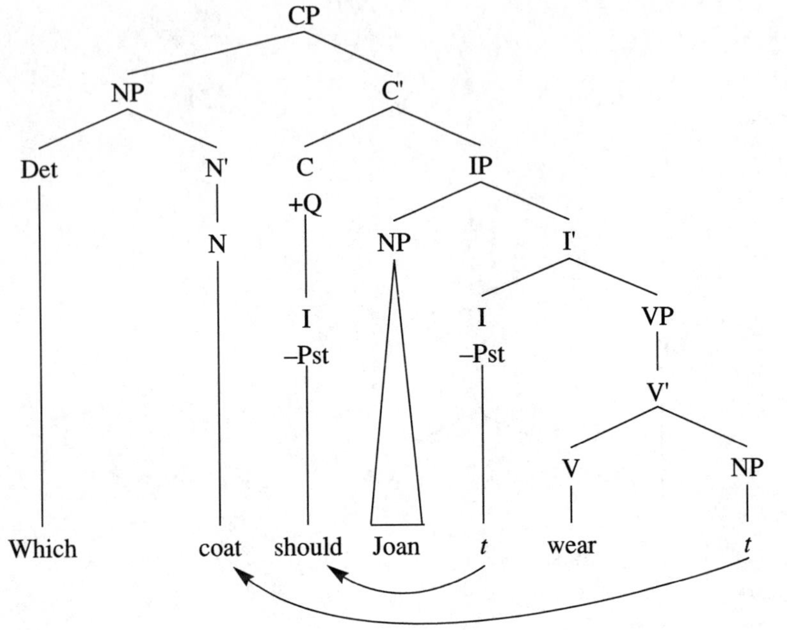

6. D-structure:

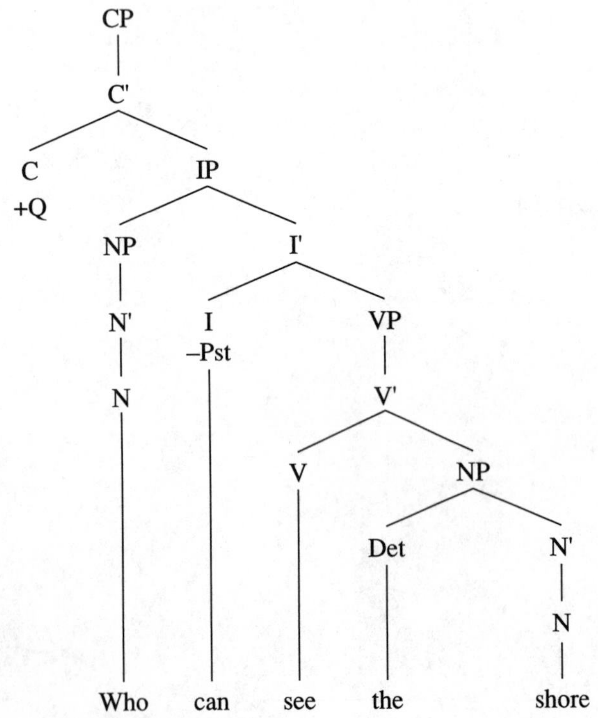

S-structure:

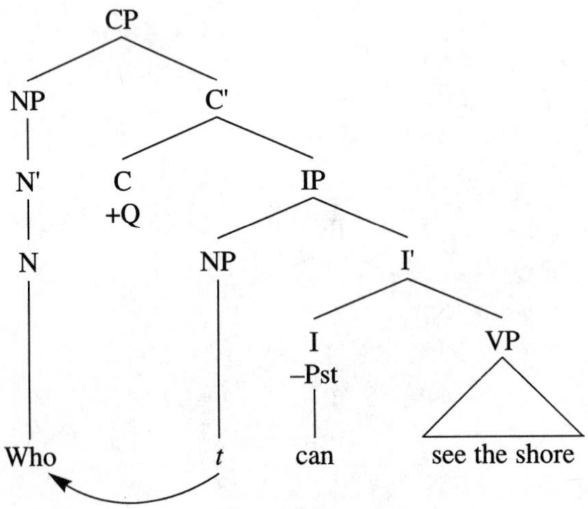

Practice 5.10

1. D-structure:

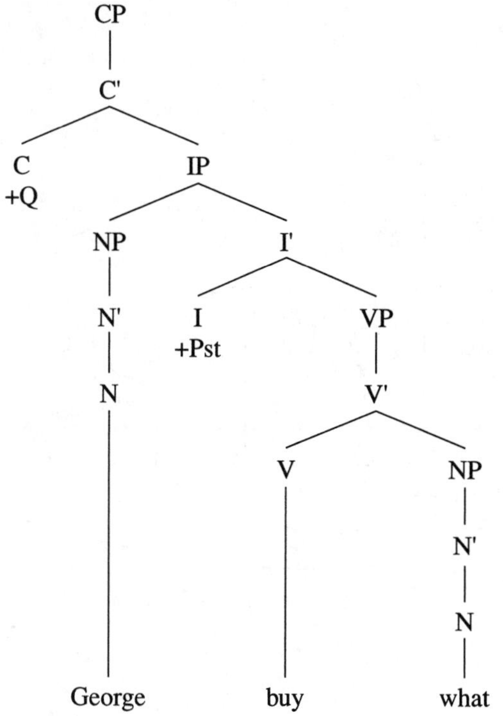

S-structure:

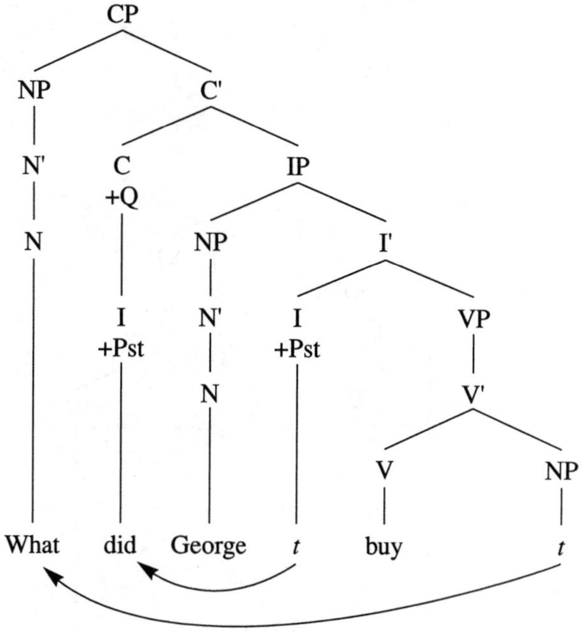

2a. D-structure:

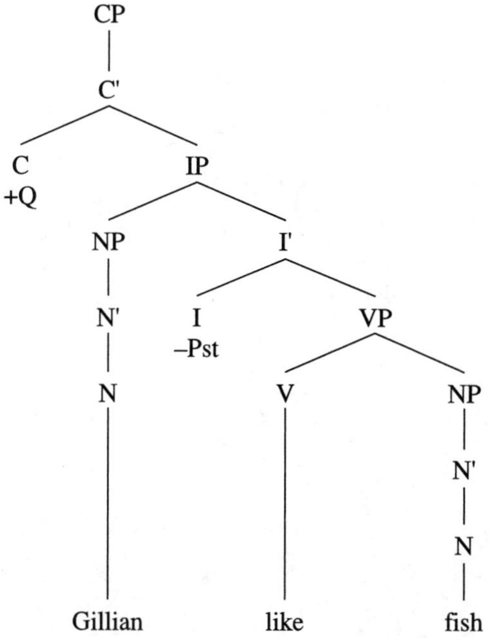

S-structure:

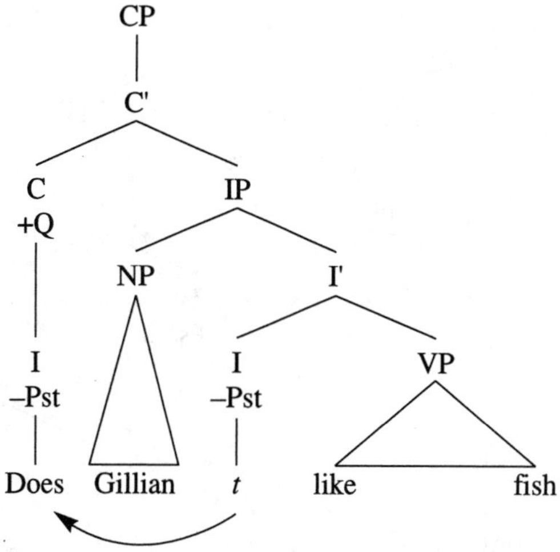

2b. D-structure:

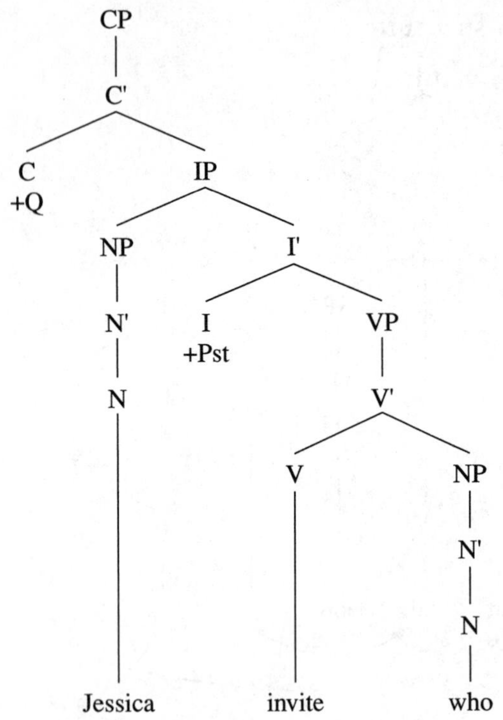

S-structure:

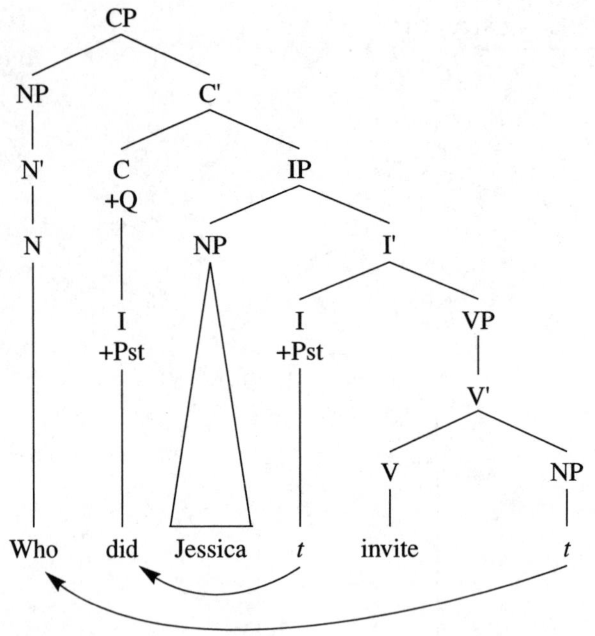

2c. D-structure:

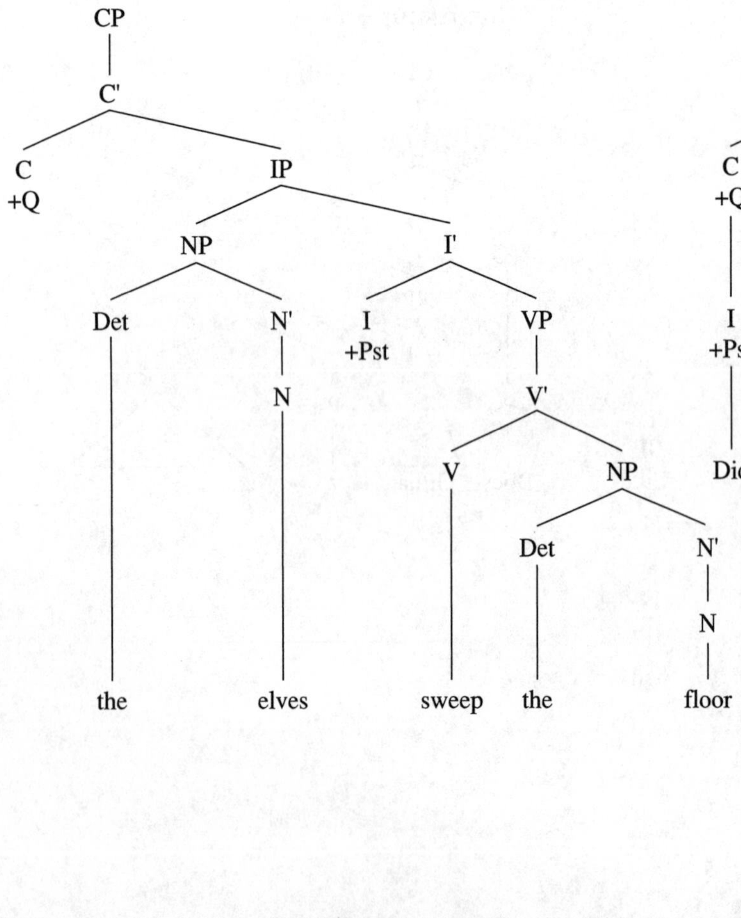

S-structure:

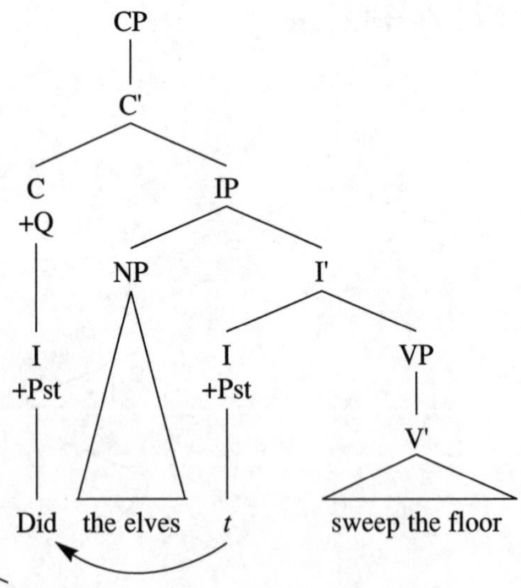

2d. D-structure:

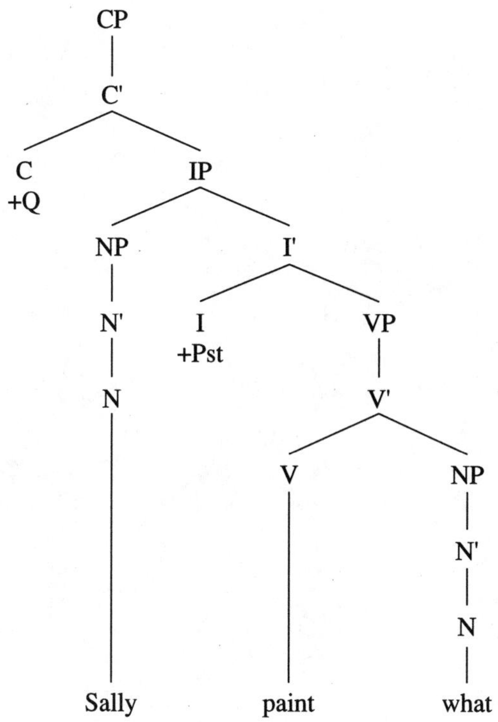

S-structure:

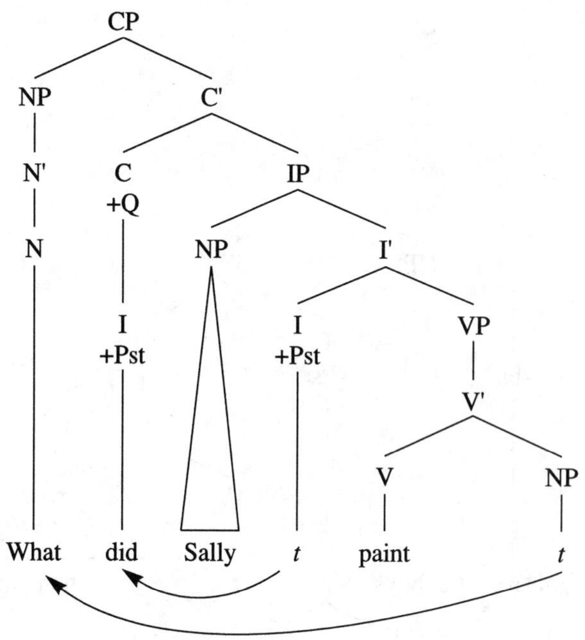

2e. D-structure:

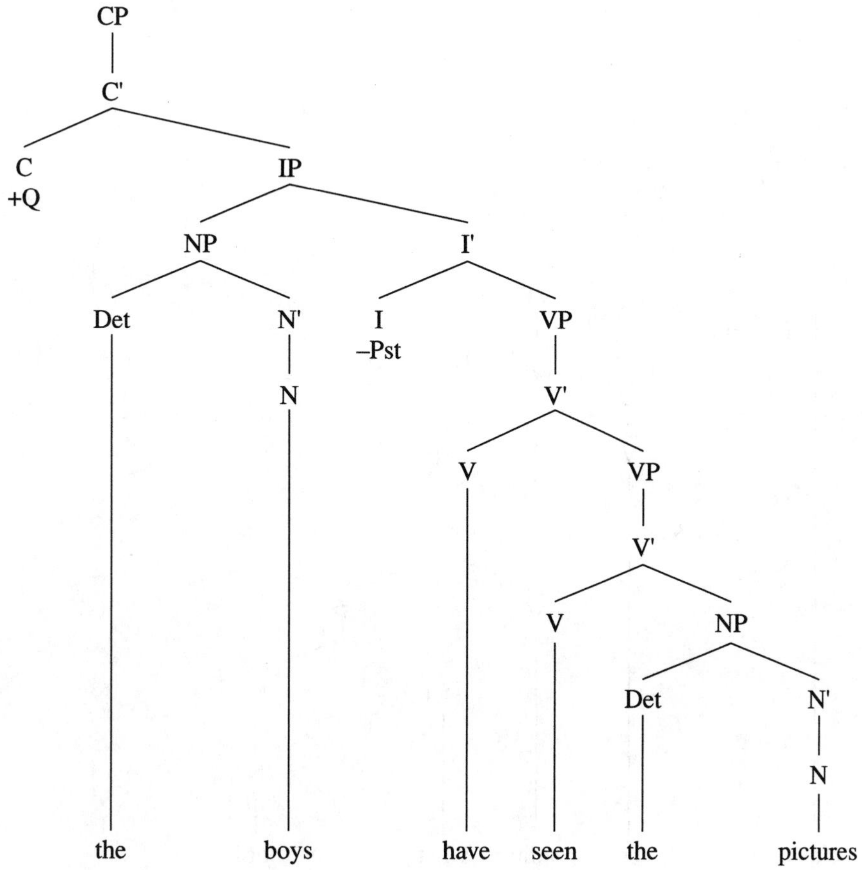

S-structure:

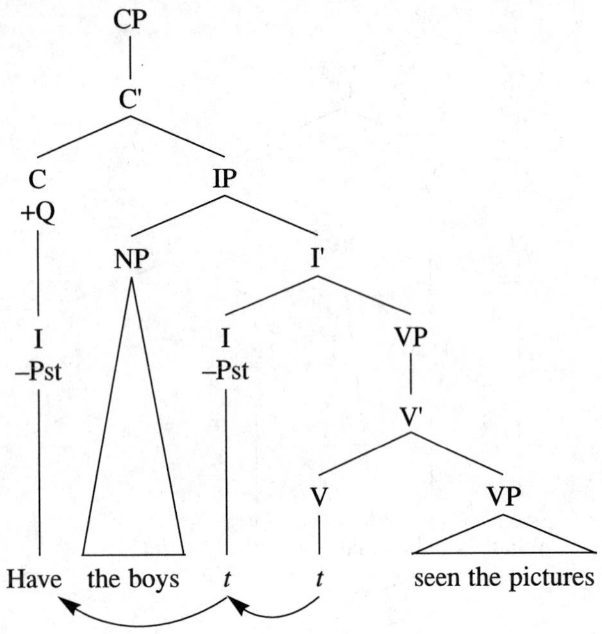

2f. D-structure:

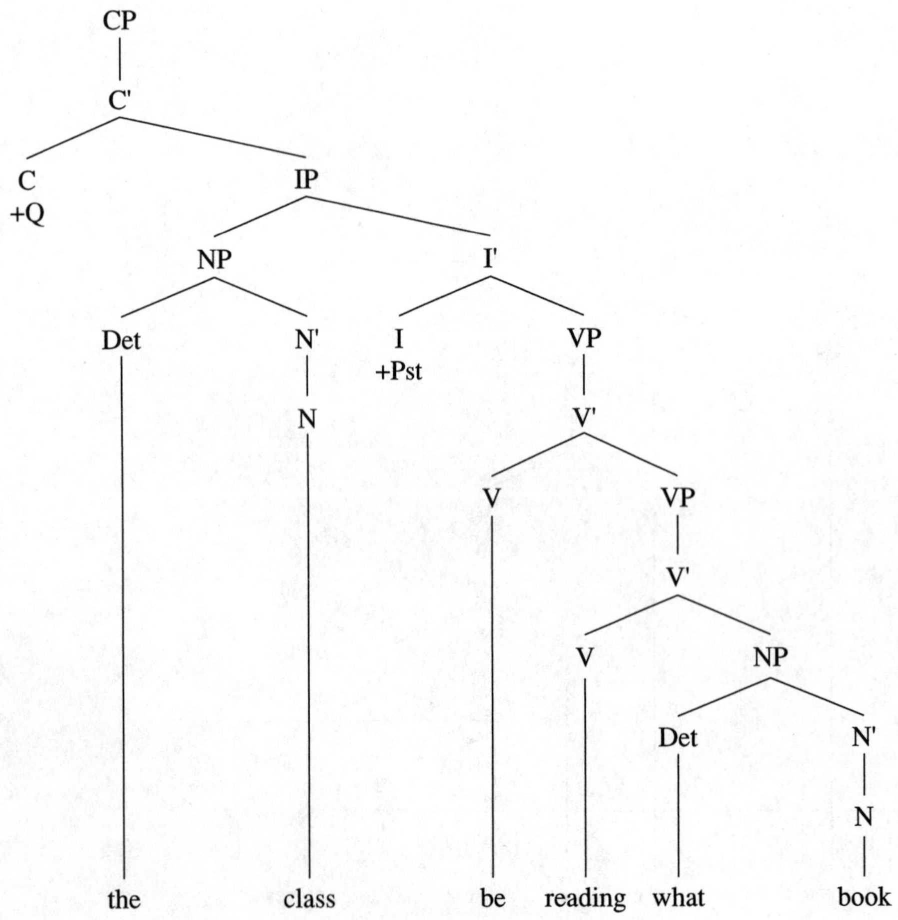

S-structure:

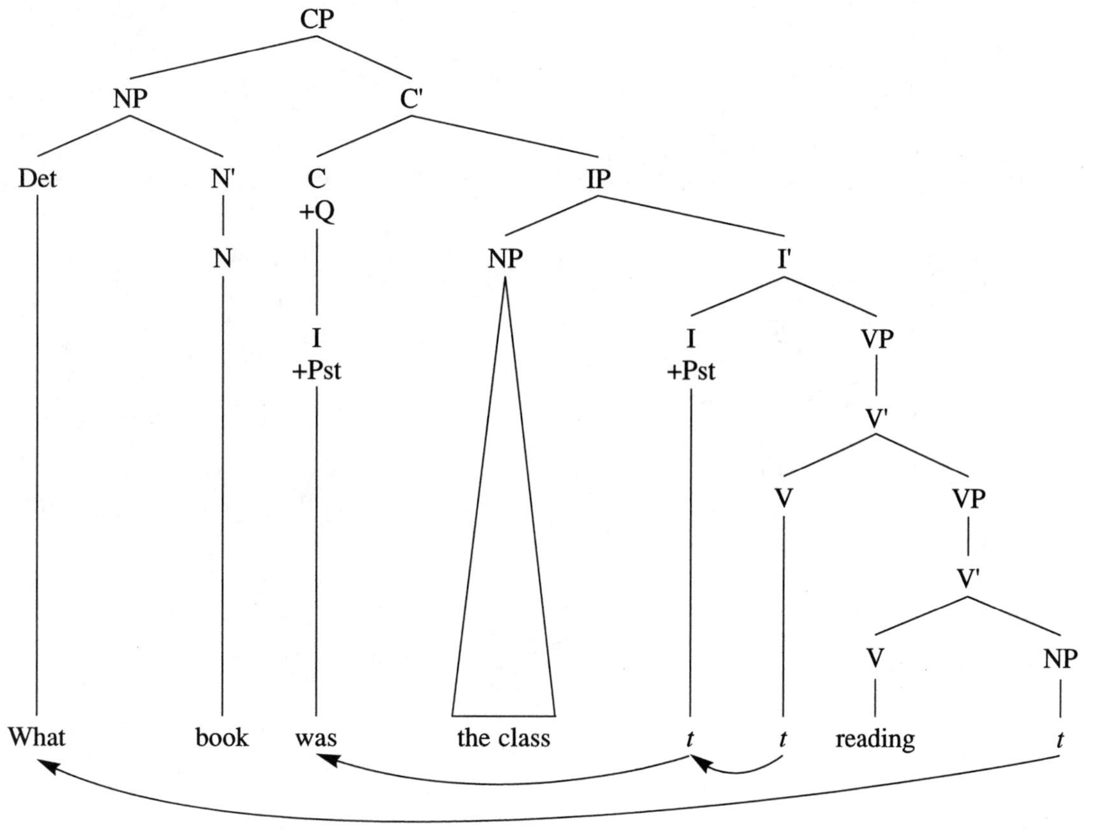

Practice 5.11 (Surface structure is shown here)

1. *Do* Insertion, Inversion, *Wh* Movement

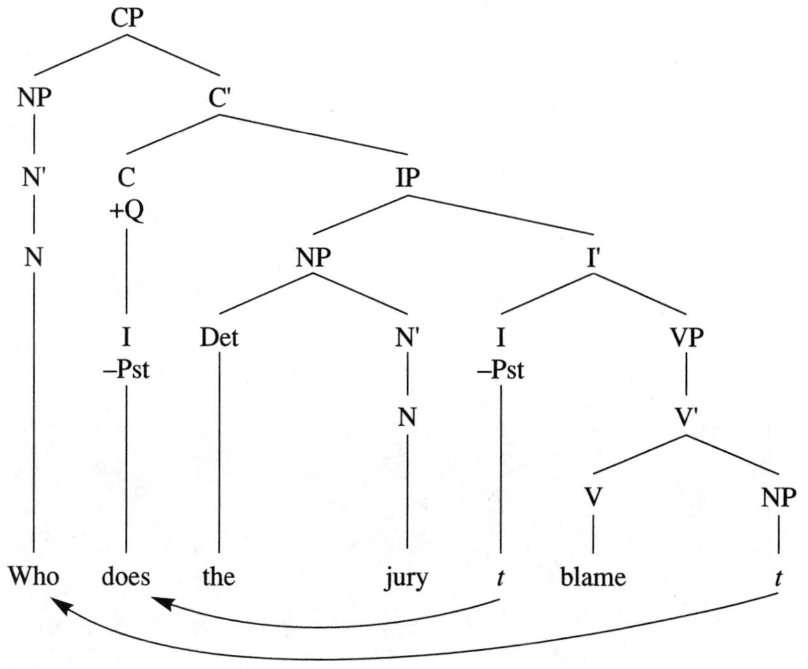

2.

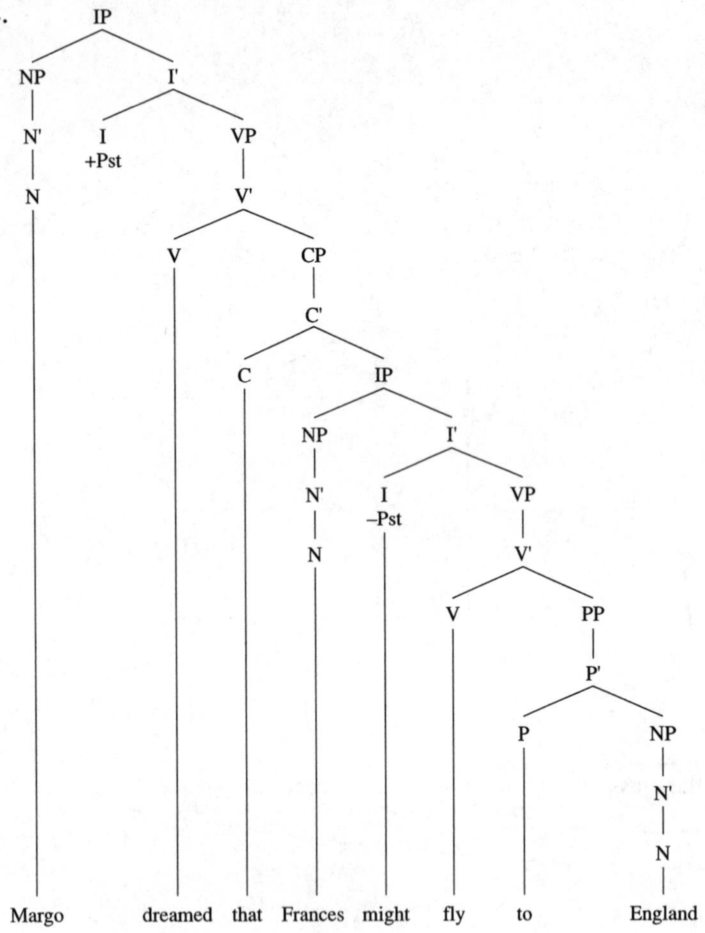

3. Verb Raising, Inversion

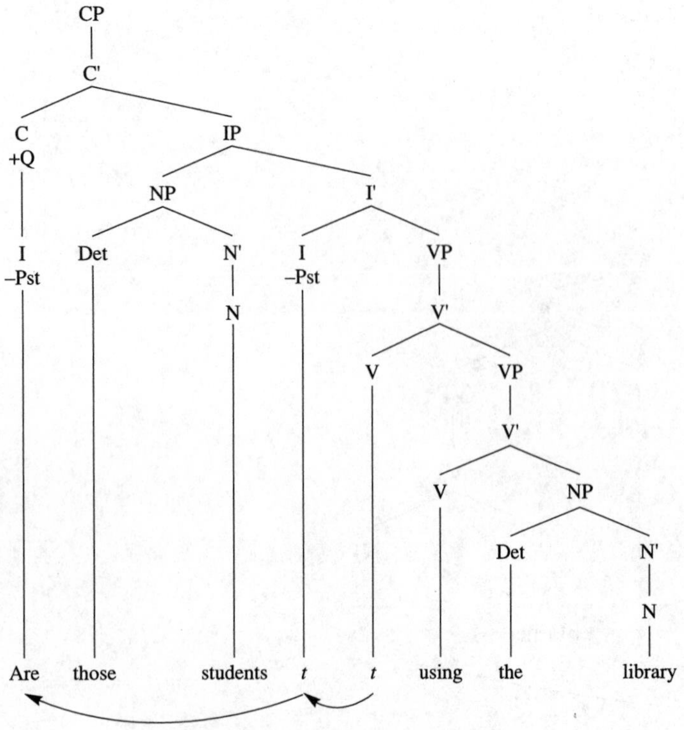

4. Verb Raising, Inversion, *Wh* Movement

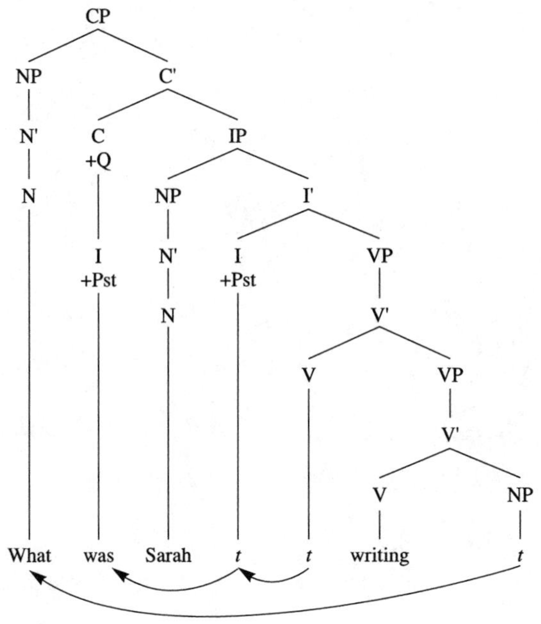

5. Inversion

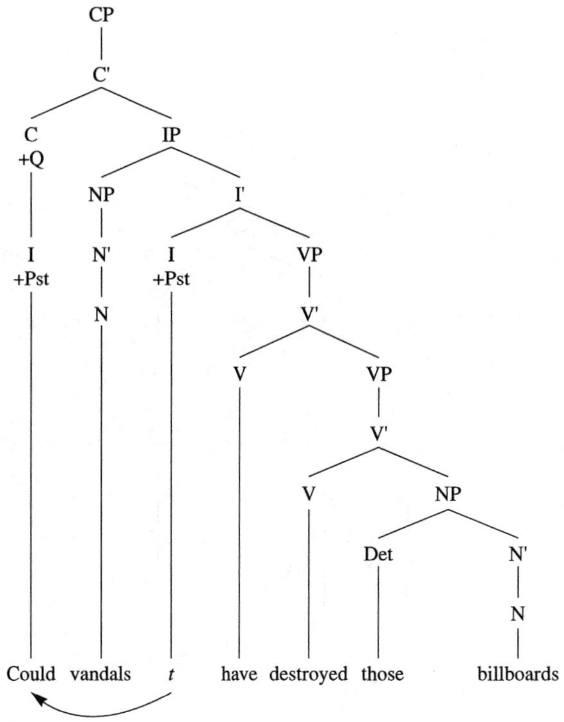

6.

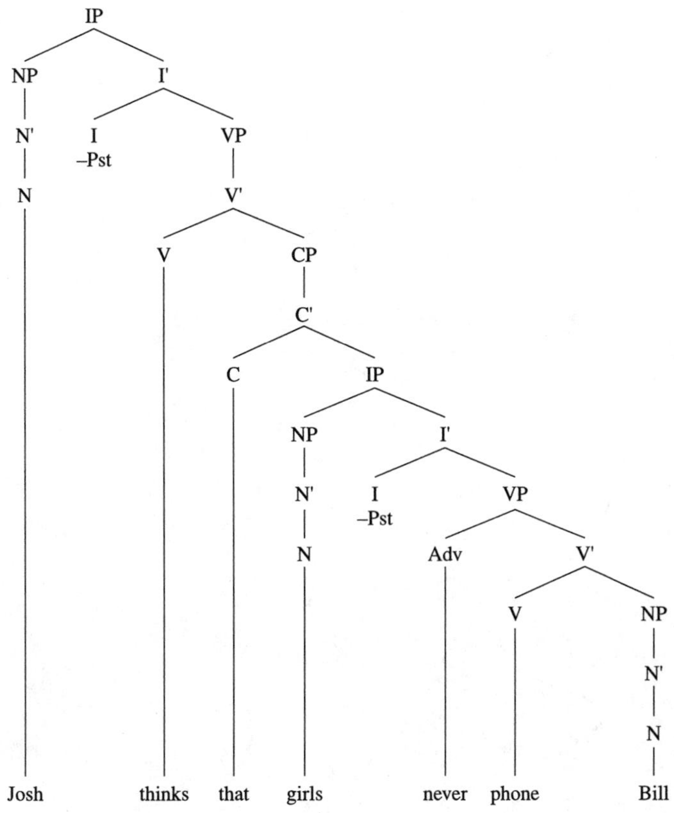

7. Inversion, *Wh* Movement

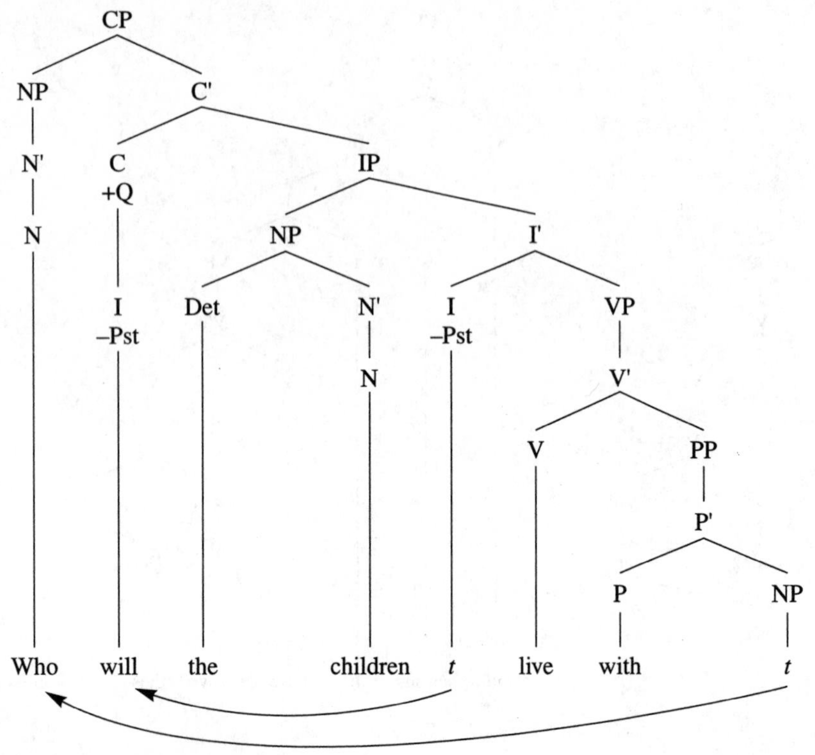

8. *Wh* Movement

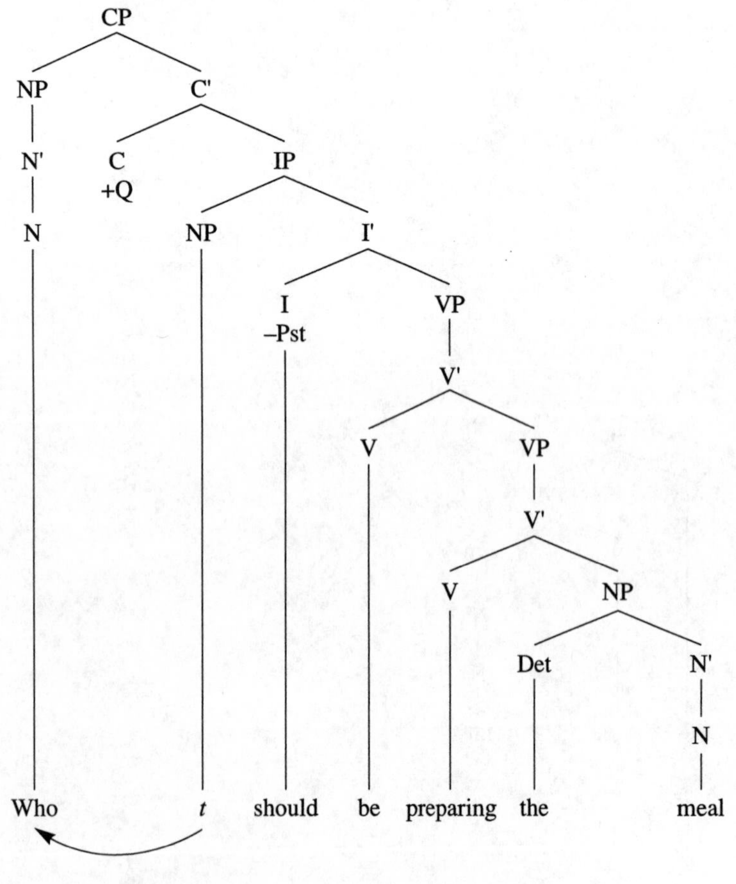

9. Verb Raising, Inversion, *Wh* Movement

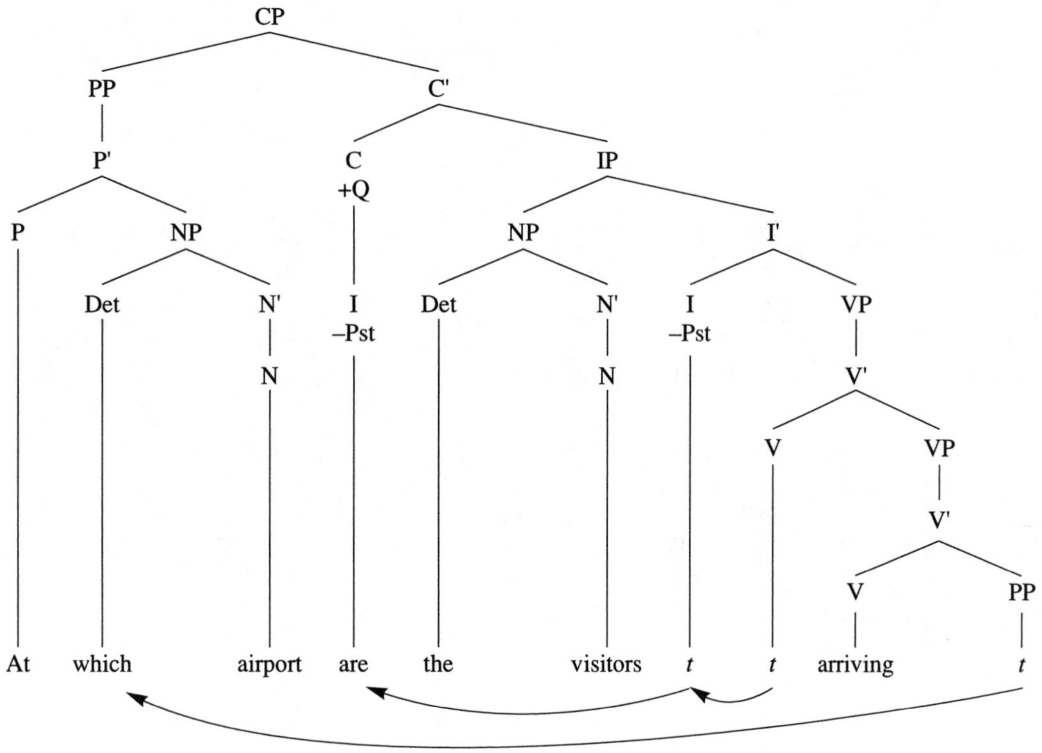

10. Inversion

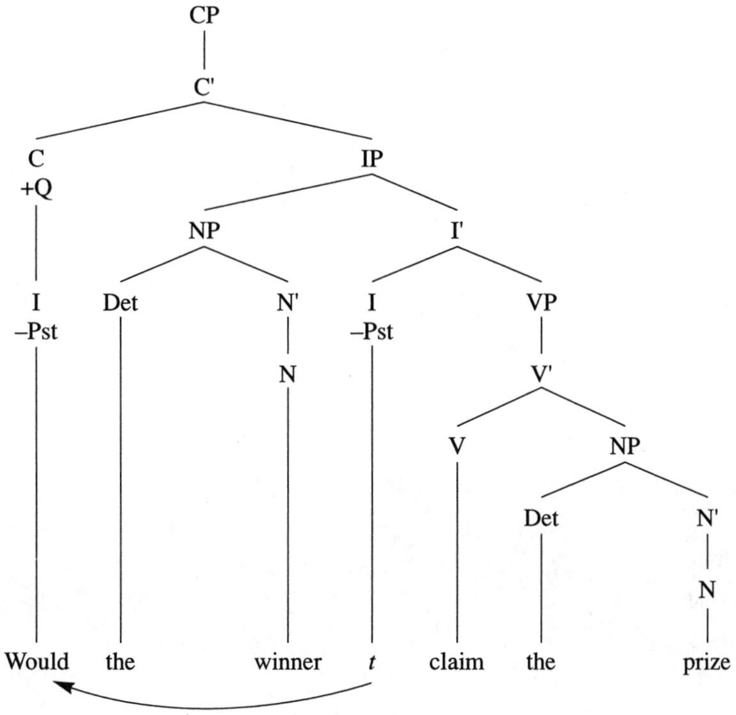

11.

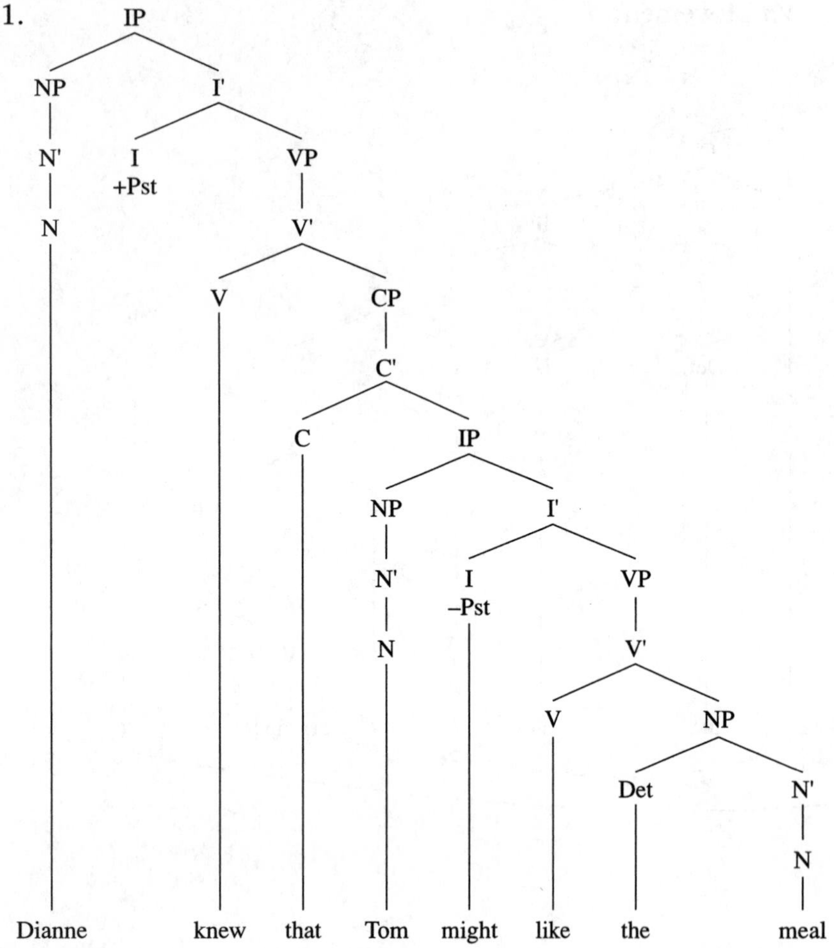

12. *Do* Insertion, Inversion

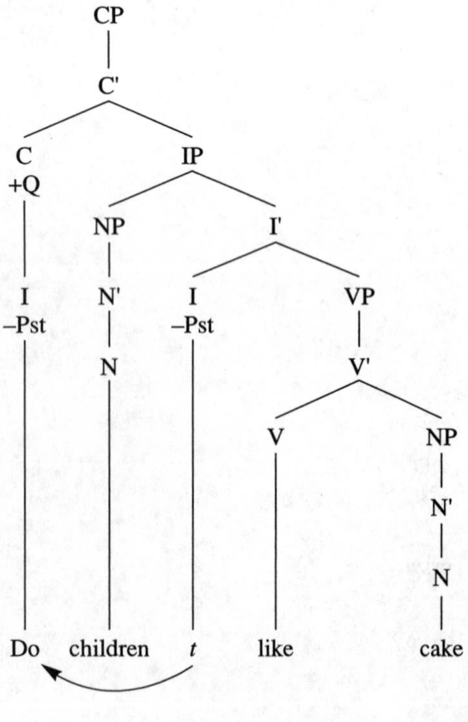

Practice 5.12

1. a. VPs joined
   b. NPs joined
   c. CPs joined
   d. VPs joined

2. a. [which Henry likes]
   b. [who won the race]
   c. [which Winston designed]

3. a. passive
   b. passive
   c. active
   d. passive

Review Exercise (Surface structure is shown for all sentences)

1.

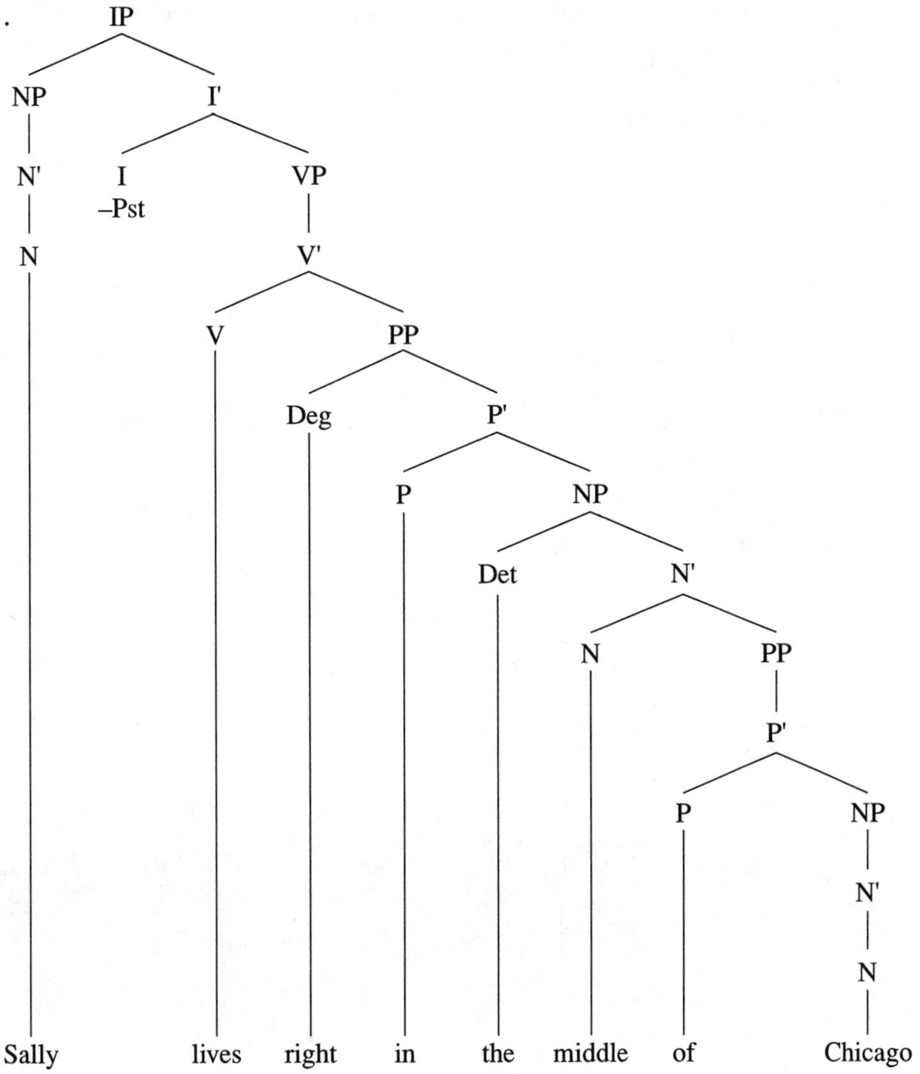

2.

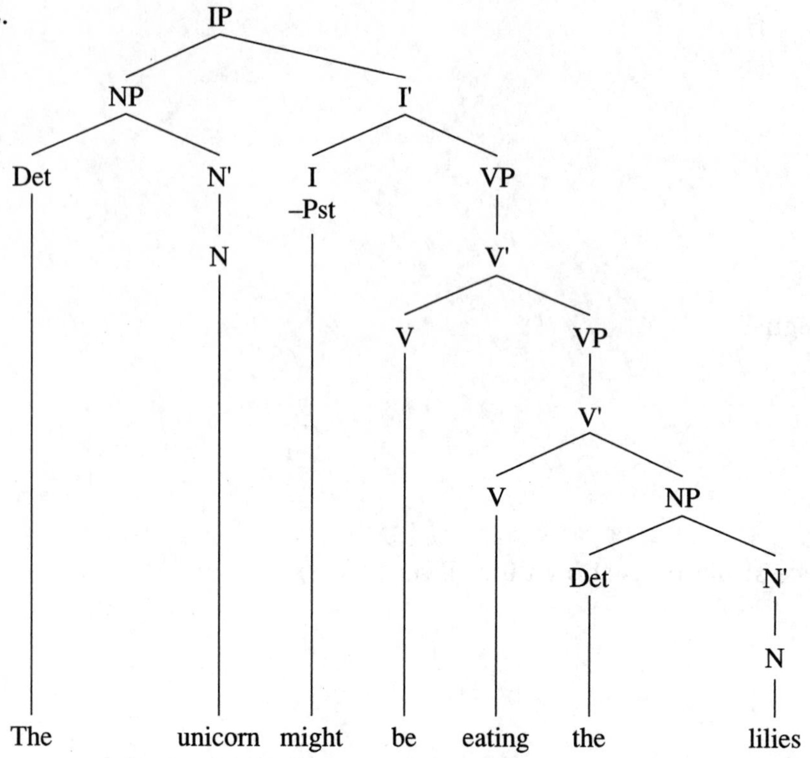
IP
NP
I'
Det
N'
I
–Pst
VP
N
V'
V
VP
V'
V
NP
Det
N'
N
The
unicorn
might
be
eating
the
lilies

3.

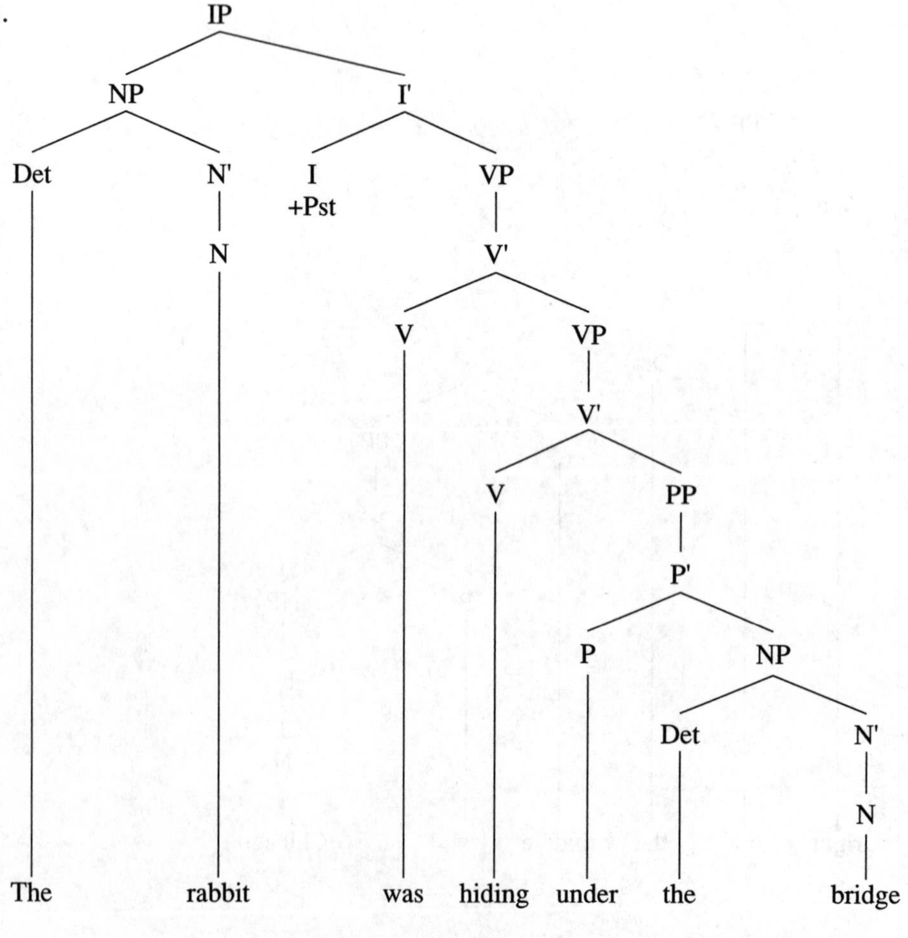
IP
NP
I'
Det
N'
I
+Pst
VP
N
V'
V
VP
V'
V
PP
P'
P
NP
Det
N'
N
The
rabbit
was
hiding
under
the
bridge

4.

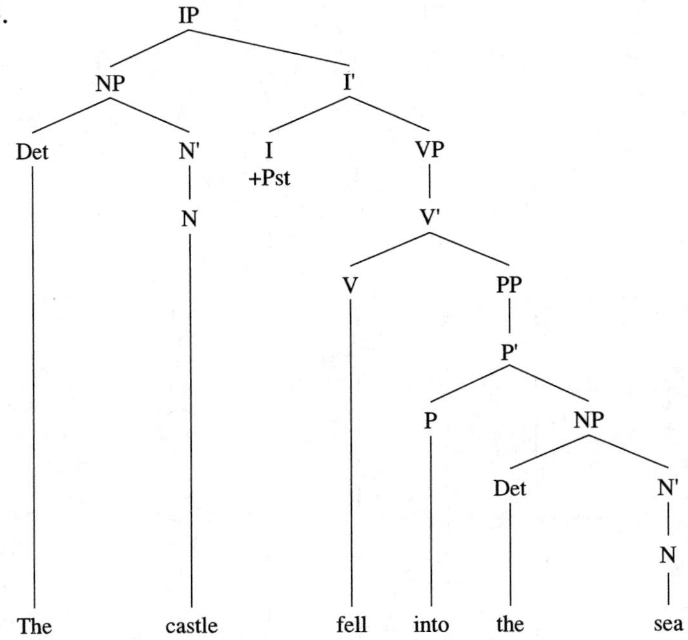
IP
NP
I'
Det
N'
I
+Pst
VP
N
V'
V
PP
P'
P
NP
Det
N'
N
The
castle
fell
into
the
sea

5.

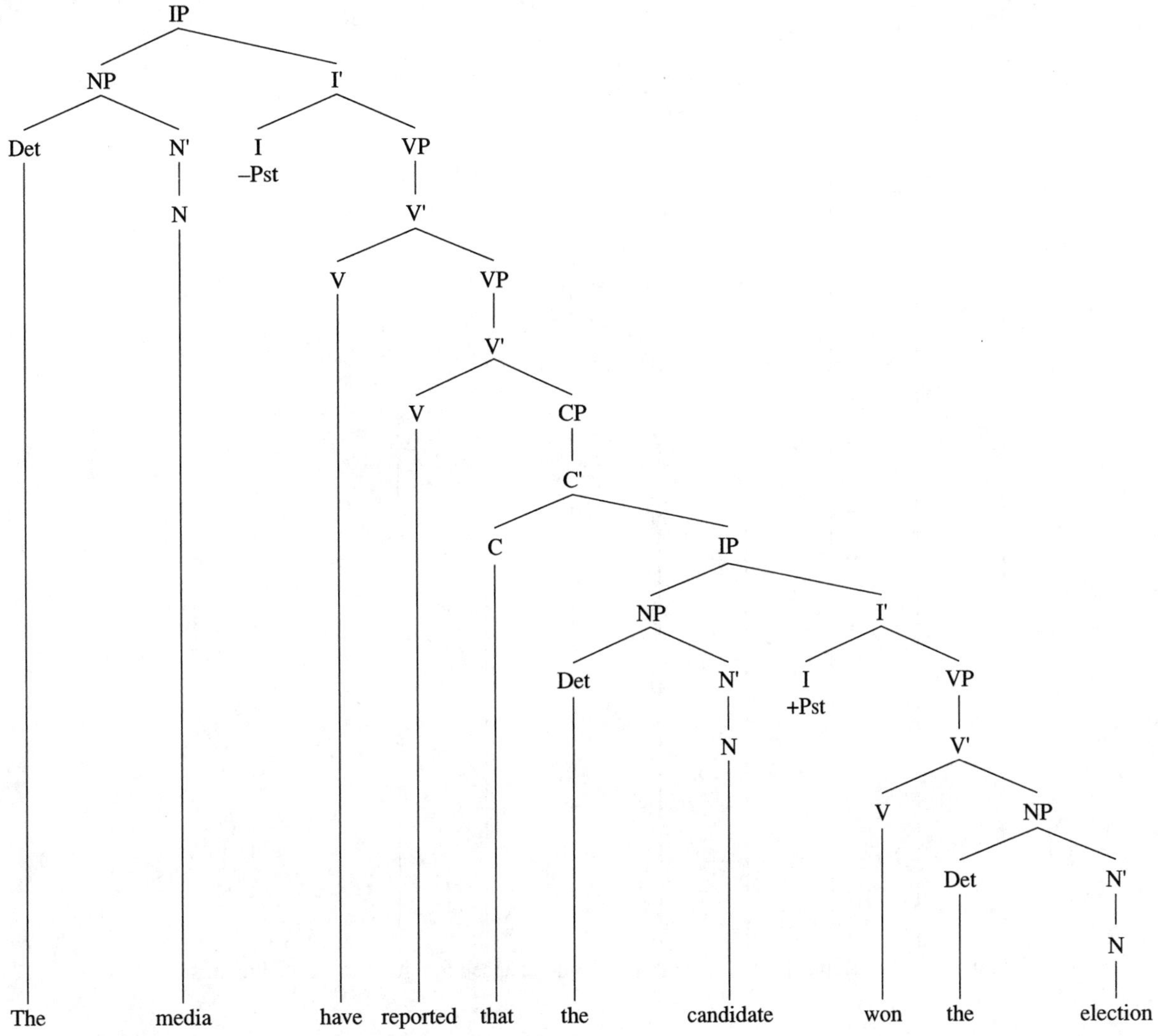
IP
NP
I'
Det
N'
I
–Pst
VP
N
V'
V
VP
V'
V
CP
C'
C
IP
NP
I'
Det
N'
I
+Pst
VP
N
V'
V
NP
Det
N'
N
The
media
have
reported
that
the
candidate
won
the
election

6.

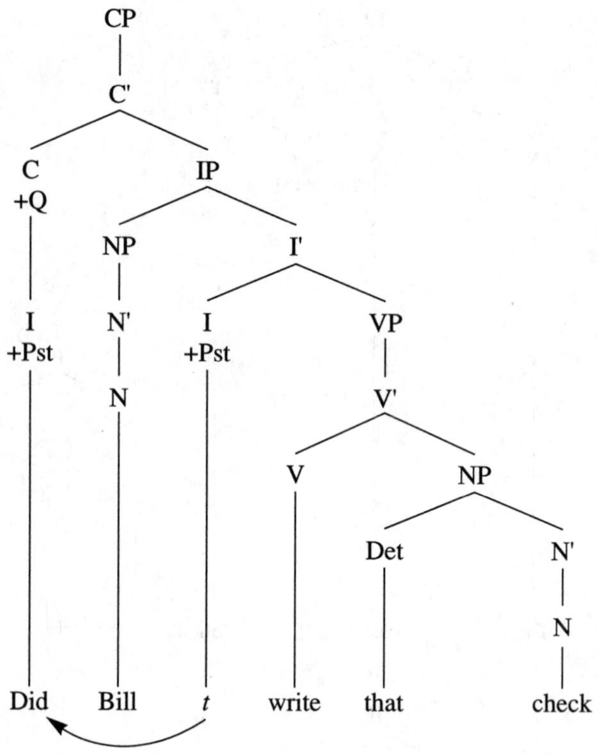
CP
C'
C
+Q
IP
NP
I'
I
+Pst
N'
I
+Pst
VP
N
V'
V
NP
Det
N'
N
Did Bill t write that check

7.

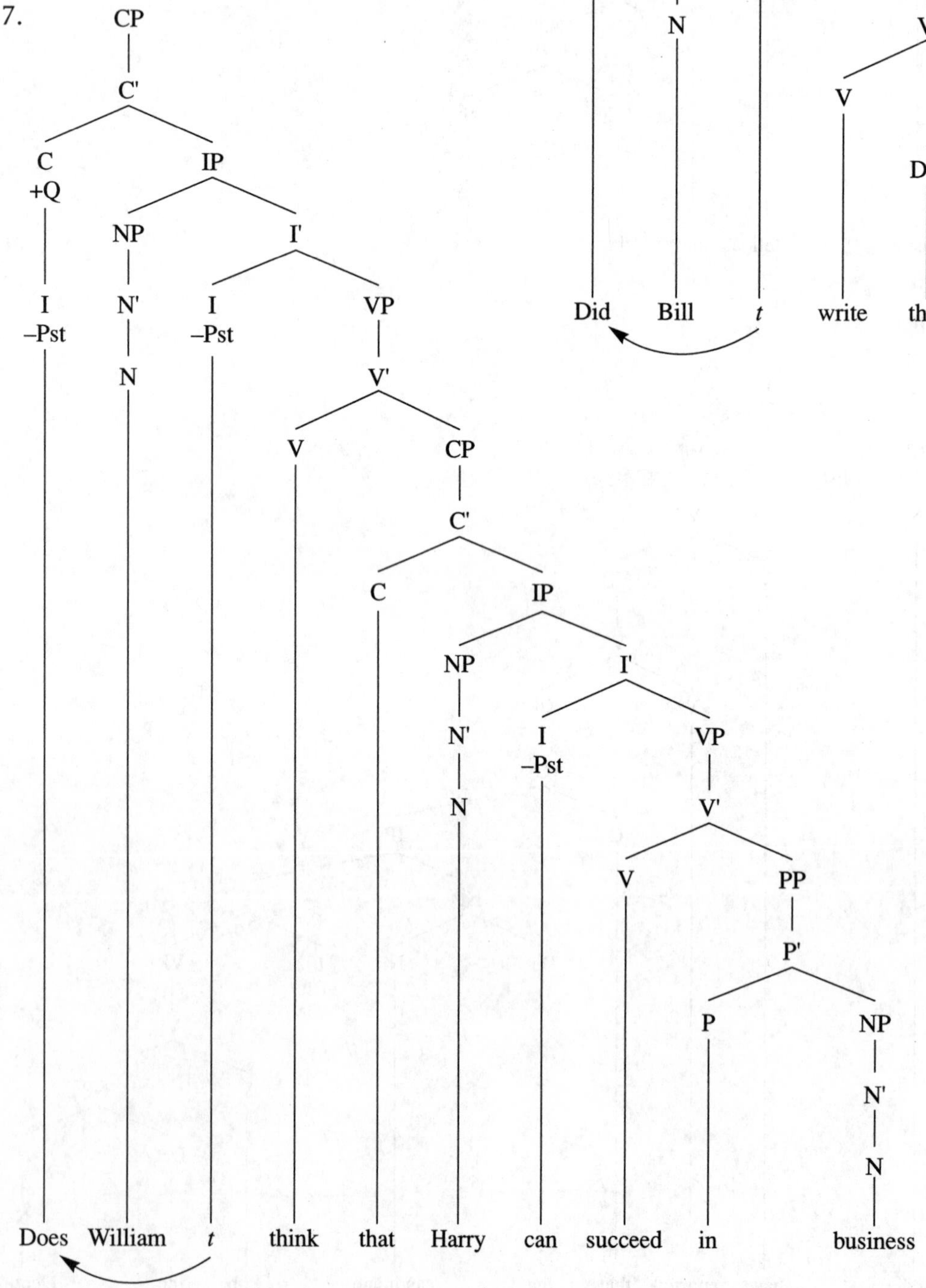
CP
C'
C
+Q
IP
NP
I'
I
–Pst
N'
I
–Pst
VP
N
V'
V
CP
C'
C
IP
NP
I'
N'
I
–Pst
VP
N
V'
V
PP
P'
P
NP
N'
N
Does William t think that Harry can succeed in business

8.

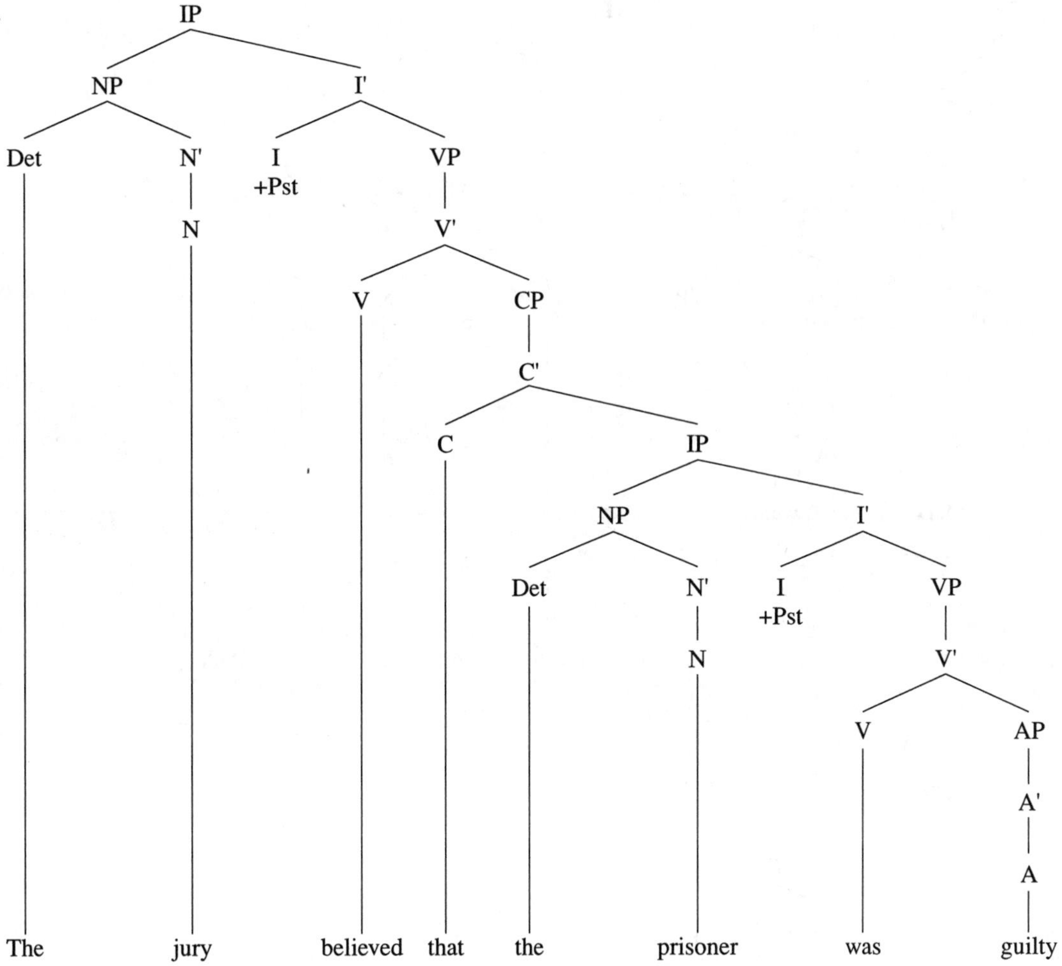
IP
NP
I'
Det
N'
I
+Pst
VP
N
V'
V
CP
C'
C
IP
NP
I'
Det
N'
I
+Pst
VP
N
V'
V
AP
A'
A
The
jury
believed
that
the
prisoner
was
guilty

9.

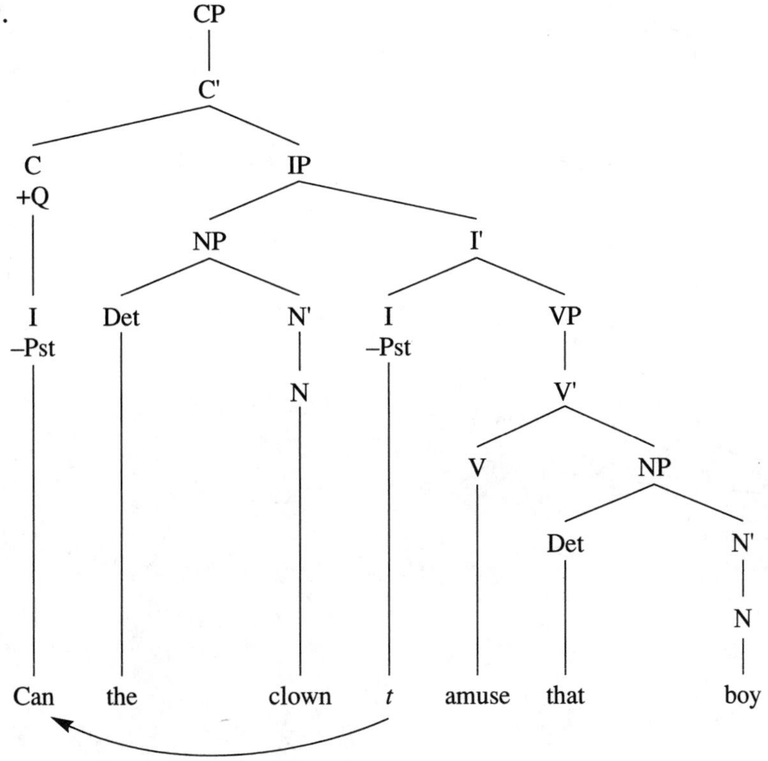
CP
C'
C
+Q
IP
NP
I'
I
–Pst
Det
N'
I
–Pst
VP
N
V'
V
NP
Det
N'
N
Can
the
clown
t
amuse
that
boy

10.

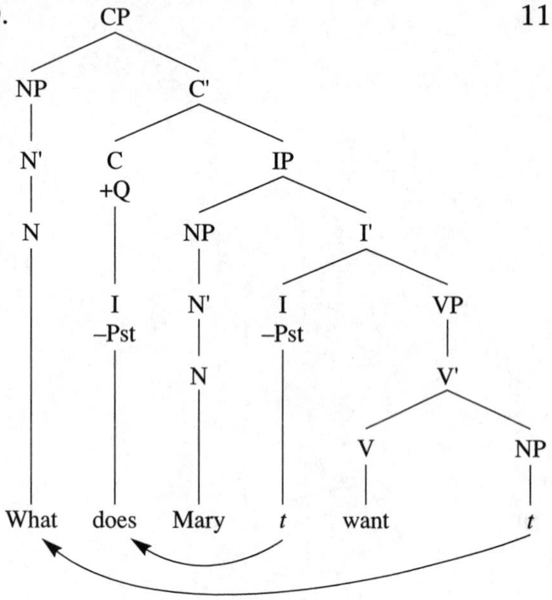
CP
NP
C'
N'
C
+Q
IP
N
NP
I'
I
–Pst
N'
I
–Pst
VP
N
V'
V
NP
What
does
Mary
t
want
t

11.

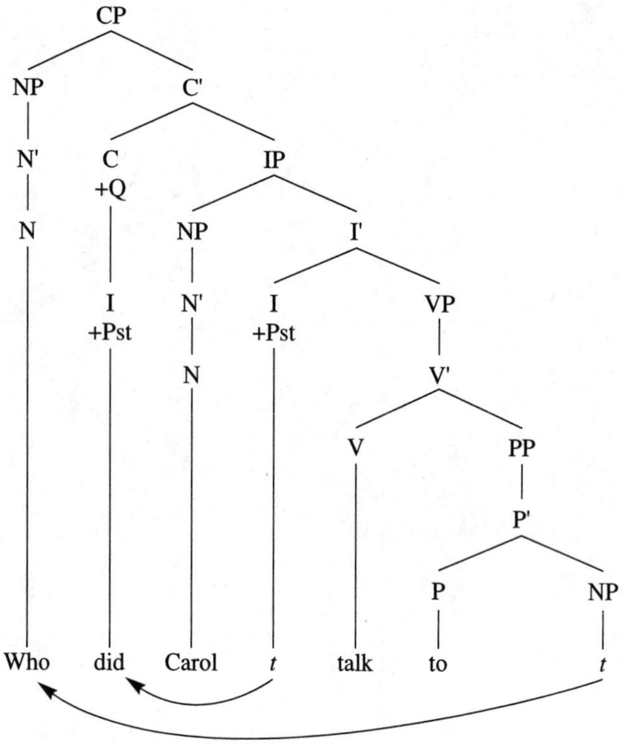
CP
NP
C'
N'
C
+Q
IP
N
NP
I'
I
+Pst
N'
I
+Pst
VP
N
V'
V
PP
P'
P
NP
Who
did
Carol
t
talk
to
t

12.

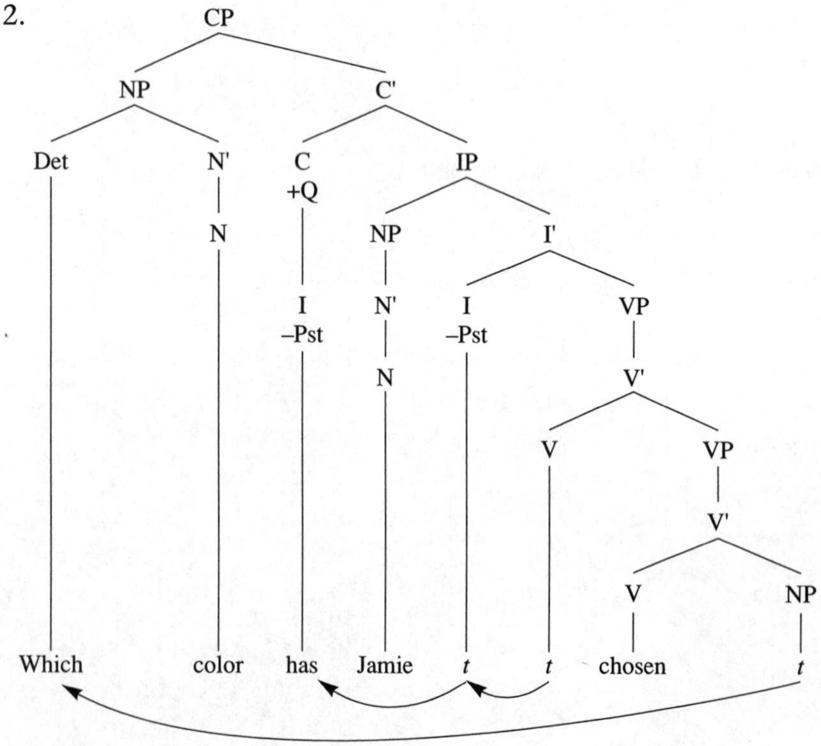
CP
NP
C'
Det
N'
C
+Q
IP
N
NP
I'
I
–Pst
N'
I
–Pst
VP
N
V'
V
VP
V'
V
NP
Which
color
has
Jamie
t
t
chosen
t

Chapter 6

Practice 6.1

1. (answer supplied in the text)
2. paraphrases
3. homophones
4. contradiction
5. entailment
6. antonyms
7. paraphrases
8. contradiction
9. synonyms
10. homophones (both are [stejk])

Practice 6.2

1. a. summer

connotation:	sunny, fun, sticky . . .
intension:	warmest season of the year
denotation:	period between summer solstice and autumnal equinox
extension:	June 21–September 20 in northern hemisphere; December 21–March 20 in southern hemisphere

b. a linguistics instructor

connotation:	wise, funny . . .
intension:	a real or imagined person who teaches linguistics
denotation:	any person in the real world who teaches linguistics
extension:	your particular professor

c. grass

connotation:	green, sweet-smelling, allergies . . .
intension:	green plant that grows on lawns
denotation:	narrow-leafed plant
extension:	the green stuff in my lawn that is not weeds

2. Verbs in A must have both a subject and an object. The subject will generally be animate and equipped with limbs capable of sweeping or kicking. The meanings of the verbs in A require an object to be swept or kicked. The verbs in B take just a subject, which is generally animate (unless the verb is used metaphorically).

3. Groups A and B are [+living, +human].
Group A is [+female]. Group B is [–female].
grandmother, grandfather, mother, and *father* are all [+parent].

4.

ewe	**lamb**	**mare**	**filly**	**colt**
[+animate]	[+animate]	[+animate]	[+animate]	[+animate]
[+sheep]	[+sheep]	[+horse]	[+horse]	[+horse]
[+adult]	[–adult]	[+adult]	[–adult]	[–adult]
[+female]	[–wild]	[+female]	[+female]	[–wild]
[–wild]		[–wild]	[–wild]	

5. The problem with connotation is that different people will have different associations for words, and associations do not necessarily get at the meaning. The problem with denotation is that it cannot account for entities that exist in an imaginary realm.

Extension and intension can account for entities in an imaginary realm, but they still do not get at what meaning actually is. Componential analysis works relatively well for words that can be classed into groups according to features, but it is difficult to specify all the features that would be needed. Furthermore, it is difficult to determine smaller units of meaning for some words (e.g., what is the feature that would set the word *blue* apart from the word *yellow*?).

Practice 6.3

1. a. grammaticized
   b. graded membership
   c. graded membership; fuzzy concept
   d. grammaticized or graded membership (hour vs. lifetime)
   e. graded membership
   (Answers concerning prototypical members will vary.)

2. Menomini
   The three types of nouns are: parts of the body, kinship terms, and objects. Parts of the body and kinship terms are "inalienable." Algonquian languages, of which Menomini is one, do not allow an unpossessed form for things that must, by their very nature, belong to someone. Parts of the body and kinship terms are typically inalienable.

3. Kiswahili
   Singular [m-], plural [wa-]: used for human beings
   Singular [m-], plural [mi-]: used for features of the natural environment
   Singular [ki-], plural [vi-]: used for inanimate objects

4. German
   Dative *dem* implies a stationary place or location.
   Accusative *das* implies movement to, toward, or into a location.
   German articles contain the idea of movement, whereas English articles (*a, an, the*) contain no such meaning.

Practice 6.4

1. Structural: a. beer that is cool plus wine (not necessarily cool)
   b. cool beer and cool wine
2. Structural: a. The woman is standing at the water cooler now. (I may have met her elsewhere.)
   b. I met the woman while I was standing at the water cooler.
3. Structural: a. The bill concerns dangerous drugs.
   b. The drug bill is dangerous.
4. Structural: a. black ties and white ties
   b. ties that are two-toned (black and white)
   c. white ties and the color black
5. Structural: a. either George and Harry together or Fred alone
   b. George plus one of the other two (Harry or Fred)

6. Structural: a. The pictures are in the attic.
b. I will be in the attic when I look at the pictures.

7. Lexical: key to the door, car, answers . . . ?

Tree structures for ambiguous phrases in sentences 1, 3, 5, 6:

1. a.

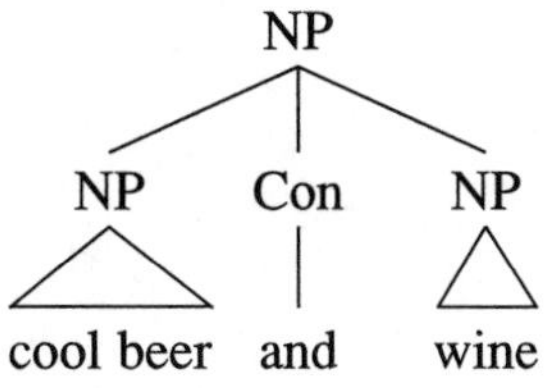

b.

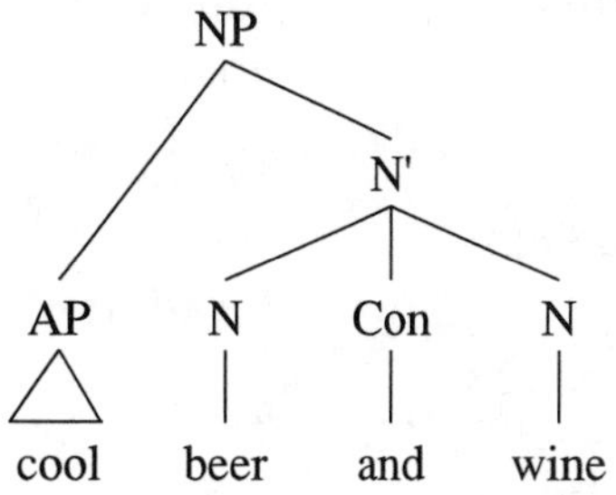

3. a.

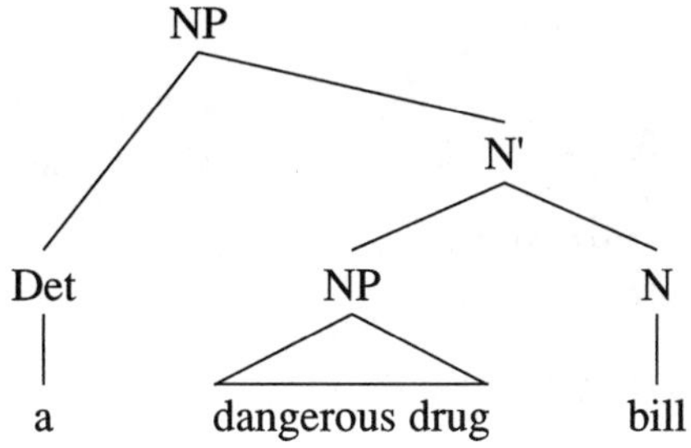

b.

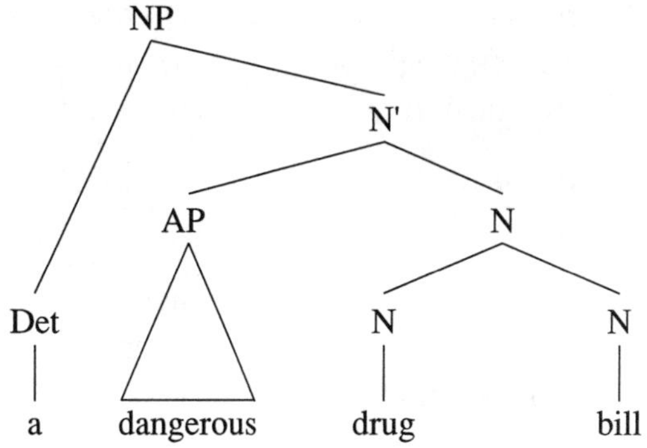

5. a.

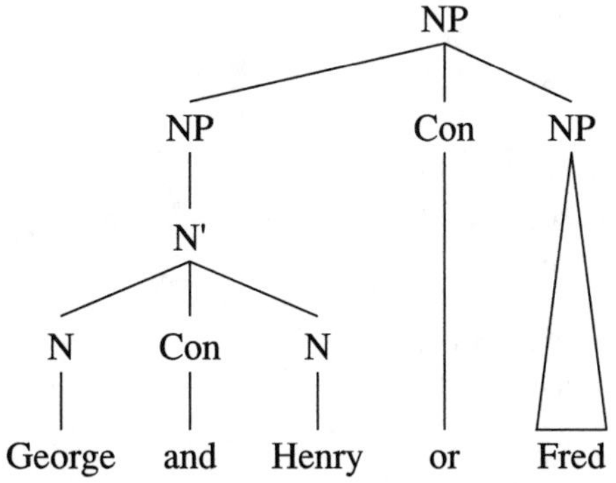

b.

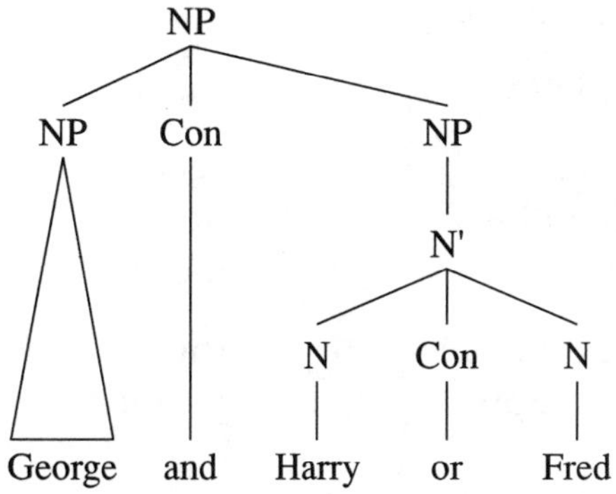

6. a.

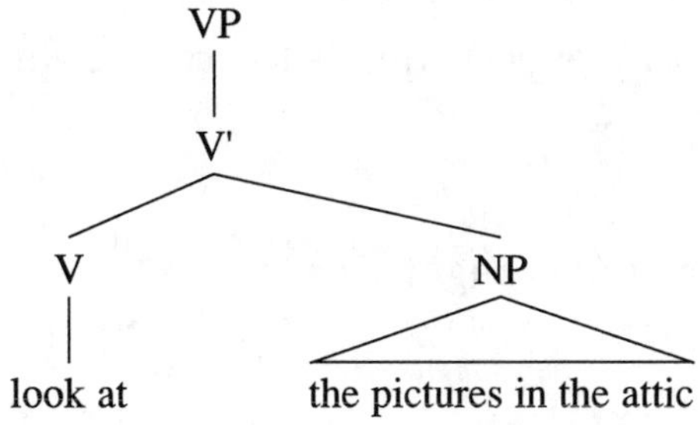

b.

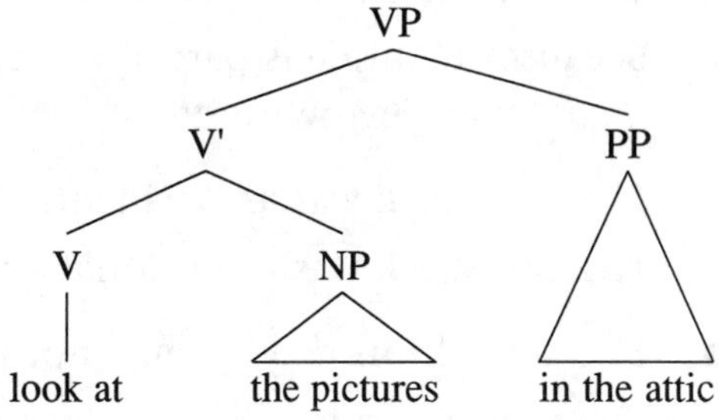

Practice 6.5

	NP	Thematic role	Assigned by
1.	Sarah	agent	drove
	that bus	theme	drove
	Indianapolis	source	from
	Terre Haute	goal	to
2.	children	agent	eating
	their ice cream	theme	eating
	kitchen	location	in
3.	you	agent	buy
	which shoes	theme	buy
	the store	location	at
4.	the cat	theme	chased
	a large dog	agent	by
	the garden	location	around
5.	the boys	agent	walked
	the park	goal	to
6.	Sally	agent	mailed
	a parcel	theme	mailed
	her nephew	goal	mailed
7.	Bill	agent	leave
	what	theme	leave
	your house	location	at
8.	the letter	theme	sent
9.	Ginger	agent	scribbled
	her address	theme	scribbled
	the paper	location	on
10.	the minister	theme	ordained
	the pulpit	location	in

Practice 6.6

1. a. Because the bride walks down the aisle, *she* refers to the bride.
   b. Because the bride is part of the couple and we expect friends to cry at a wedding, *she* refers to every friend.
2. a. The car wreck was an accident.
   b. The car wreck was intentional with malice aforethought.
3. a. The accusation may or may not be false.
   b. The accusation is actually false.

4. a. The speaker is in China.
   b. The speaker is outside of China.
5. a. We know which hospital but not the specific priest.
   b. We know which priest but not the specific hospital.

Practice 6.7

1. Maxim of Quality
2. Maxims of Relevance, Quantity, Manner
3. Maxim of Quality
4. Maxims of Relevance, Quantity, Manner
5. No violations

Review Exercises

1. The causative is grammaticized in Burmese. It is indicated by making the first consonant voiceless.
2. Answers will vary.
3. a. The witness cannot answer the question because use of *stop* presupposes that the witness has taken or is taking drugs.
   b. The implicature is not the same. The doctor is asking a genuine information question, whereas the student is making a request.
   c. The Maxims of Relevance and Quantity are being violated. As a result, the implicature of the letter is that the student does not have the necessary academic qualifications for graduate school.

Chapter 7

Practice 7.1

1. voicing assimilation
2. consonant deletion
3. vowel deletion (apocope)
4. palatalization
5. nasalization, consonant deletion
6. vowel reduction
7. consonant deletion, degemination, vowel deletion (apocope)
8. vowel deletion (syncope), rhotacism
9. epenthesis
10. place of articulation assimilation, degemination (or consonant deletion)
11. vowel deletion (syncope), palatalization
12. voicing assimilation
13. degemination, frication, voicing assimilation
14. total assimilation

Changes from Proto-Germanic [goːdas] to Icelandic [goːðr]:

frication [d] ⟶ [ð]
syncope [a] ⟶ Ø (probably preceded by vowel reduction)
voicing assimilation [s] ⟶ [z], followed by rhotacism [z] ⟶ [r]

Practice 7.2

1. Deaffrication
2. a. (1) Latin a ⟶ French e
   (2) Latin k ⟶ French ʧ (palatalization, frication)
   (3) Latin p ⟶ French f (frication; manner assimilation)
   (4) final syllable *-ut* deleted
   (5) ʧ ⟶ ʃ (deaffrication)
   Note: Step (1) must come before step (2).
   Step (3) must come before step (4).
   Step (2) must come before step (5).

   b. English borrowed *chief* before step (5) had occurred. English borrowed *chef* after step (5) had occurred.

Practice 7.3

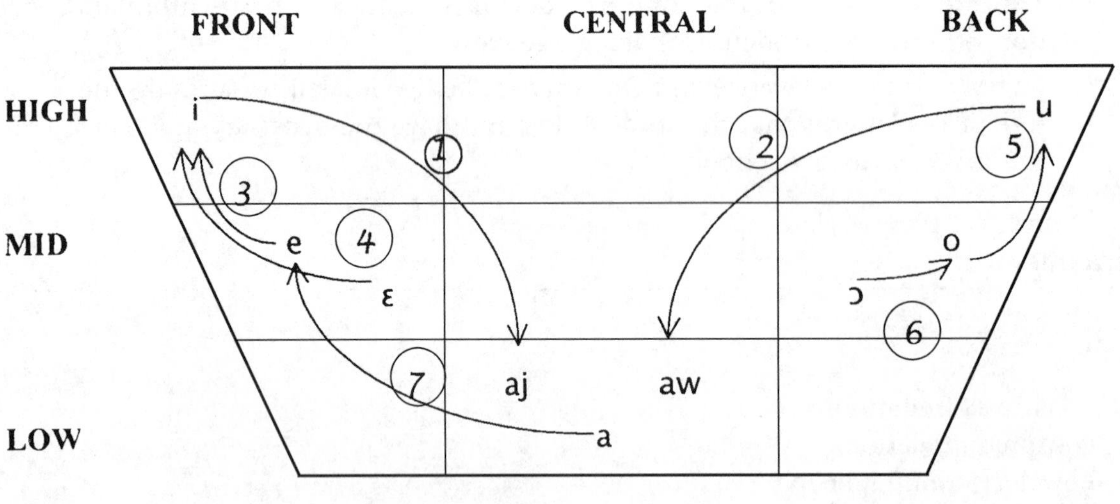

1. Long [i] ⟶ [aj]
2. Long [u] ⟶ [aw]
3. Long [e] ⟶ [i]
4. Long [ɛ] ⟶ [i]
5. Long [o] ⟶ [u]
6. Long [ɔ] ⟶ [o]
7. Long [a] ⟶ [e]

Practice 7.4

1. Reanalysis through analogy: Old English suffixes were regularized by the process of analogy, so now there is just one plural morpheme: *-s*.

2. Borrowing: Welsh borrowed plural *-s* from English.
3. Folk etymology: unknown forms were reanalyzed (incorrectly) as English words.
4. Grammaticalization: *yesterday* has given the morpheme for PAST.
5. Latin case endings were lost in Italian. Therefore, word order in the sentence becomes more important for meaning.

Practice 7.5

In these examples of early seventeenth-century English, a negative was formed by placing *not* after the verb. In the case of #2, with a pronoun as direct object, the negative is after the pronoun direct object. In contemporary English, *Do* Insertion is mandatory, and the negative is placed between *do* and the verb.

Practice 7.6

1. Scots Gaelic; attested in the early sixteenth century.
2. Old English; present before the twelfth century, reflecting Anglo-Saxon lifeways.
3. Ultimately from Old Testament Hebrew, by way of Greek and Latin translations of the Old Testament. Attested in English as early as A.D. 825.
4. From Old Norse; a case of adstratum borrowing.
5. From French, after the Norman Conquest. Superstratum borrowing.
6. Middle Latin, ultimately from Arabic. During the Middle Ages, Arabic was the language of science and technology.
7. From Italian; attested in the early seventeenth century, when Italian Renaissance architecture was becoming popular in England.
8. From Greek, via late Latin; attested in the late sixteenth century.
9. From languages belonging to the Algonquian family, spoken by Native Americans in coastal areas from Virginia through New England during early settlement of the Northeast of America. Attested in early seventeenth century. Substratum borrowing.
10. From Hindi and Marathi; attested in the late eighteenth century, at a time when the British were expanding into India. Substratum borrowing.
11. Ultimately from West African languages, through Spanish/Portuguese. Attested in English in the late sixteenth century, after exploratory voyages along the African coast.
12. This is "New Latin"—a word made from combining a Greek affix (*auto*) and Latin root (*mobile*), a fairly common way of naming new technological inventions.
13. From Tagalog *bundok* 'mountain'; attested in 1909, not long after the Spanish-American War in which the Philippines was acquired as a U.S. territory.

Practice 7.7

1. Proto-Algonquian

Fox	Ojibwa	Menomini	Evidence
ʃk	ʃk	sk	1, 6, 9
hk	kk	hk	2, 7, 10
ht	tt	ʔt	3, 4, 8
ht	tt	ht	5, 11, 12

*PA	Fox	Ojibwa	Menomini
ʔt	ht	tt	ʔt
ʃk	ʃk	ʃk	sk
hk	hk	kk	hk
ht	ht	tt	ht

2. Arabic

a.

Position	Syrian	Iraqi	Evidence
word-initial	d, t	d, θ, ð	1, 2, 6, 7, 11, 12
word-final	d, t	t, θ, ð, d	4, 5, 6, 12
between vowels	d, t	d, θ, ð	3, 10, 14
after a consonant	d, t	t, θ, ð, d	1, 8, 9, 13

b. Syrian has only d and t. Iraqi has d, t, θ, ð.

c. Protoforms: *d, t, θ, ð.

d. Proto d and ð merged to become d in Syrian, but were retained in Iraqi. Proto t and θ merged to become t in Syrian, but were retained in Iraqi.

Practice 7.8

1. Hypothetical Language Group One:

   Protoforms:

   1. munto
   2. fumo
   3. pippona
   4. nonka
   5. wusa
   6. fito

   Sound changes in Language A:

   - Nasalization of V before cluster of nasal + consonant
   - Vowel reduction word-finally
   - Vowel deletion word-finally in words of more than two syllables
   - Deletion of nasal before C

   Sound changes in Language B:

   - Deletion of nasal before C
   - Degemination (3)
   - Voicing of consonants word-initially and intervocalically
   - Palatalization of glide before high V (5)

2. Hypothetical Language Group Two:

   Protoforms: 1. puka 2. nizuʤ

   Sound changes in Language A: Frication intervocalically

   Sound changes in Language B: Voicing word-initially and intervocalically; deaffrication

   Sound changes in Language C: n ⟶ m; consonant deletion word-finally (possibly preceded by deaffrication).

Sound changes in Language D: Note that the first two changes are ordered:
(1) Consonant deletion word-finally (possibly preceded by deaffrication);
(2) Vowel deletion word-finally;
(3) Rhotacism

3. Austronesian
   *PAN. Note: Not all protoforms can be derived from data presented in the problem set. Alternative acceptable answers are given in parentheses.
   1. anak
   2. sakit
   3. hikat (probably could not be guessed from the data set; *ikat* would be an acceptable answer)
   4. uʀat (could not be guessed from the data set; *urat* or *uzat* would be an acceptable answer)

   Only changes that could be inferred from the data set are listed below.
   Changes in Malay:
   - None, or possibly rhotacism (4) (if PAN were **uzat*)

   Changes in Written Cham:
   - Vowel reduction before word-final [k] (1)
   - Substitution: Word-final stops become glottal stops
   - Substitution (or weakening through loss of place feature): Word-initial s ⟶ h
   - (Possibly rhotacism (4), if PAN were **uzat*)

   Changes in Tsat:
   - Substitution (or weakening through loss of place feature): Word-final stops become glottal stops
   - Deletion of first syllable
   - Development of tones from contact with Chinese, a tone language

4. German dialects
   Note: Protoforms are derivable from the data set given in the problem. Alternatives are given where protoforms cannot be derived with certainty from the data set.
   1. makən (or possibly: maːkən)
   2. ik
   3. slaːpən
   4. pʊnt
   5. bejtən or bajtən
   6. dat
   7. tuː

   Changes in the Northern dialect:
   - Deletion of word-final [n] in verbs
   - Possibly compensatory lengthening of vowel (1)

   Changes in the Southern dialect:
   - Frication following a vowel (1, 2, 3, 5, 6)
   - Palatalization (3)
   - Affrication of [+anterior] voiceless stops word-initially (4, 7)

Practice 7.9

	Sound	Word
1.	k	cool
2.	p	lip
3.	k/b	crab
4.	g/p	grip
5.	f	foul
6.	h	home
7.	t	sweet

Review Exercises

1. The Great English Vowel Shift

Vowel change	Modern English word
a. oː ⟶ u	noon
b. iː ⟶ aj; ə ⟶ Ø/ _#	life
c. eː ⟶ i	sweet
d. ɔː ⟶ ow	boast
e. uː ⟶ aw	gown

2. Changes in English since Shakespeare
   a. SVO is the order in contemporary English.

   Shakespeare used primarily SVO, but the last line of 1 uses SOV.

   b. Today, *not* goes between the auxiliary and the main verb. (If there is no auxiliary, then *Do* Insertion is mandatory.)

   Shakespeare sometimes placed *not* after the main verb (1, 4), but also used *Do* Insertion (3). In questions with *Do* Insertion, the order could be *do* S (*not*) V or *do* (*not*) S V. This variation suggests that the change to *Do* Insertion was in process in Shakespeare's time.

   c. Data in 3 and 4 show the variations Shakespeare used in *yes-no* questions. In 3, *Do* Insertion is used, and there is Inversion. In 4, there is no *Do* Insertion; we assume there was Verb Raising of the main verb since there is Inversion of subject and verb.

   d. Second-person singular pronouns *thou, thee,* and *thy* have fallen out of use. Along with these, the *-(e)st* suffix on verbs (*pursuest, didst*) has fallen out of use.

3. Sound changes in Romance

   Italian:
   - Frication: Voiced stops have become fricatives intervocalically (3).
   - Voicing: Voiceless stops have become voiced intervocalically (2).

   Spanish:
   - Epenthesis: [e] has been inserted word-initially before [s]-stop clusters.
   - Voicing + Frication: Voiceless stops became voiced stops intervocalically (2). Intervocalic voiced stops have become fricatives (2, 3).
   - Weakening: Geminate [l] weakened to [j] (2).
   - Vowel deletion (apocope): Word-final [e] has been deleted. (We can posit an intermediate stage where it was reduced to schwa before being deleted.)

French:

- Epenthesis + Consonant cluster simplification: [e] has been inserted word-initially before [s]-stop clusters, followed by deletion of [s].
- Vowel deletion: Word-final vowels in unstressed syllables have been deleted. (We may assume for 2 that degemination occurred before vowel deletion.)
- In 2, [ut] has become a palatal glide, articulated with rounded lips.
- In 3, the syllable [be] has been deleted with compensatory lengthening of the vowel [i].